A Double Shot of Happiness

A Double Shot of Happiness

Tim Sharp's extraordinary journey from being diagnosed
with autism to becoming an internationally renowned artist

JUDY SHARP

ALLEN&UNWIN
SYDNEY · MELBOURNE · AUCKLAND · LONDON

First published in 2015

Copyright © Judy Sharp 2015

Allen & Unwin
83 Alexander Street
Crows Nest NSW 2065
Australia
Phone: (61 2) 8425 0100
Email: info@allenandunwin.com
Web: www.allenandunwin.com

Cataloguing-in-Publication details are available
from the National Library of Australia
www.trove.nla.gov.au

ISBN 978 1 76011 256 1

Set in 12.25/18.8 pt Adobe Garamond Pro by Bookhouse, Sydney
Printed and bound in Australia by Griffin Press

10 9 8 7 6 5 4 3 2 1

Tim and Sam

As the moon with the moonbeams,
so is my relationship with you

An Introduction

My son Tim is twenty-six years old and he loves to chat to people when we go out. He's very social and very polite, and always very happy. If we go to the shops, Tim heads straight for the counter to talk to the sales assistant.

'Hello,' he says cheerily. 'How are you today?'

Before they have a chance to ask Tim how he is doing, Tim says, 'I'm good, too!' with a big smile on his face.

'Are you having a good day?' Tim says. Again, without actually waiting for the question, Tim will tell them he's having a good day, too.

I don't interrupt when these conversations are taking place. I hang back and let Tim do the talking, and I watch as realisation dawns on the face opposite him. Something about Tim is a little bit different. There is a slight monotone to his voice and he over-emphasises some words. The intonation doesn't rise on the right syllable. It's like he's been practising how to speak for a very long time, but he just can't seem to get it right.

Usually, the person standing opposite Tim smiles gently and begins to speak very simply, because they think Tim might not understand them otherwise. But most people are taken by his cheery attitude and the conversation continues.

'Have you ever been to America?' Tim asks. He's not particularly interested in the answer but he's very eager to share information about his own travels. 'I've been to America four times!' he announces, with quite a bit of excitement. Tim bounces up and down on his toes, his hands clasped restfully behind his back, and every half a minute he pulls down on the left-hand side of his shirt. If Tim's conversation partner looked closely at him, they would notice that although he is looking in the general direction of their face, his eyes will not meet theirs.

'I've been to New York, Los Angeles, Washington DC, Chicago, Nashville, Austin Texas, Memphis and Florida, too,' Tim tells them. 'I went to Disneyland in Los Angeles.'

Most people are genuinely impressed that Tim has travelled so much, and that pleases him. Sometimes I can tell people are just being polite. Maybe they don't believe him, but I can tell you that it's true. *If you think that's good, wait for the next bit,* I think.

'I am a world-famous artist,' says Tim.

It always makes me smile to see the look of surprise on people's faces. *How on earth did someone with autism become a world-famous artist*, they wonder. If I hadn't raised Tim, I'd hardly believe it myself.

1

Timmy

I knew before the doctor told me that I was pregnant. Something changed in my body, something intangible, and I just knew. I had the feeling that something wonderful was happening to me. At the same time, I felt a dawning sense of responsibility. I'd seen plenty of babies and kids in the world, but this was mine. It was mine to care for and protect, for the rest of its life.

I worried, like all expectant mothers worry. I worried that something would go wrong with the pregnancy because my mother had had several miscarriages. After the first twelve weeks passed, I felt enormous relief, but it was replaced almost immediately by other concerns. I was terrified my baby might have a disability or illness. I was terrified of Down's Syndrome, although I could never bring myself to do the test. I couldn't face making a decision if it came back positive; I couldn't terminate.

At the same time, I didn't think I had the strength to care for a child with a disability or an illness. It seemed like an impossible sacrifice to me.

In the end, I just crossed my fingers and hoped for the best. Though my body was changing and my stomach was swelling, the baby still seemed unreal. The idea of anything going wrong was unreal too.

•

My son was born on 9 May 1988, the same day the new Parliament House was opened in Canberra. The Queen had come to cut the ribbon and there was nothing on television but the ceremony, and commentators talking about the Queen's hat. They minted a special five dollar coin for the occasion and I put one aside for my little boy, in honour of his birthday. *It's a big day in Australian history*, I thought.

The birth was without doubt the most painful experience I'd ever had, but it was pretty mild compared to what some other women go through. My waters broke in the morning, but nothing happened until early afternoon when the labour kicked in and the nursing staff went into a hive of activity. I barely had time to put two thoughts together before the baby shot out of me. He was in my arms by dinnertime.

My son was the sweetest little thing, with a rosebud mouth, little turned-up nose and the most lovely, unblemished skin. I had never seen anything so perfect in my life. I had never felt so happy. I cried and babbled with absolute joy, 'Look at it!

Look at it! I've got a baby! Isn't he perfect?' I was raving like an absolute lunatic, I think—I don't believe I even heard the doctor when he told me it was a boy. They weighed him and measured him, and stuck a tiny needle in his heel for a blood test. Everything came back normal. The doctor told me that my baby was healthy and that he had good hands. He had reached for the doctor on his way out of the womb and grabbed hold of a thumb.

'He'll make a great piano player,' the doctor smiled.

I was pleased it was a boy. If I had had six children, I would have wanted six boys. Life is tough for a girl, I thought, no matter how you look at it. I wanted my child to have the best that life could offer, better than I had had. My baby was a beautiful boy with good hands! He had the world at his feet.

•

I stared at my newborn son for two days straight. I couldn't sleep, I just nursed him or sat on the bed and stared at him, touched his little toes and watched his little chest rise and fall. The nurses wanted me to rest and offered me sleeping tablets, but I told them I was fine. I didn't want to miss a second of my son's tiny little life.

He was such a placid baby, he didn't cry very much. In fact, he didn't cry at all and seemed to sleep all the time. I had to wake him for every feed and he would doze off on the breast, and I worried he wasn't getting enough milk. 'It happens all the time,' the nurses told me. 'Your proper milk will come in around day three and he'll liven up, you'll see.' They told me the birth was a bit traumatic because he'd come out so quickly; he just needed to catch up. I was fretful but I trusted them. If he didn't breastfeed, he could have formula and that would be okay too, I thought.

I was surprised when my mother-in-law came to visit the day after my son was born and told me my child's name was Timothy. 'So this is Timothy William!' she said, holding him in her arms. My husband and I had a shortlist of names but I had wanted to see the baby before we made the final decision and we hadn't agreed on a name since the birth. My husband had obviously made the decision without me. I was deeply hurt, but what could I do? I couldn't let on that I was the last to know. I thought Timothy was a terrible name for my sweet little boy, so I quietly decided to call him Timmy. Little Timmy Sharp was my firstborn son.

My husband seemed satisfied when the baby was born, yet not exactly over the moon. He had three children from his previous marriage so it wasn't new territory for him. Where I was ecstatic, he was matter-of-fact. But he was a good provider. He would always work, always put food on the table. He had a good relationship with his other children, so I assumed he would be a decent father to our child. And he mostly just left me to it. He was the sort of person that thought raising children was women's business; he'd come in and visit for half an hour a day and then he was off, always rushing away for some reason or another. When he was in the hospital room, he paced and twitched, not uncomfortable but preoccupied. He would only hold the baby for a minute or two before he handed him back. I didn't mind, because it meant my son was in my arms most of the time, but I did feel a little bit lonely. It was hard to see other couples working together with their new babies, learning what to do and how to do it, sharing all those precious first moments. The other mothers seemed to have a steady stream of visitors to their rooms, but there were very few people to come and see me. I started to get a sense of what my life as a mother would actually be like, the solitude of it. It wasn't quite what I had imagined.

•

I was in hospital for several days while Timmy got used to the world. He still wasn't feeding properly and the nurses were starting to pay closer attention. Newborns usually lose a few grams after they're born but then start to bulk up again, or at least they should. Timmy didn't lose much, but he wasn't gaining weight either, and he seemed to be asleep all the time. *He's almost too quiet*, I thought. They put him in the nursery one day so that I could sleep for a couple of hours and I couldn't believe what I saw when I went to collect him. He was very still, and sound asleep, in a room full of screaming babies.

The nurses kept a good eye on Timmy and the paediatrician told me not to panic, that there was nothing wrong. 'Babies develop at their own pace,' he said. 'Give it a few days, he'll be fine.'

Things certainly changed after a few days. The minute we stepped out of the hospital, three days after he was born, my little angel became a howler. My husband pulled the car around and opened the door, and I went to place Timmy in his car seat. Literally the second I pulled apart the Velcro tabs in his capsule, he opened his tiny mouth and began to wail. It wasn't a mewling baby sound either, but a sharp, piercing scream; he sounded terrified. It was absolutely bizarre. It was like they'd swapped my sleeping baby for the loudest one they could find, with a set of lungs like a police siren. *What on earth has upset him?* I wondered. Is he hungry? Tired? Was it the car engine? Or the sun? I had barely heard a peep out of him until that point; I had no idea what was wrong.

The ride to our home at Wynnum West took twenty minutes and Timmy screamed the whole way. 'Can't you go any faster?' I asked my husband, 'I need to get him out of the car.'

I assumed that when we arrived the baby would stop crying— that whatever was troubling him would stop and he would calm down. But no matter how much I tried to soothe him, he screamed. I tried to feed him and he cried. I changed him and he cried. I rocked him and he cried. I just couldn't settle him.

•

Once he'd started screaming, Timmy didn't stop. The second day was worse than the first and the third day was worse than the second. I know that all babies cry and all new mothers feel out of their depth. *Say goodbye to sleep*, they say. I had spoken to the mothers on my street and they had told me what to expect, but nothing had prepared me for the reality of it. It was relentless. I'd imagined that my baby would cry if he was hungry, and I would feed him, and he would stop, but Timmy never stopped. He cried around the clock and I could never figure out what was wrong. Maybe I'd secretly been pleased with myself when I was standing at the nursery window in the hospital, feeling smug about my quiet little baby, and this was karma. Timmy was catching up on all the tears he had missed in those first few days, when the nurses had kept him happy. I was his mother but I couldn't soothe him. *He doesn't want me*, I thought. *He doesn't like me.*

My baby didn't sleep, so I didn't sleep. I'd get twenty minutes here and there, but unbroken hours of sleep just did not happen. And the more tired and distressed he was, the more exhausted and anxious I became. Timmy hated his bassinet and his pram, so I couldn't put him down. I would pace and rock him for hours at night while Timmy's father tried to sleep in the next room. In the morning, I would make breakfast, bouncing Timmy in my arms while he cried. I still had a household to run, I had to cook and iron and do the laundry, but virtually everything was done one handed, now, with a screaming baby in my arms. The sound he made wasn't just a grizzle, either, there was an intensity to his crying that really scared me. I felt totally panicked and there was no one to turn to for help, not even Timmy's father. He wasn't the type of man to take the baby so I could eat my dinner or catch a couple of hours of sleep, and he was ropable if Timmy woke him in the middle of the night.

I had a terrible infection after I gave birth that ran halfway down my thigh, and the lack of sleep only made it worse. I inflamed it by pacing back and forth holding Timmy. With him always in my arms I couldn't sit down to a proper meal with a knife and fork, so I was surviving on biscuits or whatever I could quickly shove into my mouth. Timmy still wasn't feeding well, either. I was worried that he wasn't getting enough milk, but feeding seemed to distress him just as much as anything else.

It was very isolating. I didn't feel comfortable talking to the neighbours about what was happening—there were five women with new babies in our neighbourhood, but none of their children was behaving like mine. I found it easier to be on my own and avoid their questions, and not be the one who stood out. I would get anxious when Timmy cried too much and just want to get home, away from their pity and judgement. I hated it when friends came to visit too, because I felt so exposed. They all noticed how much Timmy cried and I was sure they thought it was my fault.

'Is he hungry?' they would ask.

'Has he got reflux?'

'Is he teething?'

'Is it time for him to sleep?' *It's never time for him to sleep*, I thought.

'You should put him down, you shouldn't carry him so much,' they told me. 'You're making a rod for your own back.' *You do it*, I thought to myself, *it only makes him scream louder.*

I was so tired and I already felt so guilty, and the people who were trying to be helpful were only making me feel worse. Every time somebody suggested something obvious, I felt as if there was an accusation there: *You don't know what you're doing. You're not trying hard enough.* I was exasperated and totally lost, and terrified that they were right.

My mother came over one day and I was on the verge of tears. I tried not to cry in front of her, but she knew something was wrong. 'What's the matter?' she asked. I told her I couldn't get Timmy to sleep. She took him in her arms and he settled down in about five minutes. I'd never felt so small in all my life. *I am a bad mother*, I thought. *It's my fault that he cries.*

I had no time to enjoy my son peacefully. I couldn't just sit and watch him sleep, because in the few moments he slept here or there, I was desperately trying to sleep myself or trying to stay on top of all the things that had to be done around the house. Those first few days at the hospital were the only chance I had to sit back and contemplate this lovely little creature who had come into my life; those days had just evaporated. The first weeks of Timmy's life were the most exhausting weeks of mine and there was no end in sight. Every morning I would stare into the bathroom mirror like a zombie, with dark circles under my eyes, wondering what was wrong with my baby. *This can't be normal*, I thought. *This will kill me.* I felt like I was on the verge of a nervous breakdown.

And yet, despite how battered I felt, I was madly in love with my baby. The upside to his nearly constant distress was that I *did* get to hold Timmy in my arms all the time, while other mothers put their babies down to sleep. *They're missing so much,* I thought. In the first few months of their lives, babies grow and change so much. It's a real miracle to witness it. I was absolutely spellbound by Timmy, and that fascination is what kept me going. There were days when I was so tired from walking with my baby in my arms that I honestly thought I couldn't take another step, but then I'd look down at him and he would take a little breath and I would find the energy to pick my foot up off the floor. The fact that Timmy needed me kept me going, too. I believed that he and I had a special bond. I was selfishly proud of the connection we had, even though I was falling apart. Despite the crying, despite how flattened I was, I still thought Timmy was perfect. He was perfect, so whatever he was going through must be my fault.

I remember so well the first time he smiled, not just because it was the milestone every mother looks for but also because to me it meant he was happy for a brief moment. He was looking right at me, and his little face lit up. To me, it meant he didn't hate me. He smiled and I thought, *He must like me, just a little bit.*

•

We had regular check-ups at the maternal and child health clinic and every time we visited, I told the nurses what was happening. They didn't think it was a problem.

'Babies cry. You'll manage,' they said, 'Just hang in there.'

By the time Timmy was six months old, I was nearly hysterical.

'He doesn't sleep,' I told the doctor desperately. 'He won't go down for more than half an hour.'

The doctor was concerned enough to suggest that we go to a sleep clinic. 'It will help you get into a pattern,' he told me. 'He needs to learn to soothe himself.'

The idea seemed ridiculous to me. Timmy was inconsolable and he would only get worse if I left him to cry. It's like he never ran out of steam. He was also my little baby; I couldn't walk away if he was distressed. But the main reason I didn't want to go was because I was ashamed. Motherhood was supposed to be natural and I couldn't do it. I thought if I went to a sleep clinic it was like admitting defeat, like telling the whole world that I had failed. I was also worried about Timmy's father. He didn't like anyone knowing our business and if I went to a sleep clinic, he would be angry. We'd just have to figure it out by ourselves.

•

People told me to be patient. They said it would get better as he got older, but the longer Timmy was in the world, the more things seemed to upset him. He seemed so scared and so distressed, so much of the time.

When Timmy was three months old, I tried to dress him in a little jumpsuit that a friend had knitted for him. It was powder blue, made of lovely soft wool, and he was finally big enough for it to fit him. It was such a beautiful little outfit. *He's going to look so cute in this*, I thought, *I'll have to take a photo*. But Timmy started kicking violently as I pulled the suit over his legs, and he screamed so loudly that I thought I must have stabbed him with the nappy pin. I ripped the clothes off him as fast as I could and checked the pin, but it was absolutely fine. *Maybe there's a bug in his clothes and he's been bitten?* I thought. There was nothing I could see.

While I checked him, Timmy had stopped crying. He went from howling to perfectly calm in a heartbeat, which seemed really odd. He'd been almost purple a second before. I started dressing him again, but the minute I got the jumpsuit on he started wailing, so again I undressed him and checked his nappy; I took the whole thing off this time. Once undressed, Timmy went quiet. When I started dressing him a third time, he erupted in tears and little agonised screams, like something was causing him pain. I was confused. I didn't know what was wrong with Timmy and I worried that he might have some internal issue, something I couldn't see. I chose a new outfit, dressed him and carried him away. It wasn't until much later that I realised it was his jumpsuit that had made him cry. It must have been the feel of the wool against his skin.

●

I began to notice other things that bothered Timmy, things I slowly came to recognise would drive him over the edge. From the day we took him home from the hospital, he hated being in the car. He would start screaming as soon as he heard the engine and he wouldn't stop as long as we were driving. He hated the Velcro strap that secured him in his car capsule; he was too young to hold himself up but I'd felt him jump in my arms as I pulled the Velcro tabs apart and a flood of tears would follow. Getting around in the car was such a huge ordeal that I avoided it as much as I could. I didn't leave the house unless I absolutely had to.

I couldn't avoid the weekly shopping, but the car seat was only the beginning of our problems there. For some reason, Timmy couldn't bear the sound of coins clinking together. I'd have him in my arms and he would seem okay, but the minute I opened my wallet to pay for the groceries I'd feel his little body tense up and he'd begin to scream. I thought at first that it was the sound of metal, but it didn't bother Timmy if I rattled around in the cutlery drawer—it was just the coins that drove him crazy. Ring-pull openings on cans of beer had a similar effect. Timmy's father drank a lot of beer and each time Timmy heard the pop and hiss of a can opening he would almost jump out of his skin. Once I'd figured out that it bothered him, I tried an experiment: I went down to the shed with Tim in my arms and had his father stand at the front of the house and open a can, some thirty metres away. I didn't even hear it but Timmy twitched with shock and immediately started crying, as though he was terrified. I couldn't believe it.

It took a while for me to make these connections because the things that set him off were so ordinary, so unnoticeable to me. But once I'd figured it out—if I could figure it out—there was an obvious pattern. The things that upset him upset him every time, like clockwork. It troubled me that these things never got any easier for him. I could understand if Timmy heard a new sound and he was startled, but each time was like the first, completely terrifying. He didn't adjust to the things that frightened him, which made me think it was more than just discomfort. Just like with the woollen jumpsuit, the way he screamed made me think he was in pain.

•

I worried constantly about my son. I cried all the time in that first year of his life, especially when I was alone in the house; motherhood was completely overwhelming to me and I was convinced it would never get any better. But at the same time, I had this determination about it. *Right, we've stuffed up today, there's nothing we can do about it. We'll just have to try again tomorrow.*

And Timmy did make progress, eventually. As time went on, I could lay Timmy on his bunny rug for five minutes and he would be calm. He stopped wailing every time I took him out of the bath and I managed to get him into the pram, although we couldn't really go anywhere—he still screamed if we tried to leave the house. After twelve months, he was sleeping an hour at a time and he spent only half of the day in screaming tears, but I took a little bit of strength from his progress. Half the day was better than a whole day. I assumed he would continue to get better.

The doctors were happy because Timmy's growth milestones were textbook: he smiled when he was supposed to, sat up when he was supposed to and walked when he was supposed to, although he skipped the crawling stage. He went from sitting up to taking off, with his little hand wrapped around my thumb, and he'd walk for hours with me bent over beside him.

He was a beautiful little child and I had started to find things he liked in the world. He loved water and I knew he liked to play in mud, although he never wanted to play with me. He wouldn't hand me a spade and ask me to dig, he would sit and focus on what he was doing. But if I started to step away, Timmy stepped with me. It was very empowering for me, a sign that my son wanted me close. He didn't play with me or answer me when I called, but he always seemed to know that I was there.

Timmy would put his arm around my neck sometimes or stand beside me and lean against my leg, and he was always giving me kisses and patting my arm. He had such lovely eyes, but they looked sad to me. I would stare into Timmy's eyes, searching for a clue about what lay behind them. I was always wondering how to make him happy.

2

Sam

When Timmy was fifteen months old, my doctor sent me to see a psychologist. I was so worn out by then, it was written all over my face. I kept asking for help with my son but instead they talked about prescribing me anti-depressants. I told the doctor I wasn't depressed, that I loved my baby and I was happy; I told him I was just tired, but he disagreed. I didn't take the drugs. There wasn't the same range of anti-depressants available in the 1980s as there is today and they were a lot less subtle back then in terms of how they worked on you. *The last thing I need is to be zonked out when I can already barely function*, I thought.

Another doctor who went to the same church as my parents told me I should have a hysterectomy to avoid having any more children.

'Some people just aren't cut out to be mothers,' he said.

His words cut straight through me, I just couldn't believe it. More than anything else I wanted another child. I loved my little baby so much—I loved being a mother so much—that I was thinking about getting pregnant again. It was the strangest thing; I couldn't explain it. After Timmy, you'd think I would never want to hear a baby cry again, that I didn't have an ounce of energy left to give to another child, but it was just the opposite. The one thing I was completely sure about was that becoming a mother was the greatest thing I'd ever done. I had never felt so wanted or needed and I had never felt so much love for another person. I knew I had more love to give.

As it turned out, though I didn't know it, I was already pregnant with my second son. It wasn't until I was four months along that I even realised what was happening. I was so exhausted from the lack of sleep and that general sick feeling that I missed all the signs. But when I found out, I was over the moon. I worried that the new baby might have the same issues as Timmy, but I hoped that it wouldn't. And if not, if it was hard, at least I knew I could survive. That magical rush of love would get me through.

We returned to the obstetrician who had looked after us when Timmy was born. He was a lovely man from South Africa, with a singsong voice and a very gentle nature. He congratulated me on the pregnancy but warned me it wouldn't be easy; the ultrasound revealed that I had a condition called placenta praevia, which was dangerous for me as well as the baby. In the early stages of pregnancy when the placenta forms, it attaches itself to the wall of the uterus. Placenta praevia means it attaches in a bad position, close to the opening of the cervix. The condition affects less than one per cent of women, causing bleeding throughout the pregnancy, but it has different degrees of seriousness. I was a grade four, the worst, which meant the placenta had formed directly over the cervix; as the baby grew, it would push the placenta out. Because the placenta is like a major artery, with all the blood in my body passing through it in order to nourish the baby, it meant I could bleed to death.

It was awful news but the doctor told me not to worry. He was a very reassuring man and he said there was a very good chance that the placenta would move before the birth, and he would be watching me closely until that time. I was grateful for the comfort.

The baby didn't move around as much as it should have and I worried that I was going to lose it; so many women seemed to have miscarriages. It was actually far more serious than that. At twenty-eight weeks I started to bleed and my husband took me to hospital. Luckily the doctor was able to control the bleed very quickly. It was a close call, he said. I would have to stay in hospital under observation to ensure that we made it to at least thirty-two weeks, when the doctors could perform a caesarean, giving the baby the best chance of survival—if they waited any longer, my life and the baby's life would be in danger.

I didn't want to stay in hospital. Timmy was twenty-two months old and he relied on me for everything. I was incredibly distraught by the separation and he didn't fare much better.

When his father brought him to visit, Timmy was beside himself. He screamed and cried, but I couldn't settle him—he didn't want anything to do with me. I fell apart when it was time for him to leave. The nurses had to sedate me because they were worried I'd trigger more bleeding. I cried hysterically, half out of my wits. I was terrified that the separation would traumatise Timmy and only make him go backwards; that we would lose everything we had gained. I was also worried about how his father would cope, when he didn't understand Timmy's needs. I was gripped by the fear of losing the new baby, but I wanted to go home. Despite being told so seriously and so sternly of the risks, I didn't acknowledge how dangerous the situation was. Sheer bravado made me think that the worst-case scenario would not happen to me. I begged the doctor to let me go home and against his better judgement, he agreed.

There was a long list of instructions. If I was to go home, I had to stay in bed. We had to ring the specialist every day and there were medications for me to take. Someone had to be with me, day and night; I was never to be left alone. If I went to the bathroom, I had to take a bell with me, leave the door unlocked and have someone sitting right outside in case something happened. The ambulance services were alerted and placed on call; if the bleeding started, I had to get to the hospital as quickly as possible. Every second counted; the difference between life and death.

I could see the concern in the doctor's face, but I was happy to be going home. I just wanted to be with Timmy.

•

Timmy's father had taken the warnings seriously and called friends and family in to help. If he had been a bit absent after Timmy was born, he made an effort to look after me when I got back from the hospital. He also did his best to take care of Timmy. I was happier at home. Even if I was bedridden, I knew my son would be better off with me close by. He spent his time sitting next to me on the bed or playing on the floor by my bed and he was much more settled.

I lasted a few days at home, following the doctor's instructions religiously. The first of April came and went and I was glad to get past April Fool's Day without feeling a twinge. By 3 April, I was feeling much more confident that everything would be fine. *We'll get to the thirty-two-week mark without a hitch*, I thought.

That night, my husband and I sat eating our dinner alongside Timmy, talking civilly about nothing in particular. Then suddenly, without warning, I ruptured. There was no pain, no twinge, not a feeling, no forewarning. It was like someone had turned on a tap and the blood gushed from my body. I felt the dampness and looked down in shock. There was so much and it was flowing so fast.

'If you start bleeding, every second counts,' the doctor had said. I had twenty minutes to get to the hospital before all the blood drained from my body. Seeing it pouring out of me, I knew he hadn't been exaggerating.

My blood seeped out across the floor as we waited for the ambulance to arrive. My husband was frantic and Timmy was hysterical, terrified of the pooling red liquid, frightened to hear his father begging and pleading on the phone. There was nothing we could do to stop it; each towel my husband brought me was soaked through within a minute. I sat with my head on the kitchen table, too weak to lift it. I could feel the life slipping out of me. I felt hopeless and certain that it was already too late.

I wasn't afraid of dying, it seemed inevitable and as if it was my time, but I was desperately sad that I would not be with Timmy to protect him as he grew up. And I was angry at myself for putting my unborn baby's life at risk. How could I have been so selfish and stupid? I prayed and prayed and prayed that the baby could be saved.

•

We knew that I had very little chance of making it; we had been told many times that most women don't survive that kind of condition unless they are in a hospital with access to immediate medical attention. We lived thirty minutes away from the hospital. When the ambulance arrived, sirens wailing and lights flashing, I was rushed inside it while my husband stood on our front lawn with Timmy in his arms. I caught a glimpse of my son as they closed the doors and I was convinced that would be the last time I would ever see him. My heart broke. I loved Timmy so much more than I ever thought possible.

I thought I would die in the back of that ambulance, without anyone I knew or loved beside me. The paramedic next to me was very kind but he was focused on saving my life. I could see that he was worried. He kept saying 'oh no' and urging the driver to go faster. There was a team waiting for us at the hospital and they leapt into action when we arrived; I wasn't even out of the ambulance and they were putting drips and needles in my arms. Even in my stupor, I could hear the urgency in their voices. I was conscious but I was so weak that I couldn't fight and I couldn't do anything to help. My life was in their hands.

They rushed me to the emergency room and someone yelled, 'More blood! For god's sake, get more blood!' Then the surgeon on duty came into the room. He introduced himself to me. He told me there were paediatricians and lots of specialists waiting to take the baby when the caesarean was performed. It was more than ten weeks early and they were concerned it would not survive such a traumatic birth. They would do everything they could.

'I'm going to take care of you,' the surgeon said gently. He held my hand. I gathered enough strength to speak. 'Just save the baby,' I told him. 'Let me go if you have to, but save the baby, please.'

•

The next thing I knew I could see a white light. I didn't just see it, I was hurtling towards it at a speed that should have torn the flesh right off my bones. But I was perfectly calm and perfectly safe. I was in darkness, moving towards the light, which seemed to be at the end of a tunnel, this brilliant shining circle.

All of a sudden everything stopped. The motion stopped and I heard a voice, a deep male voice of authority. 'What have you done?' it said.

I was scared to respond. I didn't know what to say. I didn't know what the right answer was. I wanted to be with my baby, and with Timmy, and I was so disappointed with how my life had ended. *What have I done?* I thought. *I wasted my life.*

The next thing I knew, I was floating above the operating table, watching doctors scramble over me with bags of blood and instruments. I felt nothing about it, nothing at all. Then everything went black.

•

I woke up in the intensive care unit, with a nurse beside me checking all the monitors and tubes that were attached to my body. I felt so dreadfully ill and weak, the worst I had ever felt in my life. And there was pain; I couldn't move. I couldn't make a sound to get her attention, to find out what had happened. Finally, she glanced over and saw I was awake. She must have seen the desperation in my face. She knew what I wanted to hear.

'The baby is all right,' she said. 'You have a little boy.'

I was too weak to speak but I cried tears of joy. They had taken a Polaroid photo of my son for me and she held it up for me to see. He was in a humidicrib in the neonatal care unit, hooked up to a lot of machines. It was heartbreaking to think of him all alone up there. The nurses were doing a great job, I was sure, but he needed someone to love him. I had to get better as fast as possible so I could meet my son.

•

Sam was born just over ten weeks early. He was so tiny, only 1873 grams—four pounds, two ounces—and he struggled to breathe on his own. Timmy had been so healthy and strong when he was born, it was terrifying to know that Sam might not make it. I didn't think ahead, I just prayed that Sam got through each day. His heel was black and bruised from all the tests they gave him; he didn't have enough flesh on his arms for a needle to be inserted. There were tubes all over his body and heart monitor sensors plastered to his chest and his back. To try to prevent damage to his sight, the doctors had covered his eyes. To keep him warm, his crib was sealed in a plastic wrap. The feeding tubes caused hernias the size of golf balls and he had to have surgery to have them removed.

Yet underneath the tubes and wires, I saw a perfect little boy. Just like with Timmy, I was fascinated by him. It broke my heart that I couldn't hold him, but Sam's eyes fluttered the first time he heard my voice and I knew that he knew me. I couldn't hold him until he was thirteen days old. It was my birthday that day, when I first held Sam in my arms, and it was the greatest gift I could have received.

Sam was in the special care nursery of Brisbane's Mater Hospital for six weeks. I was discharged after a week and went back to visit him every day with Timmy and his father in tow, at least twice a day. I was very weak, barely recovered, and it was devastating to see Sam in his humidicrib, but in a way I felt lucky. I saw some traumatic things in the neonatal ward—babies born at six months who were severely disabled or blind, who weighed less than a pound, fragile things that wouldn't survive. Sam at least had a chance.

Timmy had fallen to pieces while I was in hospital, far worse than the first time. He didn't want to have anything to do with me and he was really unsettled. The nurses and doctors in the special care unit often asked me about his behaviour. Timmy was always trying to escape from the hospital room and he cried constantly. He did like the baby, though. When Timmy looked at his brother there was wonder in his eyes. Nam, for Sam, was one of the only words he said.

•

By the time we brought him home to Wynnum West, Sam weighed nearly five pounds and he was doing well. The doctors said he could have problems, that he could be developmentally delayed or have issues with his vision or hearing, but I didn't worry about those things at the time; it was enough that he was alive.

I was incredibly weak after everything I'd been through. My doctor told me they'd 'lost me' on the operating table, which I already knew, of course. I didn't talk to anyone about it, but the near-death experience I'd had was still weighing on my mind.

I had a second chance to live a good life and I didn't want to waste it. I felt like the world had changed in some way. It had been a spiritual experience that left me feeling more content and exalted than I had ever been in my whole life, and those words, 'What have you done?' remained with me. I did not consider that it would be my mission to go out in the world and do something significant, I just felt it meant I had to make the most of every day with my boys. Life was precious.

If I had a quiet moment, I'd sit in the backyard with Timmy and Sam, and stare up at the trees. My body was battered and I had two children now demanding my attention, but in those moments I felt a real sense of peace and happiness.

3

Autism

My babies were beautiful. Timmy looked like a baby from a TV commercial; people often commented how gorgeous he was. He had sturdy little legs, like thick, juicy legs of lamb, but Sam wasn't so plump. There was no fat on him at all, in fact. He didn't have a bottom! Sam had sandy-coloured hair and his face was longer than Timmy's, and he was so tiny and fragile and feeble, but he was just as perfect.

I was so happy with my new family. We didn't have the usual problems that you get with a toddler when there's a new baby in the house—Timmy loved the baby and he accepted that Sam had to come first sometimes. Whatever upset my eldest son, Sam was never to blame. But unfortunately, as Timmy grew, his problems seemed to grow with him.

Timmy relied on things happening in a particular way, at a particular time. He needed the TV to be on all day, on Channel 7, whether or not he was watching it. In the afternoon, I had to switch over to Channel 9 for *The Bugs Bunny Show*, which was his favourite program. But it took me forever to understand that that was what he wanted. Other toddlers might cry and point at the television, or say the words 'Bugs Bunny' to give you a clue. Timmy would stand in the middle of the lounge room, screaming, while I frantically tried to figure out what had suddenly gone wrong.

The TV helped Timmy to make sense of the day, I think. *Thomas the Tank Engine* was on after breakfast. When a particular talk show came on, it was time for lunch. When the news came on, we had dinner. Timmy knew when Bugs Bunny was supposed to be on, and if it wasn't he couldn't understand why. It threw his whole world out of order. But it's not like he could explain it to me and it's not like I could console him. I couldn't reassure him and I couldn't comfort him; he didn't seem to remember anything I told him about what was going on.

I couldn't figure out a pattern to Timmy's behaviour because there were so many things that seemed to set him off. And sometimes, even when I did understand why he was upset, I couldn't fix it. Shoes were a big problem, for example. There was a successful public awareness campaign about AIDS in the early nineties, which showed a grim reaper with a bowling ball, knocking people down like they were bowling pins. *You never know when AIDS is going to strike!* We were terrified of stray needles hiding in the grass at the park so I couldn't let Timmy wander around barefoot. Unfortunately, he hated wearing shoes. I'd have to hold him down to get them on and he would scream like I was burning him, every time I tried. It made us both miserable.

Even without the shoes, Timmy was rarely happy to leave the house. He would cry from the moment we left until we got back again, as though he was terrified of the outside world. As he got older, his distress was even more pronounced—specific things *out there* would make him anxious. I wasn't allowed to put Sam down. If I tried, Timmy would push him back into my arms. If I tried to sit down, Timmy would tug at my hand until I stood up again. I couldn't put my bag down, because it meant we were going to stay somewhere instead of going home. If we were at the doctor's or some other appointment, sitting in a strange room, Timmy couldn't stand having the door closed; he would reach for doorknobs and twist at them frantically, trying to get out, as if he was trapped. He would wail hysterically. If I ignored him, it would only escalate.

I hated going out because it was such an ordeal, so I tried to spend as much time at home as possible. It didn't solve our problems. As much as Timmy didn't want to go out, he couldn't bear it when people came over. He didn't like visitors. He would cry and run around in a panic when someone arrived, saying 'Bye, bye, bye, bye,' and urging them to leave, pushing them towards the door. Other times, when people arrived, he would fall asleep as though he'd been stunned. He would start screaming and then drop to the floor, curl up and pass out, then wake up the minute I was waving our guest off. It was absolutely bizarre.

I was torn between needing help and wanting to hide what we were going through. As Timmy grew, there were just so many things that didn't seem right, like the fact that Timmy wasn't interested in other little kids. There were small children up and down our street but Timmy didn't interact with them, he always played by himself. He couldn't ride a tricycle or a bike and he didn't muck around with toys the way that other children did. He was only interested in specific things and it was hopeless to try to draw his attention away, and there was a strange kind of order about everything he did. I knew the rules existed, but only Timmy understood them.

At nearly three, Timmy still wasn't toilet-trained. He still didn't sleep through the night, he didn't speak, and feeding him was a nightmare. He had started on solids quite early because he'd had all sorts of tummy trouble as a newborn and was forever vomiting or having diarrhoea—I was concerned that he was malnourished. By two and a half, his entire diet was made up of chocolate, bread and chicken. If I tried to get anything else into him—vegetables or pasta or a little bit of fruit—he'd scream the house down. It wasn't just that Timmy was an unhealthy eater or that I spoiled him, it's that other food seemed to frighten or distress him. He wouldn't go anywhere near lollies, for example. He wasn't interested in juice, ice-cream or milk. It wasn't just the texture of things that bothered him, but often the colour. You could see the sheer repulsion on his face. He was especially horrified by red food for some reason, and I wondered if it was all the blood he'd seen the night that Sam was born.

From the moment I had brought Sam home from hospital he had flourished, putting on weight and reaching all his milestones. After the fright of nearly losing him I was extra cautious and watchful with Sam, and I worried about him a lot in the first few months, but there was no need. By the time he was one year old he had caught up to other babies his age and never looked back. He babbled and chuckled away, and was mostly a happy and content little fellow. He was also very affectionate. I liked having sons; I thought that boys were very cuddly.

The biggest issue for Timmy, as far as I could tell, was that he didn't speak. There was a little girl named Sarah who lived next door and she'd started babbling when she was very young. She was only six weeks older than Timmy but she was already like a little encyclopaedia, rattling off whole sentences. 'Happy Birthday, Judy,' she'd say politely, 'I hope you have a nice day.'

Meanwhile, Timmy had barely uttered a word. He said 'Nam' for Sam and 'Ba' for a drink. He made distressed sounds, but I couldn't understand what they were supposed to represent. I was desperate to understand him. I knew everything would get better when Timmy could talk, when I didn't have to play detective to figure out what he needed. How much easier would it be if he'd just open up his mouth and *tell* me?

We had a beautiful red cattle dog called Razor Blade Sharp and Timmy would always laugh as he trotted past. *What's so funny?* I'd think, but how could I tell? Why was Timmy happy to sit and play in the bath one day and then the next day start screaming and refuse to get in? Why did he eat a whole plate of roast lamb one day then refuse to ever touch it again? And every day, over and over, why was he so upset? I'd open the fridge and offer him things, open every cupboard door. I'd hold up Weet-Bix, Rice Bubbles, biscuits, chips, but he couldn't tell me yes or no, his screaming just got worse. I'd stand in front of the taps—*do you want water?* He gave me nothing. He didn't point, he didn't try to act out what he wanted or give me a sign; he couldn't tell me if it was a noise that was driving him crazy. I never knew if he had a pain or if he felt sick. I had no idea and I felt so hopeless as I watched how desperate Timmy would become.

It was so mystifying, so exasperating. I could see that Timmy wasn't doing it to hurt me or to defy me; he had reasons for his behaviour that he knew but nobody else did and no matter how hard he tried to step outside of that behaviour, he just couldn't. It was so awful to watch. No toddler's life should be that complicated or frustrating. If he wanted a packet of chips he should've been able to say it: 'Chips!' It made me so sad to see him struggle with everything he needed, every single day.

The upside was that I felt very close to him sometimes. In a way, I was quite proud of the fact that I was the only person in the world who *could*, sometimes, figure out what Timmy wanted, because I was the only person who knew him well enough to see the patterns in his behaviour. I was proud that I could occasionally make him happy, when he seemed so inconsolable. But I was exhausted by all the time I spent getting it wrong.

•

People saw that Timmy was a handful but I think they assumed that he was just a bad kid or that I was a bad mother. I knew he was good so I could only blame myself. What else could it possibly be? I was in and out of our local GP clinic, begging for answers.

'He's not talking,' I told the doctors, but they said it wasn't unusual; I should wait until he's three. 'I think there's something wrong with his gut,' I said, but they tested and found nothing. 'I wonder if there is something wrong with his sight, he doesn't seem to see the things I point out to him,' I insisted. The doctors found nothing. 'He doesn't sleep,' I cried, but a lot of babies don't sleep and perhaps, they suggested, I needed counselling.

I think the receptionists would groan every time I turned up. I was sure they were thinking, *Here comes that lousy mother with the crying kid.* Timmy was always hugely distressed and he always wanted to leave. I think the doctors thought I was crazy, too, wondering what I would complain about this time, what solution I wanted for a problem I couldn't define. I asked the doctors for help and they told me everything was normal, I just had to learn to cope. I wasn't coping, but I didn't know where else to turn.

It wasn't until I took Sam for his first round of vaccinations that a doctor suggested there might be something seriously wrong.

We went to our local clinic for the shots but our regular doctor wasn't available so we saw an older GP who wasn't familiar to me. He happened to see Timmy at his very worst. My shoelace had come undone and so had Timmy's, which always made him hysterical. I had to put my bag down to hold Sam so the doctor could give him his needle. The door was closed and Timmy was running to the door to open it, back to me, bending down to lift up the shoelaces, picking up the bag, pushing at the baby and pushing at me, sobbing and screaming uncontrollably the whole time. I tried to comfort him and I couldn't, then Sam got upset and Timmy's wailing increased. It was one of the most traumatic, difficult days I had ever had with Timmy; it must have looked like madness. The doctor tried to help, but it only made things worse.

'How often does this happen?' he asked me.

I was close to tears. 'Every day,' I told him. 'I don't know why.'

The doctor looked at me with genuine concern. 'You can't go on like this,' he said. 'I've never seen anything like it. This child will kill you.'

He sat down immediately and wrote Timmy a referral to a paediatrician. He wasn't blaming me and he knew where to go for help; he believed there was something we could do. I felt so incredibly relieved that he understood what I was going through. I was also relieved to get out of his office, one son tucked under each arm. The sooner I got the boys home, the sooner I got Timmy's shoes off and switched on the TV, the sooner he would settle down. It had been a very hard day.

The paediatrician we saw was a lovely man, gentle and caring. He had a Thomas the Tank Engine toy on his desk and Timmy was happy to go and stand beside the doctor and play with it. Timmy handed the train to the older man and smiled when the doctor spoke to him in Thomas's voice, 'Hello, Timmy!'

I was glad that the paediatrician was seeing the Timmy I knew, a beautiful child with a beautiful smile. Timmy was just like any other little boy. He just didn't speak.

After chatting to Timmy for a while and watching him play, the doctor asked me about the problems we had, listening very carefully. When I finished, he ran through some of the things that can affect a child's behaviour. He mentioned the word 'autism' but dismissed the idea just as fast as he brought it up. 'I don't think that's a possibility,' he said. 'Timmy seems to understand what I say and he's interacting with me. He seems happy enough.'

I had seen a current affairs program about a young man with autism and it stayed with me, although I really didn't understand the condition. Before that program, I had never even heard the word. The boy's mother was crying with such heartache, while her son threw himself about on the lawn outside. He made anxious, incomprehensible noises and he seemed to be in pain, grabbing at his head and then banging it on the ground. Their house had been destroyed by his outbursts. The mother had been hurt and her marriage had been affected, but there was nowhere to go for help. It was such an unusual condition that no one knew what to do.

I remembered that story vividly, though I wasn't sure why. I think I wondered how I would possibly cope if that ever happened to me. When the paediatrician said autism, I felt a pang of fear, but then relief. It wasn't autism, he had said, just a developmental delay. Timmy was a late bloomer; it happened sometimes. The doctor recommended that we wait until Timmy was three, see if his speech had developed, then perhaps go and see another specialist.

'It will be fine,' he said kindly.

I left that appointment happy and reassured. But as the months went by it became clear to me that the speech wouldn't magically arrive by Timmy's third birthday.

•

I knew there was an intelligent little child in there. From the time he was three months old Timmy loved books. He loved the pictures. He would sit and stare at a page for hours, wrapped up in what he saw. He just couldn't or wouldn't tell me what he was looking at. *Is it the bunny?* I'd think. *Is it the fire engine?* I would ask him questions, but he wouldn't respond, not even with a grunt or a look. He didn't point at things or try to share things with me. He didn't try to involve me at all, he was happy just to sit and stare at the pages.

I had Timmy's hearing tested because I wondered if he was deaf or hearing impaired. He didn't follow my voice or my gestures. He wouldn't respond when I called his name. I was looking for an explanation and hearing problems seemed to make sense, but we tested him and it revealed nothing; Timmy's hearing was perfect. He just seemed to exist in his own little world.

I looked for things that Timmy would be interested in and repeated their names as much as I could. 'Bird,' I'd tell him. 'Sky.' I knew he loved Bugs Bunny so I bought him books about Bugs Bunny, hoping that would trigger some communication, but there was nothing. I tried refusing to give him something until he said 'please'. I tried to get him to ask for things instead of standing in the middle of the room wailing his lungs out. I spoke to him in this endless stream, hoping he'd catch on. I never shut up; it must have driven him nuts. It certainly didn't work. He didn't speak. I didn't know what he was thinking. I didn't know what he was feeling. I had no idea what was going on inside that little head and it drove me absolutely crazy.

Every now and then I had a glimmer of hope. There was a mobile in Timmy's room with sea creatures hanging off it and he would reach out for the right one when you asked him to. 'Where's the octopus, Timmy? And where's the fish?'

There were times he seemed to know exactly what was going on around him and what I was saying. 'We're going for a swim, Timmy,' I'd tell him, and he'd go and grab a towel. If his father was working on the car, he could hand him a screwdriver. I could see that he was learning things and that things were getting through, but there was nothing coming back. It went in and got stuck there, like a one-way conversation.

I assumed Timmy was shy. I assumed it would take longer for him to speak than it did for most children; that he needed encouragement and a gentle, guiding hand. But I thought he would get there. I believed that he would. There were tiny advances in his behaviour and communication but it wasn't moving fast enough. I thought a specialist would help us to help him catch up.

We had to wait six weeks for an appointment with the specialist but I managed to book it in for 10 May 1991—the day after Timmy's third birthday. *The sooner we see him, the sooner we can work it out*, I thought. I was keen to get the ball rolling and finally get some answers. I wasn't nervous at all, in fact I felt relieved to finally be getting the help that I had been searching for from the very beginning.

Tim's birthday was lovely. He couldn't tell me what present he wanted but every time we went to a toy shop he would sit in front of a toy police motorcycle until it was time to leave. It had flashing lights, a siren, and handlebars that you could steer as you pushed it around. Timmy was over the moon when he unwrapped it. We didn't have a party because we had tried it the previous year and it only distressed him. I made him a chocolate cake and played Bugs Bunny tapes on the video recorder all day, and promised myself I wouldn't try to get him to do anything that upset him. It really made him happy.

The next day, we went to a clinic that specialised in speech therapy and developmental delays. Our appointment was with a child psychologist recommended by our doctor; he was supposedly the best in town. Things were different then—you didn't shop around for doctors the way you do now. Specialists were like gods, all-knowing and powerful. You didn't question their experience or their motives; you listened carefully and did whatever they told you to do.

It was a cold morning and we were the first people to arrive: my husband, Sam, Timmy and me. The centre was in an old house, surrounded by jacaranda trees, with a central reception room and doors running off either side. It wasn't really designed for children, but Timmy was happy enough to be there. He sat quietly while we waited and played with some of his birthday toys. We seemed to be waiting a while.

A man passed through the room several times, stopping briefly to check his reflection in the mirror as he did. He had thick hair and a big barrel chest, and wore a very smart shirt and tailored pants. He was the psychologist, but I mistook him for a clerk. He looked awfully young.

We were there nearly half an hour before he saw us, which made me very anxious. Waiting with Timmy was always precarious—I never knew when he would go from calm to upset, so the longer we dragged things out the more likely it was that he would explode.

If I was nervous about the long wait, things didn't improve when the young psychologist finally ushered us into his office. The conversation didn't start well. I smiled warmly and greeted him, made a comment about the weather, but it was frostier in his office than it was outside. He was straight down to business; I don't think he actually said 'hello'.

'What brings you here today?' he asked.

I was a bit shaken by his tone but I answered him directly, 'My son Timmy isn't developing speech.'

The psychologist nodded and asked if I had any other concerns.

I had been to see so many doctors before that moment but I was always too embarrassed to be completely honest with them about Timmy's behaviour. *This man is the expert*, I thought to myself, *it's now or never*. I told him Timmy didn't sleep through the night. I told him Timmy didn't eat much. I told him about the shoes and the sound of the vacuum cleaner, and what happened when visitors came around. I told him about the television and the distress around other children. I told him Timmy cried all the time and I didn't know why.

When I had reeled off about half-a-dozen things, the psychologist took some sheets of paper from his desk and began asking me a series of very specific questions.

'Does the child respond to the mother's voice?'

'Does the child respond to their own name?'

'Does the child repeat motions like rocking or spinning?'

I had a sinking feeling as he ran through the list, a feeling of shame. I didn't know half the things he was asking were a problem. Did that mean I had failed somehow? Timmy did spin around in the backyard and he never got giddy; it had always fascinated me. He often wanted me to spin him around but I thought it was a game. It made him happy.

'Does the child gesture or point to communicate?'

'Does the child avoid making eye contact?'

I don't know, I thought miserably. I honestly didn't know if Timmy avoided eye contact—if he did, I hadn't noticed. What kind of mother doesn't notice a thing like that?

'Does the child harm himself?'

'Does the child harm others?'

'Is the child distressed by particular noises?'

'Is the child upset by changes to their environment?'

I could feel myself shrinking in my chair, getting smaller and smaller as the psychologist went on. I knew that I had said 'yes' too many times. I was ticking the wrong boxes. My child should call me 'Mum' when he spoke to me; he should come and ask for things; he should look me in the eyes. I knew it wasn't right that he wasn't interested in other children and certain sounds made him scream in fright. I had just never looked at these things side by side before, a whole long list of problems. The questionnaire was pages long and by the end I was overcome with fear. 'Stop, please!' I wanted to say. 'Isn't it obvious by now?'

I knew something terrible was coming.

The way the psychologist read the questions, so clinical and dispassionate, made me sick to my stomach. He hadn't explained why he was asking these questions. He didn't look up at us as he went through the list. He didn't use Timmy's name once, he just referred to him as 'the child'. I felt my anger rising the longer he went on. *How dare you treat us like this*, I thought. *Who do you think you are?* His tone was utterly clinical; he didn't have one ounce of kindness in him. *Look at Timmy*, I silently urged him, but the psychologist kept his head down towards the page.

He didn't see Timmy, just a diagnosis. He was trying to shove my perfect son into an ugly, broken box.

Timmy sat with Sam at my feet, as calm as he had ever been. I reached down and touched his lovely blond hair and fought back the urge to cry. *You don't deserve this*, I thought. *This is wrong. We shouldn't be here. This is all wrong.* I hoped that Timmy wasn't listening. I didn't want him to hear it, all the negative things stacking up against him. I wanted to cover Timmy's ears and block out the psychologist's voice. I wanted to shove all the questions he'd asked right back down his throat.

When he finished the questionnaire, the psychologist stood up and walked to the front of his desk and looked directly at Timmy for the very first time.

'Timothy,' he said, and then paused. 'Timothy,' he repeated.

There was no response.

'He's never been called Timothy in his life,' I said. 'Can you call him Timmy?'

The psychologist seemed to ignore me. He said, 'Timothy, can you hop?'

Timmy didn't hear him, didn't look up; didn't speak.

Why didn't I teach him to hop? I thought, feeling despondent. He could kick and splash in the swimming pool, he could jump on a trampoline, he could climb a tree house, he could run, but I hadn't taught him to hop, it just hadn't occurred to me. I knew Timmy couldn't do it and it was the nail in his coffin. He was going to fail the whole test because I had let him down.

The psychologist walked back to his chair and began making

notes. As he did, Timmy wandered to his desk, rested his little arms on the ledge and peered over to watch the man write. *Look*, I thought, *look at him! He's paying attention now, isn't that a good sign?* But it was too little too late, and the psychologist wasn't interested. It was hugely significant for me but it meant nothing to him.

When the psychologist put his pen down, he looked up at us and said, 'Timothy has autism.'

Timothy has autism.

The psychologist had paused, like he was waiting for a reaction, but we stayed silent. 'If he doesn't have speech now, he won't develop it,' he said. 'Whatever words he has now, he will probably lose.'

The psychologist didn't offer his condolences or try to soften the blow, and he didn't stop to ask if we had questions. He didn't explain what autism was but he said that there was no cure. There was something wrong with Timmy's brain, he said. Timmy couldn't learn and he would never go to school. Timmy wouldn't be able to take care of himself because he couldn't learn basic life skills.

I had just wanted some help getting Timmy to talk; I thought he might need some speech therapy. It was like I'd gone to see a doctor with a sore thumb and he'd amputated my arm. The pain was unbearable. It didn't make sense. 'He's three years old!' I wanted to scream. 'How can you know?'

I think I was in shock. We didn't speak, so the psychologist continued. Everything in Timmy's life was the way it was because of autism, he explained. That's the way it was, and it wouldn't get any better. He said that Timmy couldn't connect with people, so he wouldn't ever make friends. He could only use people as a tool to fulfil his own needs and desires. He would be a burden for the rest of his life and he would end up in an institution. He told me I should put my son away and forget about him. There was no hope.

'Autistic children cannot love.'

I wasn't naive enough to think that my children would like me—kids have their own way of seeing the world. But I believed in that bond, that unshakeable love between mother and child. I had never loved anyone as much as I loved my children. That love was the only thing I had. It was the only thing I wanted. Yet, with a few words, the doctor had ripped it away. It was like a knife in my heart, it hurt so much. *Maybe Timmy hates me*, I thought. *Maybe that's why he cries.*

•

There was no plan. The psychologist told us that the public waiting lists for speech therapy were too long and it wouldn't do any good anyway. The underlying message was that it was a waste of public resources. 'It won't make a difference,' he said.

Timmy's father told him we'd pay for private therapy and insisted on a referral, so the psychologist made some recommend-ations. He was trying to appease us, but he was also closing the door. He would have nothing further to do with my son because my three-year-old son was a hopeless cause.

'Maybe he just has a little bit of autism?' I said desperately.

'Autism is autism,' the psychologist replied. 'You don't have little bits, you have autism.'

I was so angry. I thought he was deliberately trying to hurt my family. It was a perfect storm, in retrospect. The psychologist had a terrible bedside manner and he was completely insensitive. He said things to me that no medical professional should say, at least not in the way he said them. It was too soon for a diagnosis and he was too blunt in his delivery. And some of the things he told me were flat out wrong, not to mention heartless.

I was determined not to cry in that office but the minute I got to the front steps I was hysterical. I sobbed uncontrollably with Timmy in my arms; I couldn't catch my breath. I didn't break my stride, but it all came flooding out—the devastation and heartbreak, the absolute despair. It was like Timmy had died, though he was still right there with me. Everything I had dreamed for him was gone.

I wanted my son to live without guilt or shame or fear. I wanted him to be free, to have all the opportunities that I never had. I wanted him to be safe and confident. I wanted him to be strong. I thought Timmy's life would be happy and full of great experiences. I thought we'd sit together when he was older, and argue about politics or art or sport. I thought he'd love me. I thought he'd fall in love one day and have a child of his own. It was all gone.

4

Therapy

They diagnose autism as early as eighteen months now. There's a test. The general wisdom is that earlier intervention is essential to help a child realise its full potential.

In the early nineties, when Tim was diagnosed, the presentation of autism was about 1 in 10,000. Today they say it's roughly 1 in 70, depending on your definition. To me, it sounds like everyone is going to develop autism by Christmas, which seems unlikely. But anyway, it's common now. It was rare back then, and a mystery to me.

I spent a day on the couch feeling sorry for myself, totally overwhelmed by what had happened. Overnight, the life I had dreamed for Timmy had disappeared and there was an unknown, frightening future ahead. Timmy would never grow into the kind of person I hoped he could be, who could enjoy all the wonderful things the world had to offer. He was never going to be the son I thought I would have. I would never be able to communicate or connect with him, and his life would be one of isolation and misery. My body ached like I had been bashed from head to toe. My heart was so empty, I couldn't even cry.

Somehow the boys seemed to sense that I was beaten; they didn't make one demand that day. Their father went off to work and we went outside to sit on the pergola, Sam on my lap, Tim leaning against me, and Razor the dog at my feet. I thought of my own personal pain and I grieved for the child I had lost. I was scared. I doubted that I was strong enough or smart enough to give my son what he needed. Then I looked down at little Timmy, felt his soft blond hair and put my hand on his perfect smooth skin, and my heart broke all over again. He did not deserve the life that had been described to me. It was so unfair, so cruel. It was for him that I was saddest.

The more I looked at him, the more confused I felt—an angry, unwilling confusion. The things the psychologist had said—the finality of it, the hopelessness—they didn't make sense to me. I knew Timmy could learn because he already had, he was already changing. He could walk, he could feed himself, he could identify objects. He wasn't cut off from the world, he was interested in things; he was just interested in different things to other children. He wasn't isolated, he loved his brother, and he had a wonderful personality when you got to know him. I knew he loved me, I knew he did. When I'd buckled him into his car seat outside the psychologist's office, beside myself with grief, Timmy had reached out his little hand and wiped away my tears.

As the day wore on, I felt some resolve building. I would do anything and everything for my son. I didn't accept what the psychologist had told me. There had to be something I could do.

•

On that first day of the diagnosis, in a state of pure panic and devastation, I had gone straight over to visit my neighbour Alison. She was the only person I could turn to and I was desperate for some advice.

'What is autism?' she asked me.

I shrugged, bewildered, and said, 'I don't know.'

'Well I think you'd better find out.'

On day two I took Sam and Timmy to the library. I settled the boys as best I could and headed for the card files—there was no computer directory, just drawers full of subjects and authors in alphabetical order. I went straight for the 'A's, and looked for 'autism'. There was nothing in the file.

A librarian noticed me rushing between the stacks, checking on the boys and looking hopelessly at the shelves, and very kindly offered to help. I told her I was looking for information about autism and she asked me how to spell it.

We found one book, a medical dictionary that listed every disease and disorder with a very brief description. *Autism*, it read, *from the Latin, meaning 'within one's self'*. As short as it was, the entry seemed to confirm everything that the psychologist had said. The disorder meant Tim was isolated, that he was locked away from the world within himself. It would be my job to find him and bring him out.

•

Timmy made sounds, from morning to night. He made a repetitive moaning noise, which changed in pitch if he was upset. If the tone climbed higher or dropped, I knew trouble was coming. To me, this meant that Timmy had a voice. He was using sound to communicate, so I knew he could speak. I was convinced that he needed speech therapy and I'd do whatever it took to get it. I wanted to forget the psychologist and focus on getting some help.

Sam had a paediatrician named David Moore and he was a wonderful man, very gentle and warm. I had a lot of faith in him. He had taken very good care of Sam after we had left the hospital and our regular check-ups with him were always reassuring because he was so thorough. Thankfully, Sam was showing no sign of any of the issues that a preterm birth could cause, such as sight problems. He was going ahead in leaps and bounds.

I called the clinic to arrange an appointment with Dr Moore and at the same time called the children's hospital to make an appointment there. I would reach out in any direction until I could grab hold of something.

Dr Moore was a measured man; he went to great lengths to calm and reassure me. He said it would take some time of observation and testing before a diagnosis of autism could be confirmed and he would manage the process for us. I told him I was terrified that Timmy would be put in an institution, but he assured me that no one was going to try to take him away. He said those days were over.

Dr Moore explained to me that autism is a condition that affects your ability to communicate and form social relationships. It's not a disease, he said, you can't see it under a microscope. It's a set of attributes that, grouped together, point to a problem. But you need to see all the attributes, not just one or two.

I still had doubts about Tim's diagnosis. Tim ticked the boxes for social and communication issues but he didn't tick the boxes for a lot of other things; he didn't have the extreme behaviours or display the violence that were described to me. As far as I could see, he could learn. I told Dr Moore that I wasn't interested in the autism; I was interested in helping Tim learn to speak. I was happy to have all the tests in the world but I wanted Timmy to get some form of therapy at the same time and Dr Moore agreed it was best. He referred us to a speech therapist and an occupational therapist; the therapists worked in the same specialist centre as Dr Moore and were highly regarded. Dr Moore also arranged a series of tests to rule out the possibility that anything else might be causing Tim's many problems. Secretly, I hoped he would find something else. I wanted the psychologist to be wrong.

It was possible that Dr Moore knew from the very outset it was autism, but he was cautious—he didn't want to leap to conclusions. Psychologically, he did me a huge favour. If the second person I spoke to had closed the book on my son, I'm sure it would have flattened me. I needed the strength to fight.

•

Our first appointment with both the speech therapist and occupational therapist was a disaster. Timmy wasn't having a good day and he just wanted to escape. He was making a lot of noise and there was nothing I could do to calm him. The therapists wanted some time alone with me and asked if Timmy could stay in the play area near the receptionist, where Sam was mucking around happily, but there was no chance. Timmy's anxiety went through the roof when it looked like I was going to leave him, but when I brought him into the office he screamed wildly, clawing at the door and trying to turn the handle to escape. He was inconsolable. The therapists tried to engage him but it was as if he couldn't hear them or see them at all. He didn't do anything they asked and he couldn't be tested.

I was terrified. He had behaved so well with the child psychologist and had such a dreadful prognosis, I was fearful of what the predictions would be when these people saw him at his worst. I could also see the sad, troubled look on the faces of the two women in front of me. I had seen it before, too many times. It was as if they were looking at the worst case they had ever seen and they didn't know if there was anything they could do. I wanted to ask them why they looked so grim, but I wasn't sure I could handle their reply.

The therapists said it would take a bit of time to do their evaluation so follow-up appointments were organised. The plan was to have weekly therapy sessions and see how things progressed. If they could get him to focus, they said, there was a chance that he would respond. They were nice women but neither of them looked very hopeful.

Dr Moore did genetic tests, chromosome tests, blood tests and physical tests. He organised to have Timmy's sight and hearing checked again, just to be thorough. He looked for bacteria, viruses and congenital conditions, and sent Timmy for X-rays and MRI scans. It was hell to try to get Timmy to lie still on those machines—we'd need three adults at a time to hold him down. But it had to be done; we had to rule everything out.

We did cognitive tests and behavioural tests with the therapists, then moved on to speech and occupational therapy. In between sessions, I worked with Timmy at home, practising word games and training that the therapists had given me. It was agonisingly slow. I had to get Timmy's attention and repeat words over and over again, making sure he was focused on the sound of my voice.

Tim started to pay attention in his weekly therapy sessions but he would never sit still. Hyperactivity was mentioned but the therapists weren't certain. Timmy was definitely active, they said, but maybe not *over*active. Neither of them could say for sure what was wrong. On the upside, as the weeks went by, we started to see some results. Within a month of starting the sessions, Timmy went from one or two words that he used sparingly to ten words—ten whole words! His new words were 'ta', 'beep beep', 'ba' and 'Nam'; 'me', 'I do' and 'Azor' for Razor the dog.

It made me very happy to hear him speak, but I wanted him to call me 'Mum'—that was the one word I wanted more than anything else. I was upset that he could ask for cartoons with 'beep beep' (the sound that the Road Runner made, repeated a hundred times a day), but he still didn't have a name for me. One self-indulgent day, I decided that if he wanted to watch *The Bugs Bunny Show* he would have to say 'Mum' first. I thought it was the greatest motivator I had because he loved those cartoons so much. So a few minutes before the program started I gave him the instructions.

'Beep beep,' Timmy said.

'When you say "Mum", I will turn on beep beep,' I told him.

'Beep beep,' Timmy insisted.

I repeated my ultimatum and Timmy responded the same way, again and again and again. We went on past five o'clock, when the show started, and still I wouldn't turn the TV on. I had started it and I had to continue, that's what the therapists had told me. Tim was sobbing, with tears rolling down his face, desperately pleading for his beloved 'beep beep'. I looked at his sad, heartbroken face and my willpower crumbled. It was one of his happiest times of the day and I was depriving him of it. I felt like such a selfish piece of work. How could I do that to a little boy? What was the point? Just to hear my name? I was ashamed of myself and riddled with guilt. I turned the TV on for Tim and went out to the backyard to cry. I was so focused on getting Timmy to talk that every minute of every day was becoming a therapy session. I felt like I was constantly pushing him, and it wasn't always worth the result. It left me sad and drained and hopeless, and if it was exhausting for me, imagine how hard it must have been for Timmy. Life was already so difficult for him and here I was making it worse.

•

The therapists didn't just work on Timmy's speech, they helped me to improve some of the behaviours that had made life so difficult. Getting him out the door had always been a problem and they offered suggestions to make that a little easier. They recommended I take Timmy for a walk every day, if only to the end of the neighbour's fence and back. He screamed and resisted the whole way, but to my surprise it got easier with time. After a few weeks he was happy walking out the front door and to the end of the lawn. Within a month or so, we went a little further and by the time the end of the year rolled around, we'd made it calmly all the way to the end of the street.

Timmy had lots of toys, but few interested him and he didn't play with them the way other kids played with theirs. He would move or twist and turn an object repeatedly, run sand from our sandpit through his fingers, or push the trolley back and forth over and over again. There was no imagination or meaning in his games, at least none that I could see. He didn't let me or Sam join in his games, though it wasn't in a possessive or nasty way. It was just that Tim was in his own world and didn't need us; he could play with the same thing for a very long time and it was like we didn't exist—that he was oblivious to our attempts to join in. He didn't yell or scream at us to get away, he was just far away, deep inside himself.

The therapists suggested I try to draw Timmy out by interacting with him in very simple, very repetitive ways. On their advice, I bought him a little car, about the size of a Matchbox car, which lit up and made a noise when you pushed its bonnet. They told me to say Timmy's name, get his attention, and then show him how the car lit up when it was pushed. I had to encourage him to take it from me and push the button to make it work. They taught me to be persistent. Sometimes I had to wait hours for him to be calm and settled enough to even try it. Sometimes I'd say his name twenty times or more; Timmy just sat in his bubble and ignored me. But I persisted. I didn't know what else to do. I must have pushed that car bonnet five hundred times, I was so desperate to interact with him. Then one day, out of nowhere, he looked, reached for the car and pushed the bonnet all by himself. I felt just like the car—lit up. I was so proud of him. Timmy gave me a big smile; he was happy with himself too.

•

It was an all-day exercise in patience and strategy just to get to that point; it was mentally draining trying to push him out of his comfort zone and not to make the rest of the day fall apart, then getting that one moment of success and realising there would be hours or days before he would do it again. But it was enough of a victory for me to keep doing it. I wanted to communicate with my son, so I showered him with praise every time he did what I asked.

I had explained to the therapists about Tim's troubles with textures and fabrics against his skin. They said it was very common in children with autism and assured me they could help. Along with speech exercises and walking, and various other things, they introduced different experiments to deal with Timmy's 'tactile sensitivities'. In our sessions, they had Timmy touch shaving cream, bubble wrap, play dough, and the foam shells that were used in packaging. They helped with other things as well, like the idea of cause and effect. We blew out and relit candles a hundred times, until there was no wax left on the candle, to get him used to the idea of doing something to get a result. It seemed silly, but it also made sense to me. We blew bubbles and tried to get Timmy to blow bubbles too, but simple things like that were often torture. It would take endless attempts to get him to try anything and a lot of the activities were hellish for him. If he managed to put his hands in the shaving cream, he'd be frantic to have them cleaned, although he did love blowing out the candle. I would light it up and he'd blow it out, over and over, for hours. It was horribly tedious for me, but I wouldn't stop, if that was what he wanted.

It was incredibly draining to ask him over and over again to try these things, to stand there and repeat my request until I got somewhere, even just a small attempt, one little finger for one little second in one little bit of shaving cream. But the therapists made it very clear that if I started something I would have to finish it—if I asked Timmy to do something, I had to get him to do it. I had to be strategic and only try things when he wasn't upset or doing something else that he really enjoyed. Meanwhile, Sam was willing and eager to try anything and everything, and could do it all easily. I was convinced with all the therapy Sam was doing he would end up as some kind of genius.

•

Within a few months the speech therapist and occupational therapist had completed their assessment, and they confirmed that Timmy had autism. They probably knew the very minute they saw him, but I was grateful they took the time to make sure, and there was no doubt they'd been very thorough. Dr Moore's report was the same—my son had autism—but the news was delivered kindly along with the assurance that he would do as much as he could to help. Dr Moore made no predictions for the future, none whatsoever, which was another sort of kindness.

I was saddened by the news, but I accepted it. It wasn't such a dreadful shock the second time around. Dr Moore had given me some information, and friends of friends had started coming forward, people who knew people who knew people who knew children with autism. By the time Dr Moore confirmed the diagnosis, I'm sure I knew what the verdict would be. I was just sad to hear how bad it was: severe, they said, the low-functioning kind.

'Why has this happened to Timmy?' I asked.

'We just don't know.' Dr Moore shrugged. He told me there were various theories. Some people thought it was environmental, some people thought it was a genetic condition. They couldn't pinpoint what was going on physically, so they couldn't really investigate the cause.

Dr Moore was honest but he was kind. I realised that nothing was going to change the diagnosis, nothing was going to change what autism was, so the only thing I could do was try to focus on Tim. The doctor agreed that my son needed as much help as he could get, as quickly as possible. There was a new deadline to worry about—Timmy's fourth birthday. He said the most crucial development in a young brain happened before the age of four, so if we were going to make a real difference in Timmy's life we had to get started immediately. Timmy's fourth birthday was less than a year away. It was like an alarm clock was set in my head and I could already hear it ticking.

Meanwhile, after only three months of working with the therapists, Tim had a vocabulary of almost one hundred words. He said 'apple', 'bath', 'cup' and 'cake'; 'please', 'yes' and 'sky'. He said 'me' and 'moon', 'book' and 'bed', and best of all, he said 'Mum'. With help from the therapists, I got him to sit with me and read books—instead of staring at them by himself and not responding when I tried to interact with him, he would point at pictures and characters when I asked him to. I was always very impressed by how much he knew, how many things he recognised. Timmy couldn't put words together in a sentence, but he could communicate. He could learn. More than anything else, this gave me hope.

•

Before the diagnosis, I thought Timmy was a sensitive little boy—a deep thinker and a loner. I worried that he was too anxious, and his many fears worried me. He was gentle and always deep in thought, and just very, very shy. I thought back through my life and remembered several kids I had gone to school with, or who were family friends, who reminded me of Tim. I had always thought that he would end up a fine, quiet man like many people I knew. I now knew that I was wrong, terribly far off the mark. After the diagnosis, I saw so many things differently. I didn't love my son any less—I think I actually loved him more—but I could see how much autism was affecting his life.

When Sam started eating solid foods it was dreadfully messy, as it is with most babies, with more food ending up on his face and his clothes than in his mouth. Timmy loved Sam—he would always cuddle him or try to carry him around, and he'd get anxious if we were going somewhere and he thought Sam wasn't coming. Timmy was happy to help me bath him and liked to stay by my side whenever I did anything for Sam, but he couldn't stand watching Sam eat. He would grab a cloth and frantically wipe Sam's mouth after every spoonful until the mess was cleaned up. Poor little Sam just sat through it, calm as anything.

There were so many issues that I needed help with. Timmy's toilet-training wasn't going anywhere. He still had trouble wearing certain clothes and wouldn't keep them on. Haircuts were almost impossible unless he was held down—Timmy was afraid of the scissors. If he got a splinter in his finger or needed his fingernails cut, he would scream so much that he wouldn't be able to catch his breath. He often fell asleep in shock, afterwards, like his whole body was just spent.

Without language there were gaps in my relationship with Timmy, but in many ways it was also the strongest relationship I had enjoyed in my life. There was closeness between us; he was my dear little mate. Despite all of our struggles, I felt it was a wonderful mother-and-son relationship, more than I had ever dreamt of. I liked just being around him. I liked that he was teaching me another way to communicate and another way to learn to have a relationship with someone, but it was challenging. I had to learn to be quiet, to stop talking and using too many words. I had to learn to watch, to see what he was looking at, to see what he was interested in. I had to look at the things around him to see what might upset him; to look for triggers that might have frightened or agitated him. I had to be patient and forget about what I wanted and just focus on Timmy, and learn about him by looking and thinking in a way that was not natural to me. I had to learn to give up my own hopes and needs, and learn to wait for his initiation and attempts to reach out to me that could take a very long time. But often it was very satisfying to be silent and just be together, the two of us.

Timmy was my constant companion, always by my side. If we were outside playing and I went inside to check on something, he would follow me, even if I told him I would only be a minute. I'd sit down and he would sit on my lap. When we were out, he would try to scramble up my legs so I would carry him; he spent most of his time in my arms. I could tickle him and make him laugh, I could play peek-a-boo and make him giggle; I could lift him by his arms and spin him around and keep him happy for hours. He was very affectionate towards me, throwing his arms around my neck and planting kisses on my face, leaning up against me or holding my hand.

Sometimes, he would come running up to me, take my face in his little hands and press his nose against mine. He'd look deep into my eyes and say, 'Numma numma no,' then run off again. He had his own language, but I was certain that he was telling me that he loved me. There isn't a person on this planet who can convince me otherwise. Those moments made me cry. It was such an earnest effort on his behalf and it meant the world to me that he had tried so hard to speak to tell me what was in his heart.

5

The Father

My feelings for Tim and Sam were pure and uncomplicated. It was the first time I had ever experienced that kind of love.

I didn't love the man I married. I said 'yes' because I didn't think anyone else would have me, because in the years we had been together, that's how he made me feel. I had a sinking feeling when he proposed, a feeling of impending doom, but I grew up in the suburbs and I didn't feel like I had a lot of choices. Before he'd even slipped the ring on my finger, I felt trapped.

I knew it would be a difficult life and I would have to make a lot of sacrifices. I had a lot of older relatives who were in what I considered loveless marriages that weren't particularly happy, but they were respectful and decent to each other. They'd built a life together that seemed to work. I was resigned to the idea that my marriage would be the same and that I could do it.

He was a good provider and he had strong family values. I just assumed that would be enough.

I'm sure my husband didn't love me either; I felt like just another one of his possessions. Before we were married, I'd seen flashes of jealousy and bursts of anger, but I didn't realise those things were a warning sign of things to come. I was too young and too naive to see what lay ahead.

Volatile relationships tend to follow a pattern, and mine was no exception. The first thing that happened was that I lost my self-esteem; the second thing was that I became socially isolated. Outwardly, my husband was a very charismatic man. We had a lot of friends in the early days. We went out a lot. I was troubled by the way he'd talk about people once they were out of earshot, though, especially the women. He thought that every woman we knew was sleeping around and that they were a bad influence on me. After our wedding, it became very difficult for me to have people over. He never said anything to their faces, but he'd say things about my friends after they left that I hated, until it was easier to stop inviting people to visit than to deal with his anger. I made excuses and stopped going out. Eventually, my friends faded away. You have to work at friendships, you have to put in the time and effort to make them grow, but for me it was impossible.

I felt totally controlled during our marriage. He made all of the decisions, including what I should wear. I could do the food shopping but I was given no money to buy clothes or shoes, or anything I might like. I'd worked in real estate before we were married but he didn't want his wife working for anyone else. I had to stay at home and do his books, though I didn't get paid. I was often left bored and lonely, but I could never go out. He telephoned several times a day to check on me. If I told him I had been to visit my mother, he would call her house to check that it was true. It was like living in a prison.

I was desperately unhappy from very early on but I think in my husband's mind we had a good marriage. He brought me flowers every Friday, fifty-two weeks a year. It was a romantic gesture that should have made me feel special, but it was so at odds with the way he made me feel the other six days a week that it seemed creepy to me. It felt very smug and self-congratulatory; *look at what a wonderful husband I am.*

'If I can't have you, no one else can,' I remember him saying. It came out like a joke but, to me, the words felt like a threat, and they made my flesh crawl. Yet there he was every Friday with flowers in his hand, as if roses could cover up the rot.

•

We lived in a low-set fibro house that was built after the war. There was no corridor, just four interconnecting rooms, nine foot by nine foot, with an add-on bathroom out the back. The house should have been knocked down—it leaned visibly and the stumps were rotten—but it was set on a beautiful block, on the highest part of the street. It was the worst house on the best street, a great investment opportunity. But the house was truly ugly, so I had it painted pink. If it was pink it would look like a little cottage, I thought, as if a coat of paint was all it took to make a house a home.

From the minute we moved in I thought about leaving that house but I could never quite work up the nerve. I didn't have any money and I had nowhere to go, but I dreamt of getting out. I had a friend who'd gone as far as she could when she left her husband. She literally found the furthest place on a map, some headland in Western Australia. I thought that sounded like a great idea and I might have done it if it had been just me. I could always find a job and I would be free of the relationship for good. But the boys weren't the only reason I stayed. I stayed because I doubted myself. The voice in my head told me I was weak and stupid, and I was scared of what would happen if I was on my own. Then when Timmy came along and everything changed I was stuck in my marriage because I didn't think I could manage financially by myself. I was stuck in that house because it was a roof over our heads. All the love in the world couldn't feed a newborn.

My husband seemed proud enough. He'd painted the baby's room and put a wallpaper frieze of teddy bears around the top of the walls. He asked his sister to make beautiful curtains with teddy bears on them and he hung those too. The room looked beautiful. Together, we bought a pram and a bassinet, all the things the baby needed. He was more considerate to me during this time, too, though I suspected it wouldn't last. He kept saying, 'You're going to have a lot of work to do, you'd better be ready for that.'

He said something else that stuck in my mind, because it sounded so ominous to me. 'You know some men just can't cope with a baby in the house,' he told me. 'It means they are no longer the most important thing in their wife's life. They have to take a backwards step. Some men don't like that.' He had three children from a previous marriage and I wondered if he was warning me what lay ahead, of what had already been his experience. It was something he repeated often and I found it really disturbing.

When we brought Timmy home, my husband left me to care for him. As difficult as it was, as tired and desperate as I got, I never remember him offering to take the baby so I could get some rest. I couldn't cook a meal or eat without a screaming, restless baby in my arms. My husband slept in our bedroom night after night while Timmy howled and I paced back and forth like a zombie. Occasionally, he would wake up and rush into the lounge room, furious because I couldn't stop Timmy from crying, because I couldn't look after him properly. He'd make me feel selfish and stupid and then storm back to bed, leaving me flattened with Timmy still screaming.

I felt that my husband was being more and more critical of me at a time when I really needed support. In front of guests he'd tell me what a good mother I was, but behind closed doors he'd say, 'You need to sort this mess out.' As I struggled with Timmy, he spent more and more time at work. When he was home, it was like there was a black cloud over the house. My nerves were already frayed, but being in the same room with my husband pushed me to breaking point. I never knew when the next outburst would be. He could be truly nasty, especially when he had been drinking. It was becoming relentless.

No one knew. He was a street angel and a house devil. Occasionally someone would tell me they had caught a glimpse of the side of him that I saw. It wasn't necessarily anything that he said or did, but sometimes people said they could feel his anger bubbling beneath the surface.

Every now and then someone who had come to see us about Sam, a midwife or a nurse who visited the house, stopped to ask if I was okay. I think they sensed that I was afraid of my husband, but I pretended everything was fine. I was too terrified to tell anyone how I really felt. I felt somehow he'd find out and it would only make things worse.

•

After Sam was born, I developed a horrible infection that persisted for weeks. I went to see a doctor with my husband in tow and he mentioned the various things that caused that particular condition. In a long list that included a virus, an allergic reaction, or a side effect of medication, my husband heard only two words, 'sexually transmitted'. He became convinced I was having an affair.

Whatever doubts, whatever fears I had about my husband, I wasn't really prepared for what followed. With two tiny boys hanging off me, a newborn and a toddler who cried half the day, it was absolutely impossible that I was sneaking out for secret meetings, or letting my lovers in the front door while he was asleep. I was terribly hurt to be accused of cheating—that was something I would never do. I slept in the boys' room to avoid waking my husband during the night, but the four rooms of our house were pressed together and the walls were paper-thin. Still, he was convinced I had a nightly visitor. He started putting sticky tape across the front door and back door each night, then checking each morning to see if it had been broken.

My husband's words became toxic to me. He routinely described the various foul acts he thought I was performing with my secret lovers, even when the children were within earshot, and constantly called me names. He'd shake me out of my sleep to tell me about his suspicions, demanding I tell him the 'truth'. It would go on for hours, until I felt like vomiting from the exhaustion and the fear. He would turn up at home unexpectedly during the day to check on me. Sometimes I would look out the open front door and see him driving up and down the street. He wouldn't call in to the house, he just circled.

He started to telephone more frequently when he was out. Timmy had developed a few annoying habits; he liked to drop wallets and watches in the toilet bowl and had started picking up the telephone to listen to nothing. Often, he wouldn't return the receiver, which would stay unhooked for hours if I didn't notice. It made my life a living hell when his father couldn't get through on the phone.

My husband decided we had too much food in the house, evidence I was feeding someone else on the sly. On that pretext, he stopped giving me money for grocery shopping. He insisted we do it together so that he could control the cheque book; I didn't have a cent to my name. I had to borrow five dollars from the neighbour to buy children's Panadol when Sam was teething. I have never felt so ashamed. Some days, he would insist that someone else was drinking all his beer. He would turn the garbage bin upside down and count the empty bottles, looking for signs there was someone else in the house.

The worst things he said to me, the things that cut the deepest, were about Timmy. Before Timmy was diagnosed, he would rant for hours about how there was nothing wrong with our son, I was just a bad mother. He said I made up all Tim's symptoms and that there was nothing wrong with him. He told me I was the one who was upsetting our little boy. After the diagnosis, when my husband got angry, he said I was nothing more than an attention-seeking woman who was living through her handicapped child.

•

I ended up sleeping in the boys' room to escape from my husband. He would get up three or four times a night and stand at the bedroom door, staring at me in the dark while I lay there pretending to be asleep. Eventually not even the sleeping boys stopped him, he would just walk in and demand that I came back to his bed. Then the next day he would act as if nothing had happened. He'd sit down to breakfast and start talking about buying another property, a bigger house with acreage where he could keep horses, and the kids could roam free. I was astounded. I couldn't believe that he would think I wanted anything to do with him, let alone these fantasies of a little house on the prairie, but I was too scared to move or utter a word. Staying silent was better than saying the wrong thing and risking his anger.

Every day was like walking through a minefield. I was exhausted from trying to stay ahead of him, trying to remember everything I had to do to avoid making him angry, knowing nothing I did would ever be good enough.

•

There were cyclone wire fences on either side of our backyard and I'd see my neighbours every morning when I went out to hang the laundry. Alison on one side had little ones and so did Bev on the other. There was a line of Hills Hoists filled with white cotton nappies, up and down the street. One morning, Alison came out with her basket and cheerily called, 'Morning, Jude.' Her kindness just broke me; I fell to my knees weeping. She was just a tiny thing, built like a whippet, but she cleared the fence in a single leap and came running to my side. She begged to know what was wrong. I told her everything. Somehow, she wasn't really surprised.

Because I couldn't believe what was happening to me, I had started to keep a diary. I wrote down everything my husband said or did, to make sure I wasn't dreaming. I went inside and got the diary from its hiding spot and gave it to Alison, and made her promise me she'd keep it safe.

As bad as I felt every day, I felt equally bad for the boys. I didn't want them to think that all relationships were like this, and I didn't want them to think badly of their mother. I also worried that they might feel the same fear that I did, the minute they were old enough to speak and had to negotiate the same minefield every day. And I was terrified they might grow up to be like him.

•

On the Christmas Day after Timmy was diagnosed, I finally resolved to leave my husband. The boys were old enough to know what Christmas meant and they were bursting with excitement when they woke up; Santa Claus had paid us a visit overnight. As Timmy and Sam tore into their presents, their father handed me my present, a new swimsuit. 'Go put it on,' he said. I had a terrible feeling about it but I didn't want to upset him, so I went into the bedroom and changed.

'I think it's a bit tight,' I said, thinking we'd take it back and get the right size. He was furious, like I had rejected him.

'You'd wear it for him,' he snarled. The day turned to ashes in a heartbeat.

On Christmas morning, right in front of our sons, he started calling me ugly, hurtful names. I couldn't bring myself to look at the boys but I could tell they were watching. They had stopped playing with their toys and had fallen silent. They had learned to be quiet when their father was angry. *Never again*, I vowed to myself.

Early in the New Year, I started making plans. I called domestic violence hotlines, but all they could suggest was that I go to a women's refuge; eventually, they might find me a new home. There was no way I could do that with Timmy, I thought. He couldn't possibly deal with the shock to his routine and I wasn't sure they would even accept him. I assumed that there'd be no tolerance for his crying and his distressing behaviour, since I could hardly find a friend or family member who could tolerate him.

We received a child endowment from the government and though it was paid into an account in my name, my husband controlled it like he did all the finances. In desperation, I withdrew some money from the account and went to see a solicitor, my little boys in tow. If somehow we could stay in the house and get their father to leave, Timmy wouldn't have to be unsettled. I'd have some stability and security while I figured out how to help him—he had just had his life-changing diagnosis.

Timmy clawed at the door and wailed throughout the meeting. 'Do you have anyone to help you with the children?' the solicitor asked.

'No,' I said, shaking my head.

She obviously pitied me, but she couldn't offer much hope. If I wanted to stay in our home, my husband would have to agree to a property settlement; the law couldn't make him move out. I went back home and sat out in the yard with my beautiful little boys, pushed them on the swing and watched them play in the sandpit. I felt barely alive and I knew that they deserved better. If my husband wouldn't get out of the house, we would have to leave.

I visited the welfare office that day and told them I was going to leave my husband, to see if there was any way they could help. I told them everything they needed to know and they signed me up for a single parent's pension; I would receive the first payment in a week. I pulled a few hundred dollars out of the endowment account, just enough for a month's rent and bond, and called a real-estate agent across town. They found me a house thirty minutes away. I could pick up the keys that afternoon.

I spent the last hundred dollars I had on a moving van. There was no money to connect the telephone or the utilities at the new house, and I didn't have anything left for food, but I planned to take as much as I could with me. I couldn't pack—I couldn't risk my husband getting suspicious—but we'd grab whatever we could when we ran.

•

My husband was out of the house every Saturday morning, for a few hours at least. He ran a business on the weekend and he had to be there to oversee it, so I knew he wouldn't come home unexpectedly. That was my chance. I did my best to act normally while I made him his breakfast but my nerves were like glass, my heart was racing. I couldn't wait for him to walk out the door.

When he finally left, I called the removalists. When they knocked on the door, I gave them a list: the TV and the video player for Tim, the fridge, the washing machine and the cot for Sam. They got to work and so did I, throwing clothes into garbage bags, emptying out one cupboard after another, grabbing anything I could think of, just as fast as I could go.

It was a frantic, scary scene, especially for Timmy. He always kept a line-up of trucks and cars across the front door—I could never understand the pattern, rhyme or reason for it, but if you tried to move it he would become hysterical. It was actually quite dangerous, as you had to step over the cars to reach the door; I had no choice but to clear them away so the moving men could work. Timmy started sobbing and screaming as I packed his cars away, pulling at me desperately to try to make me put them back. I had always tried to do what pleased him or whatever would make things easier for him, but this time I couldn't, even though it broke my heart. And my resistance made Tim feel worse. He screamed as loudly as ever and grabbed onto my legs and arms to try to stop me. He threw himself onto the floor, scared and distressed about the changes that were going on around him in the house that had always been his one safe harbour. I tried to keep packing but Timmy followed me in tears, trying to put back all the things I was moving out of the place. His little face, a blotchy red ball of terror and confusion, was more than I could bear.

I went outside and sat on the front porch. What was I thinking? It was pointless, anyway. We could never survive on our own. There wouldn't be enough money for therapy for Timmy and he needed it so badly. What if I got sick? Who would look after the boys? I didn't even know if I would have enough money to feed them. We'd just scrape by on a single parent's pension; I certainly couldn't give them the life they deserved. And I wouldn't have any support. Timmy needed so much care and I was already so worn down. It was foolish of me to think I could escape. Even if we got away, I was sure their father would find us. I was terrified of what he might do if I managed to slip out of his grasp.

I had explained to the moving men what the situation was because I didn't want them in the line of fire if my husband came home unexpectedly. 'If my husband turns up, you should get out of here, fast. Don't worry about the stuff, we'll deal with it later.' They understood why we were leaving. As I sat weeping on the porch, one of the men, the younger of two, came and patted me on the shoulder. He seemed to know exactly what I was feeling.

'Don't worry,' he said. 'Our mum raised us. She was a single mum and we turned out just fine. You'll be right.'

That was enough to get me off the porch and back inside the house. Sometimes that's all it takes, just one good person with a few kind words.

For the first time ever, I ignored Tim's crying and continued to take whatever I could and throw it into the back of that truck. The removalists followed my instructions and worked as fast as I did, and we were ready to go in just two hours. I buckled the boys into their car seats and took one last look at the house. Razor, our cattle dog, howled at me from the gate. *Poor Razor, I'm sorry*, I thought to myself. There were no fences at the new house and I just couldn't afford to feed him.

•

We left the house in Wynnum West on 1 February 1992, when Tim was three months short of his fourth birthday and Sam was almost two. I had $37 in the bank. Our rent was $280 per fortnight and the pension was $420 per fortnight, leaving us $140 a fortnight, or $70 a week, to live on. It wasn't going to be easy, but I was determined to make it work. I had to make it work because there was no going back.

Our new house was in Cleveland on Moreton Bay. It was a small brick building on a small block of land, not much to look at, to be honest. Still, it made me happy. I had a surge of pride the first time I turned the key in the front door lock. *I did it*, I thought. *I got away.* It was bittersweet pride, mixed with relief. The door swung open and the boys rushed past me, excited to explore all those empty rooms. It was like a new playground at first, but I wondered how they'd like it after dark. No electricity meant no lights at night and no TV or videos for Tim.

I managed to keep the boys distracted for a couple of days, taking them out to explore the neighbourhood, climbing on the rocks down at the waterfront, unpacking their toys. At night, I gave Timmy a lovely long bath and read him stories by torchlight until he fell asleep. For two days we survived, but when Timmy woke up on the third day and there was still no power and no television, whatever patience he had just vanished.

I went and borrowed some money from a friend to get the electricity turned on. After working so hard to keep them distracted, it was a relief to finally sit in a chair and have a rest while the boys watched Bugs Bunny videos. I'd been so anxious about how the move would upset Timmy but he seemed happy enough for the moment. I had unpacked and put as many familiar objects around him as I could—he already had his toy cars lined up across the doorway. If anything, I thought his behaviour was much better than usual and I felt reassured that I'd made the right decision. Surely it was better for him and Sam to be away from that house.

Beautiful little Sam was as happy and easy-going as ever, and just glided through it, never once asking for his father. He sat beside me on the couch while Timmy sat on the floor. They were lovely little companions.

•

With every day that passed, I could physically feel the weight lift from my shoulders. There was a new lightness in my step and I started to smile again. We went to the playground every day, or to the creek to try to catch tadpoles, and we were happy. I worried constantly that their father would find us, but at least he wasn't under the same roof.

I rang him several times to assure him that the boys were safe, but I kept the conversations very short and I wouldn't tell him where we were no matter how much he demanded. He rang my mother multiple times a day, trying to find us. He put a huge amount of pressure on her, but she did her best to keep us safe. I couldn't keep him away forever, I knew that. I just wanted to hold him off long enough for the worst of his anger to subside.

Within a fortnight, I agreed to meet him. I knew he had a legal right to see his sons, so I arranged a weekly catch-up at a local pool on Sundays. It had to be somewhere public and I had to stay with them.

The meetings always started out well. He brought lollies for Sam and a chocolate for Tim, and he made a big show of playing with his sons. But the minute the boys were out of earshot, splashing in the pool, he began his interrogation. Where were we living? When were we coming home? I was too scared to tell him that we were never coming back. I did my best to avoid answering his questions. Although I felt slightly safer in a public place, I was terrified of antagonising him.

I hated Sundays. Those feelings of weakness and vulnerability and fear that I had while I'd lived with him returned and completely swamped me; just the sight of him made me want to be sick. It was like I'd never got away from that house. I knew that to keep my boys safe, I had to make sure their father remained calm, but for me it involved huge personal sacrifice. Within a few months, when I ran out of excuses, he started coming around to the house.

I don't know exactly how he found us, but I opened the door to go out shopping one day and there was his car, driving past.

A few days later, he pulled up in our driveway on the pretence of visiting the boys. After that, our Sunday afternoon meetings at the pool became Sundays at my house in Cleveland. He leaned on me and insisted until I crumpled under the pressure. *Keep him happy, keep him calm*, I thought. He would watch videos in the lounge room with the boys while I cowered in the kitchen feeling sick. *Just a bit longer*, I'd think to myself. *Just a little bit longer and he'll leave.* Even when his words started to make me feel awful I didn't have the strength to make him leave. *It's only once a week*, I thought. But once a week became twice a week, Saturdays and Sundays, and then he started dropping by during the holidays as well. For my sons' sake, I let him in. I tried to shield them from the tension that I had experienced when we had lived with their father and I kept allowing the cause of my torment into my home so that my sons could have a relationship with their father. It's not like he ever offered to take the boys for the weekend, he only wanted to see them if it was under my roof, which meant I had to face him, week after week.

It went on that way for fifteen years.

6

The SEDU and the Autism Centre

As a single mother with limited finances and two small children, it would have been hard anyway, but with Timmy I felt like I was in a war. We had great days and we had really bad days. On a bad day, Timmy's behaviours were intense and extreme, and it could go on for hours and hours. The constant sound, the constant repetition of words and actions, the screaming, the oppositional behaviour, it just wore me down. Those days were so powerful because I never knew if it was suddenly the new normal. If one day Timmy's screaming or maniacal laughter took hold and that one day became every day, I knew I couldn't cope. My fear and anxiety only made it worse. On good days, I saw a personality that was similar to Sam's, gentle and kind. To me, that was the real Timmy. The boys weren't carbon copies of each other but both were very sweet at heart, it was just the autism that made things difficult with Tim. I was determined to find a way to help him.

A neighbour had a friend who had a relative whose child had Down's Syndrome, and the child was going to a place called a Special Education Development Unit, or SEDU. I'd heard of special schools, but not the SEDU, which was a pre-school facility for children with disabilities. *Perfect*, I thought. It was the lifeline I needed. I picked up the phone immediately and called the principal, a woman named Charmaine.

'My son has been diagnosed with autism,' I told her. 'Can you help me?'

I cried on the phone and Charmaine was very sympathetic, but she was also very positive. She responded as though it wasn't a big deal, like there was nothing at all to worry about. 'Certainly, I can help!' she told me, then made a time for us to visit.

The SEDU was in Cleveland, about five minutes from our new home. It was located alongside a state primary school and a special school for older children. The SEDU was like a kindergarten for kids with special needs, although you wouldn't have known it was different from a regular pre-school, at least not at first glance. It was a lovely place—bright and colourful and airy—which was very important to me. I'd been scared it would be like an institution.

Children generally started at the SEDU when they were four, so technically Timmy was still a bit young, but Charmaine wasn't the kind of person who went by the book. She was a loud, expressive woman, who wore bright clothes and had a big personality. She threw her arms out to greet us when we arrived and almost immediately began talking to Timmy. She didn't speak to him like he was deaf or stupid, either; she was completely at ease.

'Come with me,' she said, taking his hand. Timmy followed her, calm as can be. That never happened! I felt immediately that I could trust her.

The SEDU was filled with toys and small children, and it seemed like there were a lot of teachers. They all appeared to be on the floor with the kids, playing and having a laugh. It was the first time I had been in a facility like that, the first time I had been around so many kids with disabilities. There were a lot of kids who looked different, who obviously had genetic conditions or Down's Syndrome, but you couldn't necessarily tell just by looking at them that the children with autism were different. The thing that impressed me most was that all of the kids seemed happy. It felt like a place where Timmy could be a child, not a patient.

Charmaine introduced me to an occupational therapist, who explained how they worked with the children. They used speech therapy, cognitive behavioural therapy, occupational therapy and play therapy; everything they did was to help the children develop. They tried to reduce the amount of crying, help the kids to communicate, help with toilet-training—all of the basic skills that the children would need to be able to go to school. Timmy would need to go to the toilet, wash his own hands, and manage his bag and his lunch before he could go to primary school. He'd need to respond to basic instructions like 'come here' and 'sit down', and he'd need to learn how to sit still and listen with his class—he had a habit of running off sometimes. The staff at the SEDU would do their best to teach him these basic skills.

As the therapist talked, I saw Timmy out of the corner of my eye, walking towards a ladder.

'No Timmy, come here,' I said, and he returned to my side.

'Look at that!' the therapist exclaimed. 'We could spend years trying to teach a child to respond that way and Timmy is already doing it. That's really great to see.'

The environment was so positive and encouraging, I felt like I was in heaven. I felt so lucky, though it was short-lived. They could only offer Timmy eight hours a week at the SEDU, they told me, because that's all the government funding would cover. *Surely he needs to be here full time!* I thought hopelessly. He would turn four the following year; the clock was still ticking in my head. I assumed that if my son needed help then he would get it, as much as possible—it was a social justice issue to me. If there was a way to help him, the government should do everything it could. It was no different from a physical health issue, in my mind. In retrospect, I was very naive—the system was full of holes. Charmaine apologised but assured me that they would do everything they could to help Timmy. I was grateful at least that she was on our side.

•

Timmy's first official day at the SEDU was on 10 February 1992, just days after we had moved house. I was incredibly nervous about leaving him because our lives had just been turned upside down and he wasn't used to being away from me. But the staff took him in hand and Timmy seemed happy to go. When I got him back home that afternoon, it was a very different scene. He screamed and screamed and screamed, and for the first time ever began hitting his head against the walls. He tried to bite me and was hitting me, which shocked me completely. I knew by then that children with autism often had violent behaviour, but I had never seen anything like it in Timmy. He was gentle, that was his nature. I felt quite sickened by his outburst and terrified about what might have happened to him while I was away, so I immediately called the school. They told me they were stumped; he had had a great day. They assured me they would keep an eye on him, but I was really nervous. I considered withdrawing Timmy from the SEDU at that point but I knew I needed their help. If I didn't trust them, I was really on my own.

The group that Timmy was assigned to included four little boys, two of whom were non-verbal, meaning they had no speech at all. Timmy had a small collection of words and the fourth little boy was able to communicate well enough to get his message across. I didn't understand the logic of putting Tim in a non-verbal group. I thought it would be more productive to have him in a group where language would be used all the time, but the therapists at the centre disagreed. They said that all of the boys had similar needs, so they could develop together.

The little boy who was verbal was also very aggressive and he began giving Timmy a hard time, pinching and pushing him whenever he could. The staff members did their best to keep Timmy out of harm's way, but the little boy would often lash out and they weren't always fast enough to intervene. I cried when Timmy came home covered in scratches. It made me sick with worry, but what other option did I have? I felt sad for the little boy who was so aggressive, and also for his mum, who worried so much about her son hurting other children. I could see the embarrassment on her face. They needed the placement as desperately as we did, maybe even more—their needs were just different. Despite my concern for Timmy I knew it was an impulse the little boy couldn't control; cruel autism had robbed him of that ability. They had enough to be dealing with, without my or anyone else's judgement.

Visiting the SEDU one day, I watched Timmy climb on the play equipment and he seemed happy enough by himself, but he became really anxious when the other children arrived and he didn't want anything to do with them. He settled well in the classroom but became aggressive at morning tea, pushing other children over and taking their bikes away. I'd never seen him do anything like that before and I wondered if it was the environment—it seemed to me that Timmy was learning to defend himself from the other kids. Among the other words he developed, Timmy started to say, 'Hey, stop that' and 'Hey, get away', which weren't phrases he ever needed to use at home.

But overall, the program was wonderful. There were songs and dances, games and activities, and the kids were given a lot of praise and encouragement. But they were also very focused on learning and development. The children practised sitting still, taking turns and listening to others. They learned how to cut and glue, how to hold pencils and put away their bags, how to get their own lunch boxes at lunchtime and how to manage their own things. It was going to take years to perfect those skills but they worked on them every day.

•

I'd started a new diary when we left Wynnum West and I kept track of Timmy's moods and behaviour. I was afraid that the boys' father would challenge me for custody and I thought I should have a record of Tim's progress. On 18 March 1992 I wrote, 'The lady next door gave Timmy an ice-cream but he didn't know how to lick it.' Two days later, I was thrilled that he could sit still in a chair while I read him a story—a big step forward. I was trying to see patterns in Tim's behaviour, to try to understand his condition. I could see that a lot of the generalisations around autism could apply to Tim, but I was never really sure that they did. He once picked up a plate and pretended it was a steering wheel, a type of 'pretend play' that wasn't supposed to happen with children who have autism. Then I'd take him to a birthday party and he'd sit down to play pass the parcel, but he clearly couldn't understand the game. Other children got it instinctively, but it was impossible for Tim; he

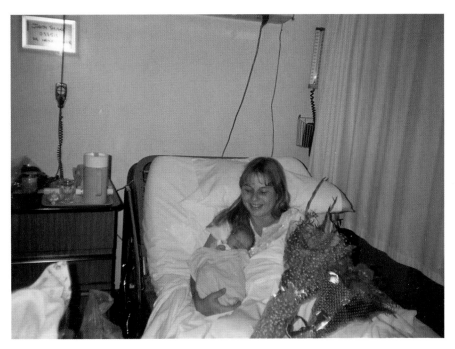

The day Tim was born, 9 May 1988. I had never known such happiness.

Tim at nine months old, holding my hand and learning to walk.

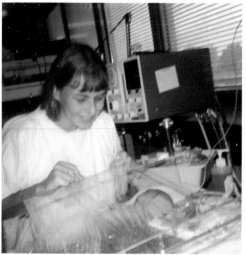

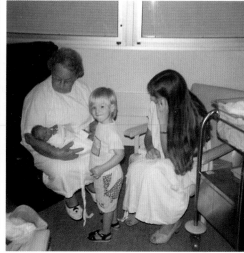

The first time I saw Sam, when he was two days old, 5 April 1990.

Tim fell in love with his little brother. Sam, in my mother's arms, is 20 days old but was still in hospital.

Playing with the boys, with Razor Sharp never far from our sides.

Struggling to take three-year-old Tim out. It was always difficult to leave the house.

Tim running towards the camera—he didn't like having his photo taken— and Sam behind Tim's carefully lined-up trucks.

Tim, so happy with his police motorcycle on his third birthday. This was the day before the diagnosis.

The boys waiting for 'beep beep'.

At the SEDU with Charmaine (in the white shirt). Sam (in the white singlet, with his back to the camera) is eating lunch with Tim's group of four boys, November 1992.

Auditory integration training with Dr Michael McDonald, August 1993.

Tim's first day of school at St Brendan's, 31 January 1995.

Tim at the school sports carnival with his wonderful first teacher, Nic Walls.

Tim and Sam with Wotta, July 2002.

The day we left the pink house at Wynnum West for the very last time in 2003.

Tim proudly showing off his high school graduation certificate, 2005.

Tim with his friend
Joyce at their high
school formal.

struggled to understand how to interact with the other children. It was so sad watching him in those moments.

In the end, I decided not to focus on the general features of his condition. I thought it was more important to focus on Tim as an individual, to figure out who Timmy was and not what the syndrome was. Someone had to. There were already too many people in his life who saw the problem before they saw the person.

Just after Timmy's fourth birthday, I was called in to the SEDU for a meeting to discuss how Tim was doing. The teachers told me that he cooperated well and tried everything at least once. He liked colours and he could do the actions when the class sang songs, but he couldn't identify animals when asked. He was also one of only two children in a class of twenty who were not able to say their own names. This came as a huge shock to me—I didn't realise he was so far behind. All along, the feedback from the SEDU had been so positive, *This is good, that's good, isn't this wonderful, he's doing well.* Then suddenly they were sitting opposite me looking gravely concerned: *the child doesn't even know his own name.*

It was a really devastating moment for me, for some reason. It was like I'd been walking around in the desert, thinking I was getting to the other side, then realising I was still lost. You think things are getting better then someone tells you things are still really bad, and actually probably worse than you thought. Timmy's fourth birthday had come and gone, and he still wasn't really speaking. Other children were having whole conversations with their parents by then. Yes, Timmy knew more words than he had a year earlier, but it wasn't nearly enough. He would need more than a hundred words to get through life.

•

We joined a playgroup that year, up at the local church. I wanted Timmy to hang around ordinary kids as well as the kids at the SEDU. I thought it might be beneficial, especially for his language development. It was a bit of a pipe dream, but I persisted. Timmy hated it; I virtually had to drag him there every week, but Sam really enjoyed himself. We had to keep going, if only for Sam.

It was hard seeing Timmy struggle in that environment. It was awful, the way he screamed outside the door, though he usually settled once we were inside. But even then, he couldn't play with the other children. He would stand outside the circle while they sang Ring-a-Ring-a-Rosie, wanting to join in but not understanding how to play. Some days he screamed throughout the whole playgroup and I could have died of embarrassment. It was such a disruption, although the other mothers were very kind about it.

I tried to be discreet in the way that I dealt with him. I spoke gently to him and reassured him, I was never angry or threatening. Often, instead of trying to make him do something he didn't want to do, I'd keep him moving, which would distract him. I was balancing Tim's needs with Sam's. It wasn't fair on Sam if we made a scene when we were out, if we had to leave somewhere, or if we couldn't go at all because it was too hard to manage Tim. Sam was entitled to experience life and have fun, and I tried my best to make sure he didn't miss out. Thankfully—and I am so grateful for this—Sam was the most easy-going, compliant kid you could possibly imagine. He was a dream. He loved Timmy more than anything and he never seemed the slightest bit fazed, even when his brother made a scene.

After all that time in isolation when I was with the boys' father, I did everything I could to make connections with people and become a part of the community. As well as the playgroup, I joined a support group for mothers of kids with autism, which was organised by a mum from the SEDU named Alice, whose son also had autism. She was a very determined woman.

Alice and her husband were very kind to us; they brought a trailer full of sand over to the house one day so that the boys could have a sandpit. They invited us around to their house several times, though I always felt unworthy. After my experience in my marriage I still felt awkward around other adults, plus I had a child who was a nightmare to take anywhere. It was like having a newborn; I could barely start a conversation before I was distracted by something Timmy was doing. He was also a bit more defiant by then and he ran around everywhere, so he had become much harder to control. Added to that, I was incredibly self-conscious about being a single mother.

When I spent time with couples, I felt constantly judged, or pitied, and I really couldn't stand it. I felt vulnerable because the boys and I were on our own. I didn't want my son to miss out on getting help because I didn't have any money, and it upset me that the parents I met could do more for their kids because they were a team and they were in a better financial position. *It's too hard on your own*, I thought.

Although I spent a lot of time with mothers from the support group, I sometimes struggled with their company. It was a very depressing circle, in many ways. Some of the things the mothers were dealing with were just horrifying—children who were extremely violent, or incontinent, or who self-harmed. There was swearing and hateful words from older children who had autism, destructive children who had wrecked houses, no place for the kids at school and so much pressure on the parents that their relationships disintegrated. It was through that circle that I came to understand how destructive and painful autism could be. The women needed to offload, that was the whole point of the group, but their stories made me very frightened of what lay ahead. There was no room in their lives for anything but autism and at times it felt like a competition to see who was having the worst time, whose child was the worst. There was so little hope.

I continued to go to the meetings as I wanted to support Alice, who was so dedicated and committed to helping others, but I preferred to spend much of my time outside, watching Sam and the other little children play. I pretended I was supervising but I really just wanted to get away. I would never survive if I gave in to the sadness.

•

Around this time, Timmy became more obsessive. It was like he was on speed some days, spinning like a broken record, laughing hysterically at nothing. He would say certain words over and over again, 'Dog, dog, dog, dog.' He'd say, 'Cup of tea, milk, sugar. Cup of tea, milk, sugar,' and 'Beep beep, beep beep, beep beep, beep beep.' It really drove me crazy. It was like he'd gone through a developmental spurt, connecting words and objects, and he had to practise every second of the day. He learned to recognise some written words and associate them with pictures, and in October he came home with his very first reader. 'My truck, my train, my car,' he would say. I was absolutely ecstatic. I always knew he liked books. I knew he was intelligent, but that really proved it. I was over the moon that someone else could see it now, too. If only he had more help, how much could he achieve?

The speech and occupational therapists we worked with initially had continued to see Timmy for quite a few months, but I couldn't afford to keep seeing them after I left my husband. They recommended, for ongoing help, that Tim go to an Autism Centre—a specialist facility that was the only one of its kind in Brisbane. They said it was state-of-the-art, but the waiting list was very long.

When I called the centre initially, they told me the wait was two years, which came as a terrible blow. *Surely if a child needs help he should get it straight away?* I thought. In two years, Tim would be six years old and should be starting school. We didn't have two years to wait. I contacted the speech and occupational therapists and they agreed with me; they pulled every string they could to get Timmy a place. It took a year just to get an interview, but I was grateful for that much. In December 1992, when we were asked to come in for an assessment, I was over the moon. *Thank god*, I thought. Be careful what you wish for.

The Autism Centre was set up in my mind as the holy grail of autism treatment. It was filled with specialists trained to deal specifically with Tim's condition. Not even the SEDU was that focused. Getting in was so difficult and its reputation was so impressive, I assumed we'd be walking into a dream. For me, it was more like a nightmare. The centre was housed in a concrete bunker, surrounded by barbed wire. It felt wrong from the minute we arrived.

Yet again, I'd been hoping for a five-day program for Tim. My main concern was that he got all the help he could, though sometimes I wondered if I just needed a break. I was torn; I wanted to be with him all the time and give him all the help and protection that I could, but I was struggling with two small children on my own. I was tired when Timmy was home but I couldn't settle when he was away, either. I worried constantly that I was doing the wrong thing. In the end, it didn't matter because there were only limited hours for Timmy at the Autism Centre, just like the SEDU. And the minute I saw the place, even limited hours seemed too much.

It was a cold, clinical place with bars on the windows; a seventies-built government building that had no humanity to it at all. It was a treatment facility for children and teenagers, but there was no colour, few toys, no posters, no bright and happy decorations. They said colour overstimulated the children, which didn't make sense to me. I thought it would be better to try to replicate the world they were trying to get these children to be a part of. It didn't look like a place for a child at all—it looked like it needed a coat of paint and a good clean-up. The playground equipment was shabby and old, there was no grass anywhere and the grounds were compressed gravel. I felt so unsettled as we walked around. I should have listened to my instincts there and then and said thanks, but no thanks. But yet again, if I refused a place, there was nowhere else to go.

I saw and heard things that really disturbed me. The centre was filled with all kinds of screaming and howling, distressed noises from non-verbal children and teenagers. The older ones were aggressive and more frightening. There were teenage boys pacing back and forth like caged animals, wearing large chain necklaces around their necks. They often tried to escape and the chains held their personal information. They had to be secure enough so the boys couldn't rip them off. There were locks and bolts everywhere, and bars and chains to protect the kids from the world, but there wasn't a lot of separation between the older children and the younger ones.

Later, I saw how aggressive some of the younger children were as well. Aggression can be a common feature of autism, but because Timmy wasn't like that I found this behaviour really alarming. I was assured that there were enough staff members per child to stop the small children being hurt, but I worried. I was fearful of Timmy being in such a sad place and the possibility of him being hurt by some of the other children, but it seemed like the only opportunity we had. It was a specialised centre for a condition that my son had—I just had to accept that that's where we belonged.

•

The staff members at the Autism Centre were professional but very cold. They were clinicians, very focused on the condition. They never asked me what I knew about Timmy, which bothered me. I had lived with him for four years and observed his behaviour; surely that knowledge was useful in some way? But the prevailing attitude, for our very first interview, was that they knew everything and I knew nothing. They were the experts and I should stay out of their way. I tried to trust the process; I didn't feel like I had an option. I asked at the SEDU and the only other facility that anyone recommended was down in Tasmania, impossible for us. So, early in 1993, Timmy started at the Autism Centre two days a week, from 9 a.m. until 3 in the afternoon.

Fundamentally, the Autism Centre was trying the same things that the SEDU had been working on, but it was more specialised care. There was speech and occupational therapy to get Timmy ready for school, and some behavioural therapy to deal with his crying and emotional outbursts. They would introduce things that were difficult for my son, like wearing shoes and toilet-training, eating different foods, and dealing with Timmy's challenging behaviours. By that point, Timmy was very oppositional—the term they used at the Autism Centre was 'non-compliant'. I couldn't get him to hold my hand or follow instructions; it was impossible to get him to sit still for a haircut or an examination at the doctors. These behaviours were so intense and so constant that it was impossible to live a normal life. The therapists would try to improve them. As part of his social training, Timmy would go out to public places with his therapists, like a shopping centre or a park, and practise walking, holding hands and eating, all necessary skills to get him through life.

Every morning, a bus arrived from the centre to collect Timmy and the same bus brought Timmy home each afternoon, and all communication with the therapists came through a notebook in Timmy's bag. His therapists would write reports in the book each day and I had to pull it out of his bag and read them, writing notes back if I had any queries. It was quite bizarre. It made me quite sick to put him on that bus for the one-hour trip to the centre; he was only four. One morning I put him on the bus and waited to wave him goodbye. As I watched, the boy sitting behind Tim grabbed his seat-belt straps and yanked back on them, and Tim started to cry. I tapped on the door and asked for the aide to go and check what was going on; I wondered why the aide was sitting up the front, too far away to intervene.

I was really involved at the SEDU so it was difficult for me to put Timmy on the bus for the Autism Centre and not see him for a whole day. I didn't know what to do with myself; it felt like I'd lost a limb. Tim was so vulnerable and I felt such a powerful urge to keep him close, to protect him. It terrified me to let him go. It's not that I thought Timmy was at serious risk at the centre, I just didn't trust people in general. I felt threatened by the world; I didn't see it as a safe place. I think because of my experience with my husband, I was constantly on guard. I was always tense, waiting to defend my sons from threats that I imagined lay around every corner.

•

Once or twice a term I was invited in to the Autism Centre for an assessment day, to see how Tim was progressing. It made me very sad. I could see that he was doing well, that he heard what was being said and followed instructions, but where I would jump up and down to congratulate him, the therapists would barely acknowledge his achievements. They said if you gave him too much praise it would overstimulate him. I was scared to challenge them about this, but it didn't make sense to me. It didn't seem right.

After a few months, the therapists recommended that Timmy come to the centre three days a week instead of two because they felt he needed additional care. It was clear they saw him as a severe case, which upset me a lot. They wanted to teach Timmy sign language but I refused to practise at home. The teachers at the SEDU had also mentioned it and it struck me as a strange coincidence—I was paranoid that they were colluding with the therapists at the Autism Centre. Regardless, I thought it was the wrong path to go down. The therapists argued that Timmy wasn't developing speech fast enough and it would help to settle him if he could communicate better, but I felt that it would end up being a prison. If he started to rely on sign language he could only speak to other people who knew sign language; we should focus on developing his language. Tim could make sounds, he had a voice; he could ask for a drink, he could ask to go shopping. I believed he could learn to speak. Why did the therapists want to push him into the margins of society? It felt like they were already giving up.

I wanted to work with the staff at the centre to help Timmy but they didn't see us as a team. They didn't share much with me and they weren't interested in hearing about the things Timmy did at home, whether he'd learned to button his clothes or push his brother on the swing. My diary entries were full of frustration: *They don't tell me much, they don't seem to listen.* Everything I offered came to a dead end. In fact, I sometimes found them downright hostile. I asked to change the day of our assessment visit once because Sam was sick, but they refused; there was no flexibility, no eagerness to have me involved. I joined Timmy's group on one of their social outings one day and the kids were sitting in a food court making disruptive noises, behaving a bit oddly, like children with autism do. On a table behind us, a group of adults started mimicking the children and laughing at them. It made my blood boil. The staff from the centre told me not to say anything and I did as they asked, but I knew it was the wrong thing to do. Someone needed to stand up for those children because they were *just children*. They couldn't defend themselves.

•

One of my major concerns was Timmy's eating, because it was still hopelessly limited: chocolate, bread and chicken, and the odd snack here and there. I was convinced he would get scurvy if he didn't eat more fruit. He was constantly sick and things still weren't right with his bowels, so I wanted to introduce more vitamins into his diet. Timmy had an individual plan at the Autism Centre and that was one of the goals. I would always send a piece of fruit along in his lunch box, hoping that they could encourage him to eat it, though they hadn't had any success. With citrus fruit in particular, it was like holding up a crucifix in front of a vampire—he'd recoil in terror. Maybe it was the smell.

I came to regret asking for help with eating. The staff members at the centre were very forceful with food, much more than I would have been. Timmy came home from the centre one day with juice stains all over his T-shirt and I knew there had been a battle to get him to drink it. I was deeply concerned, but I didn't say anything.

Timmy had been at the Autism Centre for the better part of a year when a strange report came home in the communication book. I say strange, but it was actually quite devastating. I felt sick to my stomach when I read it. On 2 November 1993, the main note in Timmy's book was nothing out of the ordinary. He'd had a good day, responded well to this or that. Then below, in a post-script, it read: *Brought up 2 mandarin pieces at morning tea, which he was told to re-eat (sounds terrible I know but Timmy's rejection is totally behavioural and he is only trying us out).*

They had forced Timmy to eat a piece of fruit and when he vomited it back up, they forced him to eat the vomit. *What kind of person would do that to a five-year-old child?* I thought. What kind of people had I trusted to take care of my son? Full of rage and guilt that I had put Timmy in that situation, I rang the director of the Autism Centre.

'I was expecting your call,' she said.

'If you were expecting my call, why didn't you have the decency to call me yourself?'

She was on the back foot immediately, apologising for what had happened. She agreed it was unacceptable to force a child to eat vomit and assured me they had updated their policies. The teacher involved had been reprimanded, she told me. 'It will never happen again,' she said.

I told her I didn't care; it was too little too late. I could only imagine Timmy's pain and distress in that situation and it made me want to scream. How did they even get him to swallow the fruit in the first place? Did they force it into his mouth? Timmy did not have the words to tell me what had happened and how he felt, or how scared he must have been. And those people were supposed to protect him; it wasn't a prison, he wasn't there to be punished. What right did they have to try to bend

Timmy to their will, to treat him like some kind of animal? Worse, I thought, if this was what they were willing to tell me, what had they left out? I thought of all the other times Tim had come home upset and wondered how far they had gone to cause that. I could see then that my instincts were right. There was no apology I could accept or any words the director could say that would allow me to trust them again. Timmy would not be going back.

I felt in that moment very similar to how I had felt the day Timmy was first diagnosed. I felt overwhelming shame and sadness, like I had failed my son. I was incredibly angry at what had happened to him and I felt completely lost. When the boys were sound asleep that night, I took a mattress off the bed and leaned it up against the wall. I punched it and punched it and punched it until I couldn't punch any more then I fell to the floor, heartbroken, bawling my eyes out. I blamed myself for what had happened. I had sent Timmy to the centre every week when I knew it wasn't the right place for him. I should have known better, I should have tried harder and I should have been stronger. I convinced myself that I only used their expertise as an excuse to send him there, that I should have stepped up and helped Timmy myself. I couldn't look at myself in the mirror, I was so disgusted, and I vowed I would never let my son down again.

7

Sound

I was always looking for new information about autism, hoping for a breakthrough. There were daytime talk shows like *Donahue* and *Sally Jessy Raphael* where you might hear the occasional story; magazine articles or flyers that you'd come across. If you heard of someone in the field with some expertise, you could call them or write them a letter and they would more than likely respond. It took longer without the internet, but information still got around. I just think we had to work harder for it.

Word of mouth was a really important communication channel. Part of the reason I stuck with the support group is because everyone shared whatever they had heard about autism, particularly anything to do with treatment. In early 1993, one of the other mothers mentioned a new therapy going around called auditory integration training. It was one of the few treatments that seemed to be effective because it targeted one of the biggest problems faced by people with autism—sound.

Though no one really understood why, it was obvious that our children were highly sensitive to different noises. Timmy's problems had started with Velcro and coins, but there was a vast number of sounds that distressed him and it took forever to figure out what each of them was. I tried to help Timmy get used to the things that bothered him, but it was an agonisingly slow process. I would leave the vacuum cleaner lying around and encourage Timmy to ride it, pretending it was a horse. I hoped that one day I'd be able to turn it on without causing him to run away crying. The blender and Mixmaster were left out too. I would coax him into pushing the buttons to turn them on and off, hoping the control would help Timmy to overcome his fear of them. He seemed a little less terrified when he realised he could turn the noise off by himself, though it didn't make it any easier for me to cook or do the vacuuming.

I used to push Timmy up and down the yard on the powered-off lawnmower, which was something else that really scared him when it was running. He was happy to do that a hundred times a day, but as soon as the engine started up he screamed and ran away as fast as possible. He just couldn't bear the noise. I was always tense, not knowing what would set him off, and it was often worse when we were away from home, when he had less control over his environment. I often took Timmy to a big shopping centre near our home and we'd take the escalator up to the third floor to visit the toy shop. When we got to the top of the second set of escalators he would look up, start screaming and run wildly away, always straight towards the crockery department. I was terrified that he was going to crash into the most expensive items and I would end up with a huge bill. I looked up but there was nothing to see except a large air-conditioning vent. It wasn't until much later I realised the sound of the motor, or the air coming through the vent, was the thing that terrified my son.

Fans were also a huge issue, especially in the middle of a hot Brisbane summer. We'd bought a standing fan when Timmy was two but it was left unused for a few days so Tim paid no attention. When we turned it on, he instantly became hysterical. Because the fan was between Timmy and the door, he wouldn't run past it; instead he jumped on the bed and with a flying leap tried to jump right through the fly-screened window. I had to lurch forward, grab his foot and drag him back in.

I tried my best to help Timmy. After the incident with the fan, I started taking him down to the shopping centre to sit in front of an electrical retail store and look at the display window full of fans. I had to drag Tim there kicking and screaming at first. I didn't even try to take him inside. My intention was just to get him to sit on the bus seat outside the store. Every afternoon, five days a week, we went to sit outside that store. Every afternoon, as we got close, Timmy would start dragging on my arm, nervous and upset. It was weeks before I could get him to sit still on that bench, patiently explaining time and again that the fans couldn't hurt him. Eventually, he sat without complaint and so I started the next step of getting him to walk up to the window and have a closer look. It became a bit of a game for Timmy, like when you are a little kid at the beach and you see a big wave coming and you run away from it but you also look back at it and half hope it will nab you. He started to run back and forward with a smile on his face, *You can't catch me!* We'd made a tiny bit of progress against the terrible fan noise, but summer was almost over by then.

•

The more I read about autism and sound sensitivity, the more I realised how horrific it was for sufferers. Some articulate adults with autism were able to explain what affected them, and some said that snow falling could sound like bricks smashing through a glass roof. It made me wonder about some of the things that had happened when Tim was a baby. When Timmy wouldn't sleep, I walked him back and forth up the small hallway of that tiny house, walking back and forth past the fridge. It was an old fridge with a fan motor at the back. I wondered if it was the sound of that fan that caused him so much distress and kept him awake. Had I been making the situation worse by continuously going past it?

I also read that the sound of a mother's beating heart could upset a baby with autism. It was devastating to think that my heart, which only beat because of my boys, could be something that hurt Timmy. I cried a lot when I read that.

•

Although it seemed like all people with autism suffered from sound sensitivities, they weren't the exact same sounds; everyone seemed to have a different catalogue of things that set them off. Audio integration training was tailored to the individual person. Initially, the doctors ran tests to identify which decibels were most distressing for the person and then they developed a program to help desensitise them to those specific sounds. Twice a day, each day of the program, the person would listen to a piece of music that had the distressing decibels taken out. They would hear the sound frequencies *around* the ones that bothered them, and it would make them less sensitive to the sounds that were missing.

A doctor called Michael McDonald was coming from California to Brisbane to run the treatment, a ten-day program that cost $1500. It was non-invasive, but it wasn't widely used or recognised in the medical profession and there wasn't substantial data to support the results. It worked for some people and not others; there were no guarantees. I didn't care. I knew that if I could improve Timmy's sensitivity to sound I could change his life. The least I could do was try.

The problem at that point was that $1500 might as well have been a million. I was broke. We relied on the Salvation Army for food sometimes and almost every bit of clothing we wore had been given to me by friends. People actually gave me $50 here and there because they saw how much I was struggling.

Timmy's father had the money, but the chances of getting it from him seemed slim. As the weather turned cooler, I'd realised that I hadn't packed any winter blankets for the boys. I asked their father if I could take some from the old house, but he refused. I asked if he would buy winter shoes for the boys, but he said no. The only way I'd get anything from him was if I moved back there and lived with him. In the end, I had to grit my teeth and smile, and pretend I was considering moving back to Wynnum West. I felt this incredible urgency that we would miss our chance with this doctor from America, and that's what got me through having to ask the boys' father for the money. I don't know if I caught him on a good day or he felt bad for Timmy, but he came through with it. The downside was that he insisted on being with us every day of the treatment.

Before the program started, I attached two old knobs and an old set of headphones to a cardboard box, so that Timmy could practise wearing headphones at home. I couldn't even get him to wear a hat, so I knew we would struggle with the headphones. But we turned it into a game and Timmy had fun with it—he was happy to wear them so long as no sound came through. I reassured him when he put them on, over and over again, 'These will make your ears better, nothing will hurt your ears any more.'

Timmy believed me. I could see a look of relief on his face, as if he believed it was possible for me to take that pain away. I was certain that he understood every single word I'd said. I was certain that he understood my intent and what I wanted for him, and I was moved by the look of trust I saw in his eyes.

•

I had no idea how they were going to test Timmy because I wasn't sure of the accuracy of Tim's answers, but the doctors assured me they'd been through the process so many times that they knew what they were doing. Sure enough, when they gave me the test results, it was like they'd been in the house with us. *This frequency is often produced by refrigerator motors, this one is associated with metal-on-metal contact.* It was really uncanny. *These frequencies cause your son physical pain.*

The training was completely exhausting, and not just because Timmy's father was there, quizzing me endlessly about getting back together. Timmy screamed when they put headphones on him and he had to be held down. He sat in my lap and I wrapped my arms around him and he screamed, squirmed and fought to get away from me. It sometimes took four adults to hold him still and stop him from pulling those headphones off. I hated using force with him, but sometimes I didn't have a choice. If we didn't get through it, there was no chance for improvement.

People had come from all over Queensland for the treatment and I was distressed to see how much suffering there was in that community of people affected by autism. I sat on the front steps of the training centre one day and played toy cars with a 21-year-old woman with autism who had never spoken a word. I watched children and adults throw themselves on the ground in violent fits, reacting horribly to the treatment. I saw a 50-year-old woman be escorted in to the centre with one of her sisters on each arm, holding her tight for security. She wore headphones even before she came in, to block out all the sounds that hurt her, and dark glasses to block out the light. She also wore a crash helmet. It was a very sad sight. I heard scared little children like Timmy screaming and crying behind closed doors, full of fear and pain, and I spoke with their parents, who were all just as anxious and as desperate as me.

I questioned the American doctors as much as I could to learn about what was happening overseas. They were lovely people, very caring and concerned about Tim, but they were unable to make any promises. It was reassuring in a way that they could admit that the treatment didn't always work. Since Timmy's diagnosis, I'd discovered that the world was filled with people who were happy to promise you the world in order to make money. There were people spruiking fad diets and vitamins; there were a lot of naturopaths talking about yeast and milk infections, and problems with the gut and bowels. There was a doctor from Germany who recommended using stem cells from lambs to treat children who had autism and a mother at the SEDU said it was the best thing that had ever happened for her daughter, but it seemed really fishy to me. I had visited a couple of these people who said they could help Timmy but it was clear that they weren't very credible. They often claimed to cure autism, which was ridiculous. They seemed to have very little (if any) knowledge of the disorder and there was a complete lack of scientific evidence to support their claims. They just wanted me to spend a bucketload of money on their pills and potions. But I never got that impression from Dr McDonald and his team.

When you spend a lot of money on treatment, you're obviously keen for it to work. You are looking so hard for results that you end up seeing things that aren't really there. But with Timmy, the results were obvious. They were big changes, almost overnight. We were in the waiting room one day when Tim's father bought a can of Coke and snapped it open, and for the first time in Timmy's life he didn't react at all. Before, the sound would have sent him into a fit of crying, but Tim looked completely unfazed, as though nothing out of the ordinary was happening.

When we rode in the car, Timmy refused to sit in the back seat. He wanted to ride in the front passenger seat with his head hidden below the dashboard. Then one day, just after the treatment started, I realised he was sitting up in his seat, staring out the window. 'Plane,' he pointed out. That, too, had never happened before.

The music Timmy was listening to sounded chaotic and dreadful with all the missing bits. The song wasn't really distinguishable, but it didn't seem to matter. By the end of the process, it would soothe him. It was as though Tim had been suffering a migraine his entire life and it was only just starting to clear. It had a knock-on effect that I didn't expect, including helping Timmy's sense of balance. He used to fall over all the time for no reason at all, and he couldn't ride a tricycle. Two weeks after the treatment had finished, Timmy was riding a bike!

In the longer term, his speech began to develop and he started playing with other little children. It was easier for him to just be in the world, once we dealt with the problem sounds. It was easier for him to pay attention to other things, to react to his environment and be more aware of what was going on around him. It was almost as if a blindfold had been removed and he was seeing everything for the first time. It was joyful.

We ran into one of the SEDU mothers at the shops after the treatment and Timmy smiled at her and said her name. She was astounded. She wanted Dr McDonald's phone number; I could see the hope in her eyes. I only wish everyone could have had the same experience as us. I had friends who spent thousands of dollars on the treatment but got nothing out of it, and they were understandably heartbroken, although I don't think it was over the money. I think knowing that auditory integration *could* work for some people, but that it hadn't worked for them, was worse than never hearing about it at all.

•

News spread quickly about the treatment and there seemed to be even more interest towards the end of the program. Dr McDonald and his team planned to return to Australia a few months later to meet the demand. They recommended that Timmy do another ten-day program as they hoped it might improve things even further and, because he'd seen the results, Tim's father was happy to foot the bill.

It was only seven months between the first session and the second, but Timmy was like a new person. He walked into the treatment centre without crying, took his place in the chair and put the headphones on by himself. He sat there happily for each half-hour session. One day, we saw a little boy we knew from the Autism Centre called James. He was doing the program for the first time and was reacting the way Tim had the first time around, screaming and squirming in his chair, completely upset. I felt terrible for James, but Timmy's experience gave me hope that his pain might be worth it in the end. I wanted to burst out laughing when Tim turned to speak to him.

'Shut up, James,' he said, 'I'm trying to listen.'

8

School

In 1993, in Tim's second year at the SEDU, a doctor who was later recognised as one of the world authorities on autism came to visit. He made a brief assessment of Tim and declared that my son did not actually have autism, but was developmentally delayed, with mild autistic characteristics. He said that Tim could learn and develop his social skills if he spent more time with normal kids.

'If you put him in a special school, that's all he will be—special-school material,' he said.

The doctor told me Tim would be in school until he was eighteen and then he could work, although he clarified that Tim would never be fully independent. I asked him why the Autism Centre had insisted that you have either autism or you don't, with no grey area. He said that they were out of touch.

A couple of years earlier, I think this news would have been welcome. When I was casting around trying to find a way out of our situation, this doctor's words would have been a life raft, but I had been through so much since that nightmare diagnosis that he only made me angry. He watched my son playing for five minutes, didn't ask me a single question, made his grand announcement and left. His arrogance was mind-boggling. How could this man predict Tim's entire life when he barely knew my son?

I wrote in my diary that night, *I feel like they're playing emotional games with me. They all say what they want then walk away. No matter what you call it, it's still the same. They don't offer practical help or tell me where to go to get it. I'm sick and tired of it. They're breaking my heart.*

I knew enough about autism by then to know that my son *did* have autism, but the label was almost irrelevant to me. I wanted to know what I could do to help him. I wanted skills, therapy, a program—a slightly different diagnosis didn't help. Every doctor we spoke to claimed to be an expert, but none of them seemed to have a clue how to make a real difference in Tim's life.

I think that particular doctor and the staff at the SEDU thought I was unrealistic, that my expectations of them and Tim were too great, but I don't think they were. I may have been surrounded by experts in the field of autism, but I was the only expert on my son—I knew he could have a decent life and no one could convince me otherwise.

•

Tim kept defying other people's predictions, even the idea that children with autism couldn't form social bonds. Everyone kept telling me that Tim would never be interested in other people, and certainly, most of the time, it seemed to be true. I took him to Hungry Jack's for a birthday party one day and he just wanted to be as far away from the other children as possible. He would go to the playground when they were at the table and as soon as they headed for the playground he'd run off in the other direction. He stayed at the table long enough to blow out the birthday candles and then he'd disappear again. But Tim had made a friend at the SEDU, a little girl named Maryanne, who wore glasses. They played happily together and held hands when they walked. It was pretty adorable and didn't it defy all the supposed rules of autism? When I saw them together I was thrilled.

There were other signs of progress at the SEDU, things I found really surprising. Tim came home one day covered in green paint. He didn't seem to notice it at all and I didn't have to wash it off until bedtime—a year earlier it would have driven him nuts. He could respond to instructions from his teachers and do colour puzzles, although he was still terrified of the colour red. One day, he told me that fireworks hurt his ears. It was the first time he'd been able to explain to me what was bothering him.

I clung to every bit of good news that we got, every step forward, but it was such a slow process. Whatever I had hoped or expected from the SEDU and Autism Centre, it was clear Tim still needed special care. The general consensus was that my son should attend a special pre-school the following year, and the SEDU staff suggested the one next door. Tim still had problems communicating and wasn't very independent; he still became upset easily and found it difficult to cope with many situations. Tim's level of intelligence could not be assessed because of his language level, but the SEDU teachers believed he would always need special-education learning programs. They thought regular schools were out of his reach, but I didn't agree. I wasn't worried about Tim being around children from a mainstream school for academic purposes; it was more about being in a social environment where there were certain expectations that mirrored the world we lived in. I didn't want Tim to be stuck in a bubble of disability and disadvantage; it seemed to me that his best chance of learning to cope with the world and to find his place in it was to be in with other children from all walks of life, not tucked away in a corner.

At the time, some people thought that if you put children with autism in among normal kids it would cure them, but I knew that wasn't so. Tim lived with Sam and I, and we were both reasonably normal. But, so far, living with us hadn't fixed all Tim's problems. I wished it was that easy. What I was fighting for was opportunity and inclusion.

Mid-1993, I began looking for a pre-school or kindergarten that would accept Tim, or at least let him have a trial, but none of the places I contacted would consider it. I was prepared to travel a fair distance and I contacted schools all over the city, but all I got were apologies and closed doors. I visited some special schools during my search and it's not like they were terrible places—I saw some lovely facilities and some very happy children—they just didn't feel right to me. They made me feel that my child was somehow less; I didn't understand why Tim, and by extension Sam and I, had to be set apart. The three of us went to shopping centres, cinemas, the pool and the supermarket, just like everyone else. Why should school be any different? There was something about the idea of a special school that took away our hope.

After weeks of searching, there was a crack of sunlight—a regular kindergarten located in Thornlands, just five minutes from the SEDU. It was a private facility run by an energetic woman named Penny, who was happy to accept Tim as long as I provided a support worker to care for him. I couldn't possibly afford it. I tried to find a volunteer through various community support organisations, but it was futile. I said I would do it, but the school told me it had to be someone who wasn't a relative.

I kept hunting. A woman named Libby from the Noah's Ark Toy Library—a toy library for children with special needs—listened sympathetically to my story. We'd borrowed from the library regularly since I'd heard about it at the SEDU and the staff members were very supportive and very interested in Tim.

It was always a joy to see them. Libby in particular was always very kind and she often had useful suggestions. When she heard my troubles, she recommended I contact the Uniting Church as she'd heard about a program they conducted in childcare centres, supporting children with special needs. Libby was right; I found the support worker I needed, a woman named Debbie Johnson—she was everything I needed and more.

Tim's first day at the kindergarten was really difficult because the other children knew instantly that he was different but were too small to understand why. They weren't very kind, but thankfully we had Debbie on our side. When I dropped Tim at the kindergarten, Debbie was there to meet him. She took care of him when I was away, and I trusted her from the very first moment I saw her. She was one of the most gentle, caring, positive and supportive women I had ever met. She understood immediately how important it was for him to be included and she treated him just like a normal little boy. She wasn't awkward with Tim; she didn't try to assess him or judge him; she saw Tim first and wanted him to have the same opportunities as every other child at the kindergarten. I think it was just Debbie's character; she was an intelligent and compassionate person. She always looked for the silver lining and if there wasn't one, she could find something to laugh about and treat it as a lesson learned.

In the end, Debbie and her husband David became a permanent fixture in our lives. They became my friends—an unexpected joy in my life at a time when I was very isolated and I found it very hard to trust anyone. David became an excellent example to the boys of what a good man should be and Debbie shared every sorrow and happiness with us. I never imagined that I would find such a friendship from a simple request for a volunteer.

After his first day, with Debbie by his side, Tim had a great experience at the kindergarten. What began as a trial at the end of 1993 became a permanent place the following year, three days a week. Sam started at the kindergarten in 1994 as well, which meant some long and lonely days for me at home, but overall I was pleased. The boys settled in well. Shy little Sam made new friends and Tim's language continued to develop; he came home one day and told me the police had come to talk at the kindergarten, and on another day told me all about their petting zoo, which had chickens and rabbits, and a very small lamb. In March, Tim wrote his name for the first time at home and I was truly astounded. I think it was one of the best days of my life.

•

Not long after we moved to Cleveland, when Tim was just shy of his fourth birthday, we were having one of our bad days and I'd become so desperate to communicate with Tim that I had sat down with a piece of paper and started drawing a picture. I was sketching a train when, to my surprise, Tim came over and stood beside me, fascinated by what I was doing. This was a child who would happily play with blocks or Thomas trains and carriages by himself, but would stand up and walk away if I tried to join him. He didn't connect or share in that way.

But here I was, with no artistic ability at all, and Tim was watching me intently. I was so thrilled I had his attention that I began drawing stick figures and naming the body parts as I drew them: arms, legs, eyes, ears, nose, big smiling face. Tim followed it all. *Why didn't I think of this before?* I thought, beside myself with excitement.

When I finished, I put the pencil down but Tim grabbed my hand and pushed it towards the pencil, wanting me to pick it up and continue. That in itself was a major breakthrough—he had indicated to me what he wanted through a personal interaction, by grabbing my hand. I was happy to oblige. Tim stood beside me, transfixed by my artless attempts to create more and more drawings for him. I drew anything I could think of, animals, characters from TV shows, flowers, birds, anything. I drew for him for hours with tears in my eyes, though when I offered him the pen Tim became upset and ran away.

Drawing became part of our daily lives. I kicked myself that I hadn't tried it earlier, but I just wasn't a visual person. When I ran out of things to draw for him, I started drawing the same things over and over again, trains and trees and cats and flowers. He loved trains especially, with faces just like Thomas the Tank Engine. When it was very clear how much Tim was interested in it, I decided to use the drawing as a way of communicating those things I couldn't explain. I thought it might help if he could see what we were going to do that day; maybe it would take away some of his fears.

'Today,' I would start, drawing my stick figures, 'we are going to a party. We give the boy a present, we wait until he blows out the candles and we sing "Happy Birthday" and then we go home.' I had drawings of the present, the cake with candles, some kids, and Tim, Sam and I in the car. The first time I tried this it was the easiest trip out we had ever made. There were no complaints or distress and he was not unsettled. As soon as we sang 'Happy Birthday', Tim insisted that he go home immediately and of course we did. I was so happy with how that outing went, I was pleased to do what he asked.

I started to use drawing to explain everything we did in a day, everywhere we would go and what he was to do and how he was to behave. I used it to talk about emotions, showing all the faces and relating them to incidents, and we also just drew for fun. Tim would stand beside me watching intently and sometimes use words to tell me what he wanted me to draw: *Cat, dog, train.* He rarely spoke but when he did, those moments were extra special.

It took nearly a year for Tim to pick up a pencil himself and start drawing. The very first drawing was really cute. It wasn't Picasso or Da Vinci but it had its own quirky style about it and I thought it was very good. It was a drawing of an elephant.

From then on, art was a daily activity in our house. I never put the pencils and paper away. They were always on the table or nearby for Tim to get to; it made him so happy to do it. By the time he got to kindergarten, Tim was drawing *Thomas the Tank Engine* characters and characters from the *Transformers* cartoons.

He didn't colour them in because it upset him to get crayon or texta on his fingers, but he did excellent outlines in pencil. It was one of the few activities at pre-school he could participate in with his classmates and I was delirious with pride whenever he brought home a picture. I kept them all, every single one. I didn't think my son was an artist; I was just thrilled that he could express himself. It was such a small thing for a five-year-old child, but it was huge for little Tim.

•

Tim had been at the kindergarten for almost a year when I started looking around for a primary school. At this stage, mid-1994, he was still at the SEDU and seemed to be doing well at pre-school. Primary school was a big step but I didn't want to wait any longer. I didn't want Tim to be left behind. The trouble was trying to find a primary school that would accept him.

Again, I jumped on the phone and received rejection after rejection. We couldn't afford any of the private schools and state schools didn't have the resources to care for a child with autism in their mainstream classes. *Why don't I enrol him in a special school?* I felt like I was hitting my head against a brick wall. 'No thank you,' I said. 'We're looking for something different.'

I called various government departments searching for help, and sat through more than one assessment meeting with education department representatives, who seemed already to have written off my son. Tim was given a rating 6 for special-needs assistance—the highest possible requirement for care, which I was told repeatedly the state system couldn't offer except in a special-school setting. I was close to tears, sitting in meetings with these panels of experts who were all smarter than me and all absolutely resolute. They were honest enough to tell me there was a crack in the system and Tim unfortunately slipped through it, but their honesty didn't change the outcome.

I was almost at the end of my tether when I found my way to a special-education guidance officer who had a real suggestion. 'Have I got the school for you!' she said.

We're not Catholics and I had naively assumed that Catholic schools only accepted Catholic students, so I hadn't bothered to contact any in my hunt to find Tim a place. But as the guidance officer explained, Catholic schools are very welcoming. They tend to keep an open door to people who are in need.

I cannot explain what it was about St Brendan's that made it so special, but the moment we walked in for an interview I knew we were in the right place. Even before I met the staff or saw any of the children, there was a spirit in its small environment that felt really beautiful. It didn't look beautiful—I don't think it had had a renovation in thirty years—but the vibe of the place was unmistakable. The school motto was painted onto the wall: 'We live in faith and love.'

St Brendan's was a small school, only 120 students, with a special-education unit of ten children who had a specialist teacher and a full-time aide. The children with special needs attended regular classes for subjects they could manage like religion, art, sports and music, where they got fifteen hours one-on-one with a teacher aide each week. They were involved in all classroom activities but did their reading, writing and mathematics in the large special-needs classroom, which was part of the main school building. It was just what I wanted for Tim! It had the best of both worlds—specialised support and the opportunity to be part of a regular primary school.

St Brendan's was the first and for many years the only special-education primary school within the Catholic schooling system, so they had twenty-odd years of experience under their belts. The principal was a quiet, older man, very kind and very dedicated to his school. He couldn't understand how other schools had turned Tim away; it was not something he could ever do. After a brief interview, St Brendan's accepted Tim for a six-month trial starting in the new school year, then his position would be re-evaluated by both the school and the Catholic education department. That trial period was extended every six months for three years. It wasn't a total green light but it was more than I could have hoped for. If it worked out, it meant that both of my boys could attend the same primary school, which was huge. I wanted Tim and his brother to be close to each other, as long as they possibly could.

•

We were stuck in traffic the first day of school in 1995, and were a little late in arriving. The children had all gathered down at the grotto for prayers and the three of us quickly made our way down there, Tim very keen and leading the way, looking very smart in his little school uniform. We were not a church-going family so I was quite surprised when Tim squeezed through the crowd to sit with the other children and join his hands together in prayer. It always struck me as a significant moment, one of reward for my faith in him, that he was very aware of what was going on and wanted to be part of it. He'd had three years of finger painting and baby songs and playing in the sandpit at his kindergarten. I think he was just ready to move on. He had already announced that he no longer wanted to be called Timmy; his name was Tim and every time I called him Timmy he corrected me. He was growing up fast.

Tim started at St Brendan's in Year 2. I had held him back a year at Thornlands while I tried to find him a primary school and he was a big kid for nearly seven years of age; he would have looked out of place among the Year 1 students. The teachers decided it was age appropriate for Tim to join the Year 2 class and I'm glad they did; he had a lovely teacher in Year 2 by the name of Nic Walls.

When I returned to the school to collect Tim after his first day, Nic met me at the gate. She was young but brimming with confidence, one of those people who is born to be a teacher. She was very sorry to tell me that it hadn't been such a good day; Tim had cried and made a lot of noise almost as soon as I had left. I was so disheartened. Nic was very nice about it and wanted to know what she could do to stop the disruptive noises, but I couldn't tell her because I didn't know. I was still working it out myself. I knew how wearying Tim's noise could be and wondered how much longer Nic would be nice about it, especially when she had twenty other children to teach.

Day after day, Nic met me after school and gave me an update on Tim's behaviour, though it didn't seem to be improving. But Nic never complained or said anything awful. Then one day, on the third week of school, she marched out of the school building happy and proud.

'I have stopped him,' she announced. 'I yelled in his face.' Nic seemed very satisfied and I was just amazed. 'I got really close to him and yelled at him—and I can really yell—and he stopped. He hasn't made a loud noise since. He starts to make a bit of sound and I yell "no" and he stops. He's been happy all day,' Nic explained. 'I didn't like doing it but I had to, it was driving me crazy!' *Try seven years of it*, I wanted to tell her.

I was relieved that Nic had found a way to get through to Tim, even if it was a little bit extreme. Her honesty was very disarming and I felt immediately that I could trust her. And ultimately, I was happy that she had found a way to get through to Tim; that she was able to teach him at all. It was also quite clear that he wasn't frightened of her or very upset by what had happened because he was holding her hand happily and leaning into her, and gave her a hug when we left. It was a huge breakthrough.

One afternoon Nic came rushing out all excited and told me that I was right; she thought Tim was quite intelligent, too. 'He's writing,' she said, and showed me his work. 'You know,

I think he can read quite a lot. And he understands a lot more than you'd think.'

Tim was supposed to spend most of his time in the special-education unit but Nic took him under her wing and kept him with her Year 2 class as much as she could. She kept Tim at a desk close to hers and sent work home with him, to help him learn at his own pace. She continued to meet me every afternoon after school and was happy to share everything that had happened with Tim during the day, what he was doing and how she was getting it done. She was the teacher of my dreams. Nic gave Tim the best start he could have ever had in school, protecting him fiercely, nurturing him like a mother hen and giving him every opportunity to be part of school life and to learn. Tim became Nic's little shadow and she became one of our dearest friends.

•

In many ways our lives had improved, but there were still a lot of complications. There were fees at St Brendan's Primary that I really couldn't afford, not with the rent I was paying in Cleveland. Cleveland had also proved to be a very difficult neighbourhood and I no longer felt safe there with the boys. As the boys' father was still hanging around, I asked him repeatedly if we could have the house at Wynnum West. He had always replied that I could move back into that house when I decided to move back in with him. For me, it wasn't an option. I asked him if he would sell the house so that I could buy something else for the boys and me, but the very suggestion made him livid.

In January 1995, my ex witnessed a scene at our house in Cleveland that changed his mind. We had difficult neighbours either side, including a kid that was cruel to Sam in one house and an alcoholic man in the other who was prone to rages. We returned to the house after a day at the pool to a perfect storm, with the old drunk yelling about trees on the property line and the little boy next door yelling names at Sam. The man turned the hose on my boys before throwing his beer over Timmy; it was a real nightmare. Tim's father just walked away and I was furious. 'I hope you're happy we live in this hellhole,' I yelled as he left. 'This is what your sons are exposed to, because you won't let them live in their real home.'

I would never have had the courage to speak to my ex-husband that way if I hadn't been so angry about what had happened to the boys. Something snapped inside of me in that moment and I just didn't care what their father could do to me. I wasn't afraid of him. I don't know what he was thinking or how he felt about it, but a few weeks later he called to tell me he was moving out of the house. I could move back to Wynnum West with the boys and he wouldn't be there. We had been away for three long years.

•

Leaving Cleveland was so different to when we had fled Wynnum West. I had weeks to get my things in order, proper moving boxes and time to pack, and plenty of time to prepare Tim for the move. His only concern was that his father might be there, but I assured him it would only be the three of us. I think Tim enjoyed the peaceful way the three of us had lived together at Cleveland, and he was aware of the changes in my demeanour as well. There was much more laughter and fun when their father wasn't around. I don't think he wanted to go back to living in an angry, frightening house.

When we pulled up in front of the house I felt a wave of relief. We were back in the neighbourhood I knew, in our home, in our street. My old neighbour Alison had hung balloons and streamers, and a sign across the door, 'Welcome Home Judy, Tim and Sam!' I was excited about so many things—we would have so much more money now that I wouldn't have to pay rent and we would be in a neighbourhood where we knew so many people and could have some peace and quiet. My dog, Razor, was waiting for me, the lovely old thing. I had missed him so much while we were gone.

The boys were delighted to be home and Tim shot straight out to the backyard, to his old sandpit and the swing set, with Sam following right behind. But I walked in slowly. As much as there were positives, there were also a lot of bad memories in that place. Time for a fresh start, I thought.

I couldn't stop their father from coming round every weekend, but I did what I could to make the place ours—mine, Tim and Sam's. I bought paint and changed the colour of every room. I rearranged all the furniture. I tried my best to forget all the things that had happened to me there and focused on a new beginning.

9

Positive Parenting

Even though Tim's first year at school had started beautifully, academically he was behind in his class and there were a lot of things he couldn't do. His speech was getting so much better and so many things were improving, especially our ability to go places as a family, but our home life was still incredibly challenging. Tim was still crying all the time, resisting me and getting very upset, and he was starting to become very angry sometimes. On occasion, he would lash out physically. He particularly hated it when I spoke on the telephone or tried to talk to anyone outside of the house, and he had hit me once or twice to try to make me stop. We were able to leave the house but the focus of Tim's distress had now moved to what happened when we went out, and he had very strict time limits for how long anything could take. When we were out with people, he would push me towards the door and say a hundred times or more, 'Home, home, home, home.' If we didn't leave, it would end in disaster.

At seven, Tim still wasn't fully toilet-trained, which terrified me. I didn't want him having accidents at school and risk teasing from the other children. Of all the battles we had to face with Tim's autism, it was one of the most upsetting and draining for me; I hoped it would get better but I could never be sure it would. There were also ongoing problems with food, with sleep, and with the feel of certain kinds of clothes and shoes. Often there was huge distress and crying for seemingly no reason at all. I am sure observers would have thought that Tim was just naughty and throwing a tantrum, and in fact a surprising number of strangers saw fit to tell me this, but when you spent time with Tim you saw it was more complicated than a tantrum. It wasn't just a battle of wills, with him not wanting to do what I asked; often it was the language, the uncertainty, the lack of understanding, a fear of the unknown, a fear that the unknown would never return to normal. Sometimes the problem was that he couldn't understand the passage of time or that he believed harmless things, things as harmless as shaving cream, for instance, could actually hurt him. Any change of routine or conditions, not knowing where my direction would take him next or how long it would last, these things were all disastrous for Tim.

It was like trying to pull myself out of quicksand. For every gain we had, every step forward that I remember, there were days of screaming, violence, public scenes; frustrated or pitying faces at the school; and a sense that things were always about to spiral. I struggled to keep my head above water; I was very depressed. The boys were my whole world; I didn't have any interests outside of them. There were no hobbies or lightness, and our entire lives seemed to be consumed by autism. I felt so often like I was fighting for my son: fighting the system, fighting other people's judgement. On top of that, the shadow their father cast over my life was still heavy and he made me bitterly fearful and unhappy.

I kept going because I had no choice, because my sons needed me. Tim was especially vulnerable and he needed me. I didn't have any dreams of a magic fairytale ending, I just focused on what I couldn't let happen. I couldn't let my son end up in an institution. I couldn't let him be abused. I wasn't looking for a way out, I was just trying to avoid the worst-case scenario. *Just don't let the worst happen*, that was all I wanted. It was the best I could hope for at the time.

•

Tim had put on a lot of weight and was still having problems with his bowels. His squeamishness around food meant it was difficult to feed him nutritious meals, though I tried everything I could. It hurt me when people commented on his size—he was big, and strong, for his age, but I thought he was beautiful. Still, we visited specialists to look for help because I wanted my son to be healthy.

We saw a nutritionist in Tim's first year of school who was very critical and insisted I force Tim to eat better, which made me feel miserable. *I try*, I thought. *I'm not a lazy mother.* She told me I had to make Tim exercise every day, which was virtually impossible. I couldn't make Tim exercise, any more than I could make him do maths or write poetry. I tried to explain to the nutritionist about Tim's autism, but she wasn't interested. She thought autism was an excuse for bad parenting. She was so judgemental I had to stand up and walk out of her office. I'd had enough.

•

I was also still looking for a solution to the ongoing problems with Tim's behaviour, which was becoming more and more aggressive. He was still very small, only seven years old, but I was terrified of how things might escalate if I didn't get some help. I was worried I might have to consider anti-anxiety medication for Tim because things had got that bad. While reading the paper one day, I came across a story about a Positive Parenting program run by final-year psychology students at the University of Queensland. It was, by all reports, a very affordable and effective way to help children with serious behavioural problems. Always looking for new ways to improve our lives and introduce new opportunities for Tim, I picked up the phone straight away.

When I'd called the university, I hadn't mentioned Tim's autism. I hadn't meant to conceal anything, I just didn't think I had to; it was his behavioural issues I needed help with. In our assessment meeting, I was told that Tim didn't qualify for the program because he had a pre-existing condition. The service was for kids with ADHD or regular behavioural problems; they said there were more appropriate services for Tim. *There aren't*, I thought, *I've looked everywhere.*

I pleaded with them to help me; I don't think I'd said please so many times in my life, and with such fear and anxiety. The student who met with me was really very sympathetic and relented finally; she agreed to ask her supervisor if they would accept us. As I walked back to the waiting room, I passed the supervisor in the hall and recognised him from his photograph in the newspaper. I was bold enough there and then to try to plead my case with him—it was one of the hardest things I'd ever done. We were on many public therapy waiting lists, but they could take years. I had no money, I was alone and I was desperate. I needed to take this opportunity. *Please.*

I was so relieved to get the phone call to let me know Tim and I could be part of the program. It was a lifeline for me. I had no idea what I was in for or how hard it would be but I knew I had to do something about Tim's aggressive behaviour, particularly if I wanted him to be able to stay in school and continue to learn.

In the assessment they had asked me which behaviours I wanted to target, what things I had already tried in order to deal with them, what consequences there were, what praise I used, what had worked and what hadn't. Over the course of six months, the students would develop a program tailored to Tim's specific behavioural issues.

I quickly learned that the Positive Parenting program was as much about training me as it was about changing Tim's behaviour. I described Tim's crying, screaming, whining and what I called 'naughty behaviour', when Tim was being really defiant, and the therapist working with us, a woman named Jennifer, said they called it 'non-compliance'. After filming Tim playing, and observing the way he interacted with me, Jennifer told me that Tim's troublesome behaviour was designed to communicate frustration and anxiety where Tim did not have the words to tell me how he was feeling. She explained that it was a learned behaviour. I had been there beside Tim every step of the way and had helped him and guided him for every minute. Now he was getting older and there were greater expectations on him and he didn't know how to do it on his own; he needed me, probably more than he ever had. He didn't know how else to communicate that need and didn't know how to cope on his own, and his bad behaviour was his way of trying to get his life back the way he wanted it to be: safe and comfortable. It was a way for him to get me to maintain my attention on him and help him, which was what he was used to and what he needed.

As I had started to make some friends and our world grew beyond just Tim, Sam and me, Tim had to work harder for my attention and so the attention-seeking behaviour had escalated. His inability to communicate his needs and confusion only added to his distress. He viewed me as an extension of himself, but we had to draw some clear boundaries, Jennifer said. It was time that Tim learned that he couldn't control my every movement. We were entering another stage of life and Tim wasn't quite ready for it.

Jennifer was a lovely woman, which made it easier for me to accept her judgement. She also promised that we could get some good results that would help Tim to be more settled and happier, which seemed like a good goal to me, even if it caused him pain in the short run.

In the initial phase of the therapy, I had to keep a journal of Tim's behaviour, which was a surprisingly positive experience. Without keeping track, I would have a bad day and remember it as Tim screaming around the clock, but when I looked at the diary I'd see, *Screamed five times a day in half hour blocks.* It really put things in perspective. It showed me patterns in his behaviour that I hadn't seen before and it clarified some things that might be slightly annoying to me but weren't actually big behavioural issues. Some things I thought were a big deal weren't as big as they had seemed, which relieved a bit of the pressure.

With Jennifer's help, we set up some rules, drew up a reward chart and established some consequences. One of the most vital things she taught me was how to give clear and precise instructions, which was a complete revelation. When I'd given Tim instructions in the past, I might say, 'Go and pick that up.' I hadn't stopped to get his attention, made sure he was focused on me or said his name. How was he supposed to know what to pick up? It was about being more aware, more deliberate and more consistent in my communication. I had to get up off my backside and walk over to him, say his name clearly and use short, clear sentences to ask for what I wanted. And it worked! I couldn't believe it.

When Tim did something great, I had to heap praise on him, but it had to be very specific praise. *Excellent job picking up the toys, Tim, I'm really glad you listened to me and did what I asked.* When he behaved badly, I had to stick to my guns. I had to pick my battles and make sure I was starting out with the ones I could win. Jennifer also taught me how to deliver some consequences and how to implement a 'time-out' policy when all else failed. Just learning how to do all this took several sessions, as we had to set it up so that it wouldn't fail—a time-out was seriously high stakes. Trying to keep someone on a chair, who didn't want to be on it for a single minute let alone five, was like running a marathon with your feet tied together. The first time I tried it, Tim wailed for an hour-and-a-half before he was quiet for a minute, and then the moment he was allowed off his chair he began screaming again. It was exhausting work.

We had to undo years of patterned behaviour, and I had to learn to ignore Tim when he was screaming to be heard. I couldn't give him the slightest reaction, not even a glance. 'There's barramundi attention and there's mullet attention,' Jennifer said. 'I need you to be a mullet.' The battles would rage all day and often escalate to being worse than they ever had been. Jennifer had warned me that this could happen, and

Tim's level of distress rose to a level that I had never seen it reach before. But no matter what, I was not going to give up.

It really was all about teaching me skills that I didn't have. We went out every day and every day I was trying to improve Tim's behaviour. I told him he wasn't to make whining noises when we were in public—it was okay at home, but the rule was no repetitive whining noises outside of the house. I felt it was crucial for Tim's inclusion in society that he learn to behave well in front of others. We might only last ten minutes somewhere before he started making sounds and we'd have to go home again, but I didn't ignore it. I was persistent and eventually it paid off. At times I was convinced that it was going to kill me; it was without a doubt the hardest thing I'd ever done. But I was so tired and emotionally distraught from the difficult years with Tim, and I knew that if things didn't change we would end up living in isolation. Tim and I would be shunned by the rest of the world because of his bad behaviour. We would never be able to go anywhere or have anyone over. I didn't want that. I wanted the world to see what a beautiful, gentle and interesting person Tim was, and I wanted him to have the opportunity to enjoy life the same way everyone else did, with people, out in the world. I was determined to get full advantage from this program. With this in mind, I made sure I stuck to it.

Often I would drop into bed at night, exhausted by the relentless rules, not for Tim's behaviour but for my own. I had to follow the program to the letter to ensure it worked, and some days I felt like my nerves were going to snap.

One morning, frustrated that I was ignoring his screaming and demands, Tim picked up a handful of marbles and shoved them into his mouth. I froze. *I know I have to call 000. I know I have to pick him up and turn him upside down, but in this moment I need to stay calm and ignore him.*

It was terrifying. Without turning my head to look at him, and not showing any expression or movement that revealed my horror, I watched him out of the corner of my eye. I saw him waiting for me to lunge at him and desperately remove the marbles, but I didn't. I followed Jennifer's instructions and did and said absolutely nothing, even though my heart was racing madly. I could see that it was getting uncomfortable for Tim to keep all those marbles in his mouth. They moved slightly in his bulging cheeks as he tried not to swallow. His eyes were fixed on me, waiting for the reaction he wanted. He soon realised that for one of the first times in his life he wasn't going to get my attention, even though he had raised the stakes enormously. He also realised that he could no longer hold that many marbles in his mouth without swallowing them, and spat them out onto the floor. Without saying a word I turned away, and Tim walked off to go and play with some Transformer toys. Those few seconds had tested every instinct I had as a parent, but in the end it was worth it.

After just three weeks, changes began to occur. Tim was whining less and he was getting more rewards. I was already using fewer time-outs, which was a relief. As the weeks went by, Tim was happier and more compliant. He didn't hit or try to hurt himself, and I could talk on the phone without him trying to stop me. Initially I'd get just a few minutes but over time he settled completely and I could conduct an entire conversation. I could ask Tim to do more things without resistance or upset. Nearly all the behaviours we targeted were disappearing and his life was so much happier.

It really impacted on my thinking about autism. I had put too much emphasis on sensory overload and not enough focus on behaviour. I think it's a very common assumption about children with autism that they just aren't capable of learning to behave better, but it's not always true. When I first started taking Tim to the movies, we could only get through ten minutes. By insisting that he learn to sit still, I was able to improve that time—fifteen minutes, twenty minutes, then eventually the whole film. Not all children who have autism get this opportunity; they don't learn to control their behaviour in a demanding environment, because people simply don't believe they can. It's easy to lower your expectations when you think you're being kind, but it's not always necessary. I had a little faith in Tim and he repaid it in spades.

•

I looked forward to the appointments with Jennifer every week, to report on Tim's success, ask questions and to try to learn even more. During one of these sessions, she mentioned how concerned she was about me, which made me cry. She had seen first-hand how difficult life with Tim had been and she worried about how I was coping. Despite our success, I was feeling very low. I was battle-worn, exhausted, and despite the improvements with Tim I hadn't been able to pull myself out of my depression.

Jennifer arranged for me to have an appointment with another psychologist who diagnosed me as clinically depressed. They said it really shouldn't come as a surprise, considering all I had been through. They offered me anti-depressants but I refused them because I was scared that I would stop functioning well enough to care for Tim and Sam. They asked me to check in to a hospital for rest but I refused, although I did agree to go into therapy. I began seeing a psychologist once a week and it did make a difference. Over time, it changed a lot of the bad patterns in my thinking, like my belief that I was an unproductive failure and that I could read minds; that I thought I knew for sure that everyone I met was judging me. It helped me to think a bit more clearly and be a bit kinder to myself. It was a real turning point for me.

•

With our new skills, rules and negotiation tactics, I was finally able to make big breakthroughs in many of the areas where I had been struggling with Tim, like toilet-training and learning to tie shoelaces, and especially with food. I was able to teach him social skills like saying 'hello' to people, starting conversations and taking turns to speak, and developing his manners and attention.

Jennifer visited St Brendan's and talked to Nic, and gave her some advice. Nic was just as impressed as I was by Jennifer's professionalism and care. The impact of the Positive Parenting training spread across everything. I was becoming a better communicator and making things much clearer for Tim, and he was becoming more certain of what I expected and wanted from him. To my surprise, I survived the process, exhausted but hopeful. We had truly turned a corner. From having to plead to be accepted into the program, Tim became their star graduate and my letter of thanks was used in their annual report. They said his was one of the best outcomes they'd ever had—little Tim was a major triumph. By the end of 1995, he was a different person: amazingly, happily positive. 'I love my life,' he told me one day. I could only laugh with happiness.

10

Growing Up

Razor was an old dog and had never been too keen about playing with the boys; he was protective, but not playful. Next door we had a new neighbour, a nice young man who was a little too fond of booze; he had a Rottweiler puppy named Stubby, after a stubby of beer. The puppy was a cute thing but Rottweilers had a bit of a reputation as vicious, aggressive dogs, and it made me nervous to have him so near the boys. Tim would go up to the fence and put his fingers through the mesh and the pup would come and lick them like crazy, jumping around in excitement. Tim was always delighted but it made me very anxious. I watched Tim like a hawk when he was outside and near Stubby, though I didn't want to make my son feel nervous for no reason.

One afternoon, as I watched, Tim took himself out through the front gate along the footpath and into our neighbour's yard, right up to Stubby, who was excited enough to jump all over Tim. I figured that if anything happened I could run to the fence in six swift strides and jump over it in a single bound, and release the dog's jaws from whatever part of Tim he had latched onto. It was a terrifying wait, but I decided to let Tim have some time with the pup—I'd never seen Stubby do anything aggressive.

Sam was playing in Alison's yard on the other side, with all of the neighbourhood kids. Sometimes Tim would join them when they played but he always floated around on the outskirts of the group, or went inside Alison's house to check out their video collection. It was the saddest part of autism for me, Tim not having friends. For me, Stubby was like a friend for Tim. I didn't want to drag him away if I didn't have to.

Tim sat on the ground with the pup, who was already quite big at about six months of age, and Stubby scrambled all over him and mouthed at every part of Tim he could. Tim was perfectly calm and chuckled the whole time he was there, like a happy little Buddha. He came home with his shorts shredded and holes in his T-shirt, but beaming from ear to ear; Stubby had wrecked Tim's clothes but hadn't put a mark on his body. They'd had a lovely time.

From then on, Tim visited Stubby every afternoon. He couldn't wait to go over and play with the pup as soon as he came home from school, and every day he'd come home safe and happy. It was an expensive exercise as Stubby tore at all of Tim's clothes, but I got into the habit of dressing him for puppy playtime; Tim only wore his shredded clothes when he went over the fence. For some reason, Tim loved it when the dog jumped around him, mouthing his little hands and licking his face. I don't know what it was that he loved so much, but I think it was one of the happiest times of his life. The dog loved Tim, too, and waited beside the fence all day for him to come home. He'd get so excited when he saw Tim, jumping and barking and calling out for him to come and play.

Stubby moved away with his owner after a year and it was a very sad day for Tim, who looked for him each afternoon long after he was gone. But the pup's legacy was a good one. Tim had walked over to the neighbour's yard and made himself a new friend, and their many happy memories remained. These days families pay tens of thousands of dollars for assistance dogs, as company and protection for children who have autism. It's a formally recognised therapy and the dogs are carefully trained, and it's easy to see the benefits for the children. We couldn't have afforded an assistance dog, even if they were used back then. We were lucky to get Stubby the Rottweiler for free.

•

Sam started at St Brendan's in 1996 and he looked adorable in his little uniform. He looked very handsome and very grown up, but he was also tiny, too tiny to go. 'If I go to school, who's going to look after you?' he asked. He was such a sweet little boy.

I reassured Sam and he went off happily, but the truth is I was miserable without my boys. The days were very long and very lonely; I realised then just how much I had built my life around caring for my sons. I'd given them every bit of love and energy I had up to that point, and I wasn't the sort of woman who could suddenly start enjoying 'me' time. I didn't have many friends and I didn't have any money to go shopping or get my nails done, in fact I couldn't afford the petrol to drive the ninety-minute round trip to school twice a day. To save money, I dropped the boys off in the morning and then sat in the car and waited until school was let out in the afternoon.

With nothing to do and nowhere to go, I figured I might as well start volunteering at the school. Whenever they needed classroom assistants to help the kids read or volunteer parents for the swimming carnival or sports day, I was there. Any job that needed doing, I put my hand up, and when there was nothing to be done I went back to the car, or sat on the school fence, and waited for the final bell.

One day, several months into 1996, the school principal came out to have a chat with me while I was waiting for the boys. He was a lovely man named Ian Morice. The woman who worked in the school library was ill, he said. She would need to take some time away from work. Would I be interested in covering her job? I was absolutely terrified but I couldn't say no; it was an incredible opportunity and I could earn some extra money. But I hadn't worked in years and I didn't even have proper work clothes to wear; I had to borrow some decent clothes from a friend.

I worked in the school library for a month. Everyone was very nice, but I felt totally unworthy. I couldn't even bring myself to eat lunch in the staffroom. The boys were very proud, however; they wanted desperately for me to stay once my month's employment was up. Maybe having a few extra dollars in my purse made a difference for them, I'm not sure. Maybe they sensed how proud I was to do the job. I felt like someone had given me a chance and I was determined to do it well. I had purpose and it made me feel much stronger.

In August the following year, an ongoing position as a teacher's aide came up at St Brendan's and Ian encouraged me to apply. As daunting as it was—I hadn't had a job interview in over a decade—I was familiar enough with the school by then to at least give it a try. The job involved working with children who had special needs; I certainly had plenty of experience.

I thought my heart would burst out of my chest when I got the job. It was such a big achievement for me. It wasn't a handout; I had proven myself and earned the job just like anyone else, so maybe I wasn't so unworthy after all. I worked at St Brendan's for the next seventeen years.

●

When Sam started school, he began to make friends immediately. There were no more than twenty kids in his class and all of the mothers waited out the front of the school each afternoon. It didn't take long before we became friends. They were lovely women who made me feel very welcome in their circle. I was Sam's mother first and not the mother of the child with autism, although they always made an effort to include Sam's older brother. Whenever Sam got a birthday party invitation, Tim was invited too.

It was quite a revelation to spend time with parents whose conversation was not dominated by disability and disability management. There was a lightness to it that was crucial for me; I was still climbing out of my depression. It was just what I had wanted for Tim—a world where he was included in everyday things: school activities, social events. Instead of jumping in to tell us what Tim couldn't do, we were surrounded by people who said, 'Why not?'

I became very close to a woman named Bridget, the mother of a little boy named Max. Max and Sam were like two peas in a pod, and fortunately Bridget embraced all of us. After school, we would often go to Bridget's house so the boys could play together and she and I developed a strong bond. She was a godsend for me. I don't remember ever laughing so much with anyone as I did with Bridget. She helped me to rebuild my confidence around other women—she reassured me and strengthened me.

Bridget's family owned a beach house and her mother, Barb, kindly invited us to stay for a few days during the school holidays one year. The house was perched on a hill right on the beachfront, with magnificent views to the north and south of an endless, perfect white coastline.

One day, a friend of Barb's joined us for lunch, a Jesuit priest named Father Maher. He was just as I imagined a priest should be: gentle, humble and curious. It was lovely listening to his conversation with Barb. Halfway through our lunch, Barb asked Father Maher what he was studying, as Jesuit priests are devoted to knowledge and learning. He explained that he was continuing his life's work, studying the reports of people who had had near-death experiences. My ears pricked up immediately.

Father Maher described some of the things that people reported when they were being revived. White light and a rushing feeling were common, and some people said they heard the words, 'What have you done?' My cutlery dropped with a clang onto the plate as he spoke. I felt the blood drain from my face and tears welled in my eyes. I wanted to leave the table but I couldn't embarrass Bridget or Barb in that way, so I did my best to hold the emotions in.

Father Maher had spoken that phrase just as I had heard it on the night that Sam was born. *What have you done.* I took it to heart, as a reminder to focus on what was most important in my life.

Father Maher and I exchanged letters for several years after that lunch. He was the first person I ever discussed my experience with. Although we didn't practice the same faith, we had similar beliefs. After all the troubled years he helped me to regain that feeling of peace and thankfulness that I felt after Sam's birth. Twenty-five years later, at least once a week those words still come to me and they still move me to my core. Thanks to my correspondence with Father Maher I realised what my response was to those words. It is, 'I have loved.'

•

St Brendan's was a wonderful place. They took Christian values seriously and every day the message of love and kindness was communicated to the kids. It meant that people were always working to make sure Tim and the other children in the special-needs unit had the same opportunities as everyone else, but it also meant I didn't have to worry about bullying. In all of Tim and Sam's primary school years, we rarely had an incident where Tim was called names or made to feel different. I have always been so grateful for that. A little boy named Darren from Tim's class actually called our house one day to ask if Tim wanted to have a play; he and his mum came around for the afternoon and we all had a lovely time. When another classmate of Tim's left St Brendan's, a boy called Joshua, he called Tim just to say goodbye. 'Thank you, Joshua,' Tim replied. 'I think you're a very good friend.'

In so many ways, once we had settled there, the boys had an ordinary childhood. They loved Transformers, Pokémon and Dragonball Z. Tim was increasingly obsessed with films and music, particularly The Beatles, whereas Sam loved to run and jump; he was an incredibly active little boy. One of the things we really loved doing together was going to the pool or the beach and Sam was becoming an incredible swimmer. Both boys had started swimming lessons before school but Sam was like a fish in the water, he really had a gift. By the time he was five or six, his coaches had begun to comment on it. By seven, he was swimming competitively for our local swimming club. He started training every afternoon and on the weekends we went to swimming carnivals. Tim and I would sit and watch the children swimming for hours, which brought a bit of balance to our family. It was nice for all of us to focus on Sam.

There were many swimming clubs that wouldn't let us join because I had told them of Tim's autism and they didn't think they could accommodate him. I didn't bother pushing it, I never did. I never wanted to be somewhere we weren't welcome. I preferred to find a place and people that were more accepting, and I didn't have time to waste. We found a home at a club that was happy to have Tim, where he was invited to swim in the carnivals against some other children with special needs, including little bespectacled Maryanne who we'd met at the SEDU. Tim was a great swimmer and he was often a champion in his very own category. Sam won the club championship for a record four years in a row and he began to swim in the state-level competition.

•

Tim was a different child entirely by the time he was eight years old, but there were always complications and challenges stemming from his autism. There were scenes at school fetes and end-of-year performances, when Tim was out of his comfort zone and asked to do things—dances or plays—that he didn't understand. Sometimes he would act up in the special-education unit, screaming or trying to run away. His behaviour was massively improved but every now and again he still had an outburst, and a few times the police were called to our home

Tim carrying the Australian flag during the opening ceremony of the Very Special Arts Festival at the John F. Kennedy Center for the Performing Arts in Washington, D.C., June 2004. *(Image: Australian Broadcasting Corporation Library Sales)*

Tim wearing a Laser Beak Man T-shirt outside the White House in Washington.

Tim looking at his art on exhibit at Union Station in Washington, D.C., as part of the VSA Festival. *(Image: Australian Broadcasting Corporation Library Sales)*

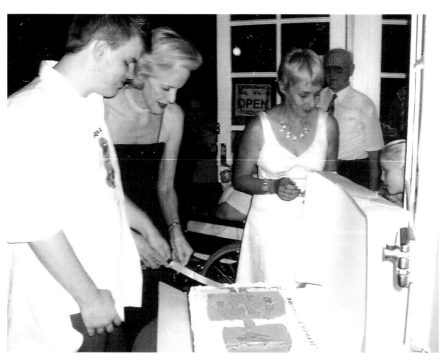

The Honourable Dame Quentin Bryce, who opened Tim's first art exhibition in 2005, cutting the Laser Beak Man cake as part of the celebration at South Bank in Brisbane.

Tim Sharp—'Laser Beak Man and the Fruit Flies'. 42 × 29 cm, crayon and pen on cartridge paper, 2004.

Tim Sharp—Laser Beak Man, 'Hubba Hubba'. 84 × 59 cm, crayon and pen on cartridge paper, 2005.

Have A
FilthY
DisGusting
Birthday

LaseR Beak Man
Says

Laser Beak Man's 'Filthy Disgusting Birthday' card.

Tim doing what few people can—making Wayne Bennett smile—
at Tim's 2006 Brisbane Powerhouse Exhibition.

Tim Sharp—'Laser Beak Man Tells the Wiggles to Shut Up'. 84 × 59 cm, crayon and pen on cartridge paper.

Tim Sharp—Laser Beak Man, 'The Barbie Queue'. 84 × 59 cm, crayon and pen on cartridge paper.

Tim receiving his second honour as a finalist in the Young Australian of the Year Awards in 2007. (The first was in 2006.)

Tim at Wollongong Beach in 2012, showing off the surfboard covered in his art.

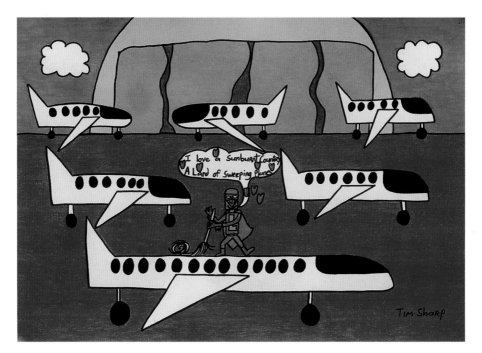

Tim Sharp—Laser Beak Man, 'I Love a Sunburnt Country, A Land of Sweeping Planes'. 84 × 59 cm, crayon and pen on cartridge paper.

Tim Sharp—Laser Beak Man, 'Wee Wee Wee All the Way Home'. 84 × 59 cm, crayon and pen on cartridge paper.

Tim Sharp—Laser Beak Man, 'The Chick Magnet'. 58 × 42 cm, crayon and pen on cartridge paper.

Tim Sharp—Laser Beak Man, 'A Double Shot of Happiness'. 84 × 59 cm, crayon and pen on cartridge paper.

when a misguided neighbour had reported child abuse because she heard Tim screaming. It was horribly embarrassing.

While Tim's language had come along in leaps and bounds, there was still so much he couldn't say. When he was nine, he contracted pneumonia and he suffered a collapsed lung, but he wasn't able to tell me that he was sick or in pain. When we went to hospital, the doctors needed to get a blood sample and Tim was terrified; it took five people to hold him down just so they could draw some blood. He was still petrified of the colour red. On the other hand, when Tim hurt himself earlier that year, running around outside, he came to me for the first time ever and told me he was hurt, and asked me to comfort him. His behaviour was often a paradox.

Sam just glided through all of it. He was a happy little boy who was always skipping or singing or humming to himself, and he never protested no matter where I took him. He came to every one of Tim's appointments and therapy sessions, and I never heard him complain. He loved the toys and always found something to play with, happy to amuse himself while I talked to the adults.

Sam never seemed to have a problem with the more unusual behaviours of the children we associated with who had autism— he just focused on playing and having fun. He was compliant and helpful, sweet and considerate of others. Even as a small child, if we were out somewhere and someone dropped something he would rush forward to pick it up for them. He was a thoughtful boy. That was just his nature.

Sam adored his brother, and even though Tim didn't play the way he wanted he never gave up. He followed him around when he was little and, when he was older, Sam always tried to include Tim when he played. Likewise, Tim adored Sam. Tim was so much bigger than his brother and he loved to pick Sam up, hug him and give him a big kiss.

•

Throughout their childhood, the boys' father still loomed over my shoulder. He still came round every weekend and at other times, even more often than he had at Cleveland. There'd been more boundaries in Cleveland, which was unfamiliar territory for him. It was a bigger house, so it was easy to confine his visits to the living room, whereas at Wynnum West it was such a small space that we were all on top of each other.

The problem was that he felt very at home at Wynnum West. After all, he and I still owned it jointly. It was legally half his house, and he certainly acted like it was. When he came round to visit the boys, he went wherever he wanted and there was nowhere I could go to hide from him. He felt like he could have free and easy access to the backyard, including the big sheds up the back where he stored his things, and the driveway where he decided to wash his car every weekend. He felt comfortable turning on the TV or helping himself to a drink in the fridge, and I was torn between sitting in the bedroom until he left and pretending to be busy with every single scrap of housework I could think of. It was a horribly confronting and uncomfortable feeling to be trapped in a room with someone who has hurt you that much.

Every week he asked me the same thing: 'When are we getting back together?' He said the boys needed a father around, although he never offered to have them over at his place for the night or take them on a holiday. And he never stopped accusing me of having secret lovers and calling me horrible names. Nothing had changed in his behaviour and I never felt safe, but I didn't know how to deal with him. People told me just to get rid of him, but I didn't know how. I was still struggling with my own feelings of depression and worthlessness; I wasn't strong enough to confront him about his behaviour. I also tolerated it for the sake of my boys.

•

Poor old Razor had to be put down in 2001, at seventeen years of age. It broke my heart to do it but his legs had gone, worn out by constantly jumping fences to go and have fun. In 2002, we went to the pound and found a ten-week-old German shepherd crossed with who knows what other breeds; she had long legs and bounded all over the place with a permanent smile on her face. Tim loved the dog but it was with Sam that she bonded best. She was very playful and loved to run, which suited Sam so much more than Tim. The puppy was always by Sam's side and would race through the house and make a flying jump onto Sam's bed when it was time to go to sleep, and dug her heels in when I tried to drag her out. We called her Wotta because we were always saying, 'What a dog!' Sam really loved that pup.

One Sunday, I heard the boys' father arrive, open our side gate and drive the car into the backyard to wash it and work on it again. It angered me; he was supposed to be there to spend time with the boys. I was standing at the sink and realised after a few minutes that I hadn't heard the click that meant the side gate had been closed and, when I looked out of the window, I couldn't see the puppy in the yard. I was just moving towards the back door when I heard Sam scream out. 'Mum,' he cried. The sound came from the street.

I ran out the front door and up the road towards Sam, who was standing beside a four-wheel drive that had stopped in the middle of the road. Near its front wheel lay poor Wotta, eyes frozen wide and blood dripping from her mouth. She was gone. Poor Sam was distraught, so I picked him up and carried him home. I was shaking with anger and hurt. It should never have happened. It was pure carelessness that caused it and the boys' father was to blame. Enough was enough.

After the dog had been buried in our backyard and the boys were consoled, I walked up to their father and told him I wanted a property settlement. I wanted to sell the house at Wynnum West and rid myself of him for good. 'You can no longer control our lives,' I told him. My anger gave me courage.

To my surprise, within the year I got a legal property settlement. The house was sold in 2003, with enough money in the split for me to buy a modern, low-set brick home in the next suburb, with a smaller yard but no maintenance, three bedrooms instead of two, a lock-up garage and a study. It had been well maintained by the previous owner and I was proud to call it home. It was the place where we finally came to rest; the place where my little boys would grow into men.

•

I think the house at Wynnum West was cursed. Just after the Second World War, the block that the house was built on was divided from the main property, a small crop and poultry farm, for a son who had come home from the war. The returned soldier built the fibro cottage that our family had lived in. He built an incinerator in the backyard—nearly every yard had one in those days. One morning, his wife went to the backyard to throw the rubbish in the incinerator. She stood too close to the flame in her nylon nightie and it caught on fire. The woman burned to death.

The soldier had serious health problems—kidney disease and cancer—but before he died he sold the house to a young couple, who owned it before us. I thought it was strange that when we first inspected the property there were at least three locks on each door, including the bathroom door. I found out after we moved in that the woman was the victim of domestic violence and abuse; the locks were meant to keep her husband out.

We were the next owners and had our own troubles. The people who bought the house from us sold it after just a few months. The following couple had it a short while before the woman was diagnosed with cancer.

The little pink fibro house is gone now, completely demolished. A new brick house stands on that block. The trees and gardens are gone, as are the fences. All the backyard buildings have gone and the driveway is now on the opposite side of the house. I went to visit Alison one day and stood on the front footpath, looking at the property. There was no sign of our life there, not one trace. It seems bizarre that the only recollection of the house is in my mind, but there is nothing else left. I hope the curse is finally broken.

11

Laser Beak Man

From the moment he picked up a pen, Tim had not stopped drawing. From the beginning, he had a strong hand; he always drew strong lines. Then when he started colouring, he was meticulous; the colours were bright but always carefully inside the lines. We made hand-drawn Christmas decorations every year and wrote our names on the back, but even when the names wore off, Tim's were easy to spot. Sam smiled if the colouring was good and would say, 'That one is definitely Tim's.'

As a boy, Tim drew Transformers and Pokémon characters, as well as Bugs Bunny and his beloved Thomas the Tank Engine. As he got older, he started to develop characters of his own and those characters began to come to life. By the time he was nine or ten years old, he had also started to develop stories. On a Monday, he might begin by drawing a gangster on the page, then on Tuesday he might add a henchman. On Wednesday, he'd add the backdrop of a bank—you could tell he had been thinking about the scene. He would sit at the table scratching away and I'd hear him muttering under his breath, acting out the characters as he drew.

Like all boys his age, Tim loved superheroes. Batman was very big around that time because the film franchise had become very successful and there was a Batman cartoon on TV; Tim and his brother were infatuated. Whenever we went to the shops, the boys would carry an action figure each. When they played, big brother Tim was always Batman and poor Sam was his sidekick, Robin. When Tim drew, he often drew superheroes, acting out the scenes as he went. He'd be the baddie one minute and then his voice would change and he was the hero, dropping his pencil periodically to throw a couple of uppercuts in defence of justice.

The thing that struck me about Tim's drawing is that he always added a little bit of humour. They were stock pictures in many ways, but there was always something unusual about them that made me laugh—the bad guys would blow up the bank but the building would collapse on them or Batman would get his cape stuck in the door.

Tim liked to laugh, and he always loved it when I giggled. He loved playing the funny man, even if he didn't quite understand why I was laughing. We'd been to see a doctor once and when the nurse came out Tim said, 'Not you again.' When she brought out the needle, he said, 'Just let me die.'

For a little person who didn't say a lot, he could certainly pick some funny words. But with his drawing, it seemed like Tim always knew what he was doing. It wasn't an accident that his pictures were funny. I think the years of watching Bugs Bunny made a big impression—from slapstick to dry wit, he had taken it all in, and blended it to come up with his own magic brand of humour.

•

When Tim was eleven years old, he told me he was going to be Laser Beak Man when he grew up. I had no idea who he was talking about—I assumed it was a character on television. He continued to talk about Laser Beak Man for several weeks.

One night, while I was cooking dinner, Tim sat drawing at the kitchen table and I wandered over to see what he was working on. The picture made me chuckle out loud.

'Who's this?' I asked.

Tim said, 'Laser Beak Man.'

Tim's superhero was drawn roughly in pen without any colouring in. He stood plainly on a white page, but there was something very cute and funny about him. He had a big cheeky scowl; you could tell he was naughty.

I could see that Tim was quite proud to show me his creation, which was unusual. He usually drew for his own personal satisfaction but never came over to say, 'Mum, look at this.' I wasn't really part of the process. Tim knew his Laser Beak Man drawing was funny and he was happy it made me smile.

After that day, Tim began drawing Laser Beak Man all the time and a cast of characters developed around him. There was a villain called Peter Bartman and baddies like Concrete Man and Tomato Man, and a vehicle that drilled under the earth called the Thriller Driller. Tim also drew a picture that explained where Laser Beak Man got his power from—rocks called magna crystals.

At first, Tim's Laser Beak Man pictures were classic good versus evil scenarios and I could see how much they borrowed from film and television, but as his character started to evolve, the stories evolved too. Tim created a character called Evil Emily, who was a baddie but also a sort of romantic interest. When Evil Emily appeared, she started to do funny little things like put chillies in Laser Beak Man's drink. In response to that, Laser Beak Man would have a funny one-liner. Tim's character had started to develop a personality.

•

Tim's art got better and better, and it was obvious to everyone that he had a talent. The teachers at St Brendan's began commenting on his work and when I saw the other children's drawings I could understand why; Tim's technique was already pretty advanced. Art became his favourite subject, all through to the end of primary school.

Tim graduated from St Brendan's in 2000 and I was very sad. It had been such a nurturing environment for us and I was nervous about what lay ahead. I was also sad to see my little boy becoming a teenager. It all happens way too fast. When he finished primary school, Tim was a happy, confident young man who was well liked and included in the community—so different from the crying and screaming child who had the constant threat of a trial period hanging over his head. St Brendan's was one of the best things that had ever happened for Tim.

I continued to work at the school and made many good friends as a result, including Ian, the principal. When it came time to look for a high school for Tim, Ian was by my side. We drove up and down the coast together, looking for the best fit. He was an amazing man; he really cared for the children at his school.

Finding the right high school was every bit as emotional as finding a kindergarten and primary school for Tim. A lot of research went into it; a lot of restless nights worrying about making the right choice; a lot of days trying to convince people and impress people, and advocating for Tim. High school was such a big thing because it was expected that Tim would be a lot more independent and I would have a lot less input once he started, so I really had to make a good decision. It was hard work and I was frustrated that I had to go through it all again. I was worn out so quickly by the drudgery of it all.

In the end, I chose Cavendish Road State High School. There weren't any options for Tim in mainstream schooling and there weren't many high schools in Brisbane that had special-education units, but Cavendish Road was a good place. The head of the special-education unit at the school was a thin, balding man named Gerry Nathan who came marching up to us the minute we arrived and jumped straight into action. *Right then, off we go.* Gerry had been at Cavendish Road for thirty years and he had started the special-education unit there. It was the largest unit of its kind in Queensland. He seemed very comfortable with autism and he instilled me with a lot of confidence.

'We do not tolerate bullying here,' he said.

Cavendish Road had over a thousand students but it had a very good name. It had a good academic record and a strong sports culture, which made me happy. Sam would be joining Tim when he finished primary school and Cavendish Road needed to suit him as well.

When Tim left primary school he was at a Year 4 reading level and a Year 2 level in maths. His social skills were good but he lagged far behind his peers. The twelve-year-old boys around him had gone off on their own paths; they were interested in sport and girls, whereas Tim still loved Bugs Bunny. The developmental gap was really obvious by that point and Tim's high school education would be focused on life skills and vocations, on finding Tim a place in the adult world.

Tim moved from a unit that had ten kids with special needs, in primary school, to a unit with over a hundred special needs kids at Cavendish Road, and a few of the other kids had much higher needs than Tim. It wasn't always an easy environment. Tim did have some trouble with bullying, but it was from students within the unit. The teachers were very quick to deal with it, though. They always kept me well informed about what was going on. I had less one-on-one time with the high school teachers so I just had to trust the program.

Almost as soon as he started at Cavendish Road, Tim began seeking out friends among the regular students. Fortunately they were an accepting bunch that always included him—particularly the girls. There were three lovely girls who took him under their wing. Tim didn't like having his lunch in the special-needs unit and he didn't understand why the other students could eat their lunch anywhere, so the girls invited Tim to sit with them at lunchtime. He just loved it. He even let them call him Timmy. He would never let me get away with that.

Tim's classmates were getting into grunge and rock'n'roll and he developed his own love of music at that time. His favourites were still The Beatles, but he was also very fond of The Offspring, KISS and Michael Jackson, and he got into heavy metal. He loved movies even more than music and he'd watch the same videos over and over again—*Home Alone, Jumanji, Space Jam* and *Milo and Otis; The Terminator* and *Terminator 2: Judgement Day*. He'd spend the morning with Thomas the Tank Engine and the afternoon with Arnold Schwarzenegger! He could recite whole chunks of dialogue from his favourite films.

•

Compared to what other parents go through with their teenagers, I got off pretty lightly with Tim. He got upset with me once and threatened to leave home but the whole thing was awfully funny. He grabbed his school bag and marched to the street corner, couldn't think of what to do so walked back home again.

I had heard so many horror stories about what happens to kids with autism once the hormones kick in and I was truly terrified of what was coming. In fact, I don't think I'd heard a single positive story about that developmental period. Many children have an extreme shift in behaviour and become incredibly violent and even suicidal. When young men get bigger and stronger, distress and bad behaviour becomes very dangerous—I knew of one woman whose son threw her through a glass window and of another house where every wall was smashed with holes from angry, violent outbursts. Inappropriate sexual behaviour was a problem too, for the poor kids whose bodies were changing, who couldn't understand or control their urges. The shame attached to inappropriate sexual behaviour seemed to hurt people even worse than the violence.

It seemed so improbable that Tim would behave like this, but it also seemed like it was the norm. I feared that Tim's voice would start to change and then his personality would change too, and all the gains we had made would just disappear. But it just didn't happen. We were very lucky.

•

Sam joined Tim at Cavendish Road in 2003 and he was happy and confident from the moment he arrived. They had more sports for him to play and teams for him to join—St Brendan's hadn't even had a football team! He seemed to make a whole lot of friends straight away.

At thirteen or fourteen, when Sam became a teenager, he had long outgrown Tim developmentally. But Sam's life was so consumed by swimming training that it felt more like he just had his own thing, not like he was different to Tim. I was thrilled for Sam that he had found the great passion of his life. He was so focused.

I nearly burst with pride the day Sam was elected School Captain at Cavendish Road. It was such a large school, with many students excelling in many different areas, so it was a huge honour and achievement for Sam to be selected. I had tears in my eyes as he gave his acceptance speech. I wasn't sure what I'd done to deserve such a wonderful son. He was a very social young man with wonderful communication skills who could show a lot of respect and restraint when needed. He had wonderful manners and maturity beyond his years, and he had the most positive outlook on life. He knew right from wrong and he was always eager to help and support others. And he was always a loving brother to Tim.

Perhaps growing up with Tim helped Sam to become an outstanding young man. He had a level of understanding and empathy that many other kids didn't have. When people asked Sam what it was like to have a brother with autism, he said, 'I don't know, I've just got a brother.' Like me, he didn't see autism, he only saw Tim. Tim's disability was never a big deal.

Maybe that helped Sam to see past the surface and find the real value in people.

•

Throughout high school, Tim continued to make gains, which I found really encouraging. He did a lot of cooking and using shopping skills at school, and because of that he was finally willing to try new foods. Tim made stir-fries, fried rice, moussaka and lasagne—he had suddenly developed a taste for ethnic cuisine. He made spaghetti and apple pie, too. He really thrived in home economics.

Tim also did very well in art and was included in the main-stream art class. He had a really encouraging and supportive art teacher named Megan Kerr, who reached out to him and did what she could to support him. Megan's greatest gift was to boost Tim's confidence. It was clear he had some talent and a very individual style, but it didn't fit the requirements of the curriculum or allow Tim to be assessed as an equal with his peers. She'd ask the students to draw something from Monet's Garden and Tim would draw Bob Marley on a lily pad. But she gave him a lot of her time. If Tim ever showed interest in something, Megan would send a book about it home with him. She introduced him to Andy Warhol, who became one of Tim's obsessions. 'He's the best artist in the whole wide world!' Tim said. 'He likes colours and he likes music.'

Megan did her best to develop Tim's skills and give him

the opportunity to make work, while encouraging him to try new things.

Tim loved all kinds of art and he threw himself into it without protest or upset. Art opened up a whole new world for him and he didn't feel the need to just keep doing things his own way. He tried sculpture and lino printing and painting at school. He used lots of different colours and it really made him happy. At home, Tim was still drawing like crazy. Half of the pictures he drew were of things and places he was interested in, like ancient ruins in Greece, and the other half were pictures of Laser Beak Man.

•

We still didn't have much money so we sometimes gave people homemade birthday cards when we were invited to birthday parties, and Tim was always the man for the job. One day, we had a birthday party for one of Sam's friends and I asked Tim to draw a Laser Beak Man picture. I couldn't believe what he came up with. It was bright and happy, with a grinning Laser Beak Man on the front and a very special greeting: 'Have a filthy disgusting birthday!'

I laughed very hard when I saw it and so did Sam. I'd never seen anything like it. The boy who received the birthday card loved it. So did his mum and his aunt. The aunt worked in the arts and she thought the card was something special. 'You should really do something with this,' she said.

She showed it to a friend of hers called Neal Price, who was the director of an organisation called Access Arts, which supports artists with disabilities in Brisbane. Neal called me and told me he thought the card was really funny.

'Tim is a talented artist,' he said. 'We need to promote him.'

'Great!' I answered. 'I was thinking the same thing.'

I put the phone down, feeling over the moon. I had spent years and years fighting for my son, trying to nurture him and guide him through his disability. I was fighting to protect him and to ensure he didn't slip through the cracks in the system, and I was fighting to get people to see him as more than just a boy with autism, as a person with thoughts and feelings and character. But this was something completely different—I didn't have to fight. With joy and enthusiasm, someone came to us and said, 'Wow, what an incredible young man!' And I thought, *Well of course he is!*

I'd known for some time that Tim was really talented, but it was amazing to have a complete stranger call up and confirm it, someone who actually knew what he was talking about, who wasn't just trying to be kind. I had no idea what kind of future my son would have and I had worried about it constantly; I wanted him to have a good life. At the high school, they were talking about sheltered workshops, which is where some people with disabilities worked. From everything I had seen, the work was menial and the environment was sterile, but it gave people a sense of purpose. I didn't want that for Tim. Neal spoke about Tim as an artist and all of a sudden a door opened. Maybe Tim's drawing could be an actual career? It seemed too good to be true.

We went to have a meeting with Neal and figure out what he could do for us. I had no idea what to expect, but he was a lovely man—he just wanted to help, although there wasn't all that much he could do at that point. Tim was too young to be a member of Access Arts; he was only fourteen and he didn't have a lot of really fantastic drawings at that point, so we couldn't have an exhibition, but we both agreed that the birthday card was great. Neal organised a small grant so we could print a proper batch and a few weeks later a box of one thousand 'Filthy Disgusting Birthday' cards landed on our doorstep.

•

The cards looked beautiful. Unfortunately, I had no idea what to do with them. I think the idea was that I would sell them to people, but I was a terrible salesperson. I was always the mum who sent half the chocolate box back at the end of a school chocolate drive. What on earth would I do with a thousand birthday cards?

Neal had been so kind and supportive that I tried my best—I took the box into St Brendan's and made all the teachers buy one, and I took them around to all of our friends, and into the swimming club. We left some at the local shops and some at Access Arts, but once I'd exhausted our immediate circle I ran out of ideas. I was also a bit embarrassed asking people to buy them—I've never been very good at asking people for money. Of course everyone we knew bought a card, but I still had hundreds left over—I swear that box was bottomless. On the upside, we'd never have to buy another birthday card for the rest of our lives.

I was so embarrassed when I ran into Neal. I told him I wasn't doing as well as he might have expected.

'Don't worry,' he said. 'Keep a hold of them for now. You'll find a use for them eventually.'

I thought, *You give me a thousand cards, I'd better sell those cards by next week!* But Neal had a long-term view when it came to Tim. He understood that Tim was a young artist and that it took a while to build a career; this was just the first little step on a very exciting journey.

The thing is, I didn't actually know anything about art. I don't think I'd even been to an art gallery at that point, so I had no idea what artists did or how they made a living, but Neal seemed to know what he was talking about. The only thing I knew was that Tim made funny drawings. Kids loved them; adults loved them. They made people smile. I thought it would be nice for Tim to share that with the world.

12

The Invitation

It was always Tim's job to get the mail. One day, in March 2003, he came in with a bundle of letters and began to distribute them, 'Here's one for you, Mum. Another one for you, one for Sam, and another one for you, and one for Laser Beak Man.'

That made me look; I didn't realise Laser Beak Man was a resident of our house and I was certainly surprised to hear that he was getting mail. The envelope in Tim's hand was large and brown, with no sender details and no letter inside to say who it was from. What it contained was information about the Very Special Arts Festival, to be held in Washington, D.C., in June 2004.

Very Special Arts, known as the VSA, was an international non-profit organisation founded in 1974 by Jean Kennedy Smith, the sister of John F. Kennedy. According to the information I was sent, the VSA was a society where people with disabilities could learn through, participate in and enjoy art.

'Nearly five million people with disabilities participate in VSA arts programs every year through a network of affiliates in forty-nine states of the United States of America and sixty-four countries worldwide.'

I was fascinated by what I read; I'd never heard of anything like it. One of President Kennedy's other sisters founded the Special Olympics and Jean founded this special organisation for the arts.

The VSA Festival was held once every five years in Washington, D.C., the home of the VSA foundation. The following June, the festival would bring together two hundred jury-selected artists from all over the world, from literary, media, performance and visual arts, who were specially selected to represent their countries.

The package included application forms for Tim.

Naturally, Tim was curious to know what had arrived in the mail for Laser Beak Man, so I began explaining to him about the VSA Festival. It would be the VSA's thirtieth anniversary in 2004 so it was going to be a time of great celebration. The event would be staged around some of the famous places in Washington, like Union Station and the John F. Kennedy Center for the Performing Arts, and participants would get to visit the White House and meet the president, George W. Bush.

Tim was very interested in facts and figures by that point, and was particularly fixated on current affairs. President Bush was in the news a lot after September 11 and Tim was very familiar with him, almost obsessed. He could list from memory all of the presidents of the United States, their date of birth, date of death and the years they were in office. He knew a lot of Bush's biography off by heart. The idea of meeting the president was incredibly impressive to my son.

I read and reread the VSA information several times that day, wondering who had sent it. I assumed it was Neal, but I couldn't be sure; why wouldn't he have sent a note along with it? It was such an incredible opportunity for Tim, it was almost overwhelming. Washington was an impossible dream for us. I couldn't believe someone had even suggested it.

Of course I wanted to submit Tim's work, but the forms made me very nervous. A lot of the requirements seemed complicated. I wasn't familiar with some of the terms they used and I was concerned because the selection committee needed interpretations and explanations of Tim's artwork. They wanted to know about his 'arts practice', his 'medium' and 'materials' as well as the themes of his work. Tim didn't verbalise the rhyme or reason of his artwork with me and I felt really uncomfortable assuming I knew what he was thinking.

The committee also required the artwork to be photographed in very specific ways and the application to be submitted electronically. We had been given an old computer by a friend but I was a total novice when it came to using it. I had no idea what I was doing. Thank god we were connected to the internet at least. Our printer was also a scanner. After the boys went to bed that night, I sat down at our desk and took a deep breath, and submitted a VSA application for Tim.

It took me a long time to complete the forms. I wasn't quite certain of exactly what they wanted; it was all new to me. I had chosen for inclusion a piece that Tim had recently completed that he was very fond of called 'Laser Beak Man and Friends'. It was a happy, colourful work that introduced people to the world of Laser Beak Man, with a few villains including Peter Bartman, a girl playing guitar, bees, flowers and a helicopter. Laser Beak Man was skateboarding through the middle, in a park in his home town of Power City.

Tim gave Sam and I a bit of information about Laser Beak Man in this artwork and it seemed to create the flavour of his superhero. It made me smile every time I looked at it. That was good enough for me.

I had nearly finished the application and was double-checking everything when I saw something I'd missed the first dozen times I'd read the application forms. The closing date for applications had passed six weeks earlier. My heart sank. I had worked myself into such a state of excitement, thinking about this marvellous opportunity for Tim, but it was all for nothing. We were way too late.

I stared at the date for a while and then shrugged to myself. *Can't hurt*, I thought. I had already done all the work so I figured I might as well send it in. Who knew what would happen, anyway. We certainly had nothing to lose.

It was well past midnight in Brisbane when I pressed the send button, but it was daytime in America. I left the computer on while I went to have a shower and get ready for bed and when I came back to turn it off there was a message from Washington, D.C. I got a reply to my email almost immediately: 'Thank you for your email, however applications for the VSA Festival are closed. Our panel of judges is convening tomorrow to assess the applications.'

I was really devastated then, but I gave it a last-ditch effort. I responded to the email, saying, 'Thank you very much. We'll try again in five years,' but I attached a picture of the 'Filthy Disgusting Birthday' card. A reply came back almost immediately.

'That really is so funny and cute!' the woman wrote. 'I will include it with the other submissions for the jury tomorrow.'

I shouted, 'Yes!' and punched the air with excitement. Sometimes it pays to be a little bit cheeky.

•

We didn't think or talk about the VSA Festival again after that night. I didn't want to get Tim's hopes up and it seemed impossible that he would be selected, really. It was such a prestigious event. Tim was young, with not much experience and with a mother who had even less. I'd probably filled out the forms incorrectly, and we were too late anyhow.

When we received a letter from the VSA in July 2003, I expected it to say, 'Thanks but no thanks, you have not been successful'. As always, Tim had collected the mail that day and he opened the letter to begin reading it.

'Dear Tim, Congratulations,' he began.

I almost fell out of my chair.

Tim had been selected to represent Australia in the drawing category of the VSA Festival. There had been over 700 applicants and only four young adults from around the world had been chosen—one from Wisconsin, one from Estonia, one from Argentina and Tim Sharp from Australia! Suddenly Tim had gone from special needs to just really special.

The thing that bowled me over was that they hadn't asked about Tim's condition on the application forms. There was a box to check, 'Have you been assessed as having a disability?', but that was all. They didn't ask what Tim's disability was or what level of care he required, or try to put any limitation on him. The field was open to anyone with a physical or mental disability, which included an enormous range of people. Tim wasn't selected because he had autism, he was selected because they loved his artwork. It wasn't a handout, it was a real achievement. I couldn't have been more proud. I was surprised and ecstatic. Sam was ecstatic too.

'Are you happy, Tim?' I asked.

'Yes,' he replied. 'When are we going to America?'

I came back to earth with a hard little bump. *How are we going to get to America?* I thought. There was no way we could possibly afford it, but obviously Tim didn't know that.

'We won't be going,' I explained to him. 'But it's so lovely that you were invited, isn't it? It's wonderful just to be asked. Doesn't that make you happy?'

'Yes, Mum, I am happy,' Tim replied. 'When are we going to America?'

•

An information pack for festival participants arrived in October 2003, along with a letter saying, 'We look forward to seeing you in Washington!'

There was information about the festival events and attendance costs, with attendees expected to contribute $1000 per person towards a hotel room, the opening and closing ceremonies, conferences, symposiums, a congressional reception, exhibition, performances, a grand ball and the White House reception. There was no way we could go without Sam—we were a trio, we did everything together. If I was even going to consider it, it would be $3000 for all of us, and that's without airfares and food. When I did the maths, I was even more resigned to the fact that it wasn't going to happen. We were talking about thousands and thousands of dollars. I was sad for Tim but hopeful for his future. That would have to be his reward.

'When are we going to America?' Tim asked.

'We can't go, Tim. I don't have the money,' I said.

'We have to get the money,' Tim replied, then walked away to resume whatever he was doing.

Simple as that, I laughed to myself, but it really got me thinking. If Tim wanted to go that much, I had to give him the chance. If he had faith, it was my responsibility to make sure it was rewarded. He inspired me to try a little bit harder, though I really didn't hold any hope. *I have to get the money*, I thought. I had no idea how.

•

There was a deadline to reply and confirm that we would be attending the festival. Without a clue how I would get us there, I went ahead and confirmed our attendance—if the invited artist could not attend the festival, they would offer the place to someone else. Shortly afterwards, there was another deadline to pay a deposit and make some financial commitment.

My first stop was a bank that I had been with for twenty years. When I had been married we had paid off a house through that bank; I'd never had any problems there. I paid all my bills on time and I didn't owe anyone any money, so I assumed I'd be a good candidate for a loan. It was a very short interview. I met with the manager of a large, central branch and told him about Tim's marvellous opportunity but his answer came back immediately and it wasn't good: 'I'm sorry, you don't earn enough money.'

I decided to try again at my local branch, where they had known me for many years. Again, the answer was fast and brutal. 'I'm sorry, you don't earn enough money.'

I was pretty disgusted with the bank's response. They were being prudent but it was totally impersonal. I knew that no matter what, I would repay the loan; I had even offered to re-mortgage the house. It didn't make a difference. I was a single parent, on a part carer's pension, with a part-time job as a teacher's aide at St Brendan's Primary School. I worked twenty hours a week and earned eighteen dollars an hour. The banks just didn't think I could afford to service the loan and I didn't know how to convince them they were wrong.

I'd read in the paper about artists getting funding from the government and it occurred to me we might get something like that for Tim. I felt sure he would get support to attend a prestigious event like the VSA Festival, where he would represent his country. If people could get funding to dip snails in paint and have them crawl across a page, surely Tim could get a grant to go to Washington. I was convinced that Tim's case was worthy of public funds—it made perfect sense to me!

I bundled together some examples of Tim's art and marched into the city to see the Queensland Government arts department. I didn't make any exploratory phone calls; I figured I should make my case face-to-face. I walked right up to the woman at the front desk and started to explain about Tim. She wasn't interested, not one little bit.

'Can I talk to someone else?' I asked.

The woman gave me a bunch of forms and told me I'd have to fill them out. She couldn't help me.

I left the arts department and went to visit the youth affairs department, the disability affairs department and even Access Arts—unfortunately Neal had moved on by that point. I visited every government department I could think of and was rejected from each one. I was walking the streets in tears. It wasn't that people had given me a definitive 'no' but no one was actually listening. I knew what a huge deal it was for Tim, but I couldn't get anyone excited about it. Tim didn't have enough recognition, they didn't fund overseas trips or his trip didn't fit into the right program. They were all very sorry, but there was a coldness to their response and again it felt like Tim was slipping through the cracks. It was so frustrating.

When we told our friends about the VSA Festival, they were as excited as we were. It was really good fun to share the joy and know that so many people believed in Tim and that they wanted us to go to Washington. A lot of friends suggested fundraising, but I just couldn't bring myself to do it. It didn't feel right. This was a great opportunity but there were so many people with much greater needs than us who really needed charity, like people with sick children. It just didn't sit well with me, asking people for money for something that wasn't a necessity. I could never have enjoyed the trip if I knew someone else had paid for it. I had to find another way.

I saw a lot of ads on television for mortgage brokers who would come to the house to discuss your loan if the banks wouldn't help because you were too high risk. I didn't know how these mortgage brokers worked—for me, all your financial business was done at the bank—but I certainly fit the criteria. I had a house; I decided I would mortgage that. I just needed someone to help me.

I rang several brokers over the next couple of weeks and four different men came to visit the house. None of them stayed long. Although they were happy to drink tea and eat the cakes I made for them, they couldn't get me the money. I wanted $20,000 to replace our old car and take the boys to America, but I didn't earn enough money. They all thought it was a great opportunity and they said we should go, but unfortunately none of them could help us.

I gave up. I had no more ideas. I had explained my situation to the VSA arts people and they were very patient, understanding and supportive. They said they could waive the $1000 fee for Tim and me, would that help? I was very humbled by their generosity and cried a lot. If they were willing to help us, surely someone else would. I thanked them and told them I'd find the rest of the money, no matter what.

Tim didn't have to worry about any of this, of course. He had an unshakeable belief that we were going to Washington and it was actually quite inspiring. I found a flyer for a different mortgage broker in the letterbox and I decided to give it one more go.

The man who came round to our house was softly spoken but he looked like a rugby player. He had huge muscles and a big, thick neck but he was very well-dressed. He didn't waste words. He seemed very honest and very down-to-earth to me, although the conversation didn't come easily. I felt like he'd be more comfortable talking about football than discussing my disabled son. But still, he listened. He asked me questions. In the end, he told me the same thing as everyone else, 'I'm sorry, you don't make enough money.'

Whenever I spoke to people about Tim, I tried not to exaggerate the situation. I didn't play the victim or cry, or carry on with any histrionics. It was extraordinarily difficult for me to ask for special favours; I didn't like to and I didn't on that day. But I did try to explain to that man the situation we were in. I told him I was on my own because life with my husband had been intolerable and that life with a child with autism had been very hard, very challenging. I wasn't looking for a handout, I just wanted to get a loan and help my son. I wanted him to have this opportunity.

The broker wasn't a very expressive man, but he was really impressed by the VSA invitation. He had played rugby for Australia and he knew how special those moments could be. He also told me that he had been raised by his mother because his father had been abusive. He shared with me his own story of growing up with a violent drunk, of his mother protecting her sons and keeping them safe. When his father became dangerous, she would wake the children in their beds and make them climb out the window and run up the street, so that he couldn't hurt them. Both he and his brother had gone on to play rugby at a very high level and he was grateful for the sacrifices his mother had made to get him there. I got the impression that he hadn't spoken about these things with many people. It was a very emotional conversation for both of us.

The broker was a very genuine man. If nothing else came out of that meeting, at least I had met someone who understood what parts of our life had been like. He also gave me hope that my boys would be all right, that the cycle of fear and intimidation could be broken. From what he said, it seemed to me that his mother was a wonderful woman.

Like everyone else, the broker told me I wouldn't qualify for a loan, but he made a few calls. 'My mum was in a bad situation,' he said. 'She needed money to support us at times and people helped us out. It's my turn now. I'm going to try to help you.'

He didn't want to get my hopes up and I respected him for being honest, but I was still incredibly disappointed. Everyone he called said no. It wasn't looking good. Then just as the broker was about to leave, his phone rang and he went outside to take the call.

'This guy owes me a favour,' he said.

He was outside for a few minutes and then let himself back in. 'I have the loan for you,' he said. Simple as that. I'm certain he knew in his heart that I would never ever let him down.

In the years that followed, I sometimes saw the broker around the local shops. He would look at me and I'd see a glimmer of recognition in his eyes, but he'd always look away. Maybe he told me too much about his life that day. Maybe he didn't want to hear me say 'thank you' again. Maybe it was enough for him to know that he had helped us. I still wanted to thank him; I always will. I really wanted to let him know what a huge difference he made to our lives.

13

Washington

Tim was excited to hear we were going to Washington, but seconds after I told him he was off to play Nintendo. He lived in the moment and Washington was months away. It was up to me to get the whole thing moving.

We had never been overseas before. We'd never been anywhere at all! It was going to be the adventure of a lifetime. I'd be paying the loan off for the rest of my life but bugger if the debt wasn't worth it. I was so excited I told everyone we knew, and then someone we knew told the local paper.

A journalist from the *Wynnum Herald* called our house and asked if they could interview Tim. The man thought his story was very exciting and he told me their readers would love it. I could see his point—I thought it was a great story too. I invited him over for a chat. The journalist sat with me and Tim and asked a lot of questions, all about the VSA Festival and Tim; how old he was, where he went to school. He asked where Laser Beak Man had come from, too. Tim answered where he could. I was happy Tim was getting attention for his achievements. I was incredibly proud.

The headline that ran with the story was, 'Tim's Art Fit for a President.' I was giddy when I saw the articles but Tim was completely unfazed.

'You're famous, Tim!' I told him with a grin.

Tim coolly answered, 'I know.'

•

I had decided that Tim's inclusion in the VSA Festival was so big that it was the equivalent of him representing his country at the Olympic Games. I decided that the nation deserved to know about it—I decided he should have some media coverage. My ideas can be very fanciful sometimes. I thought that the only show that could do the story justice was the ABC's *Australian Story*. *Might as well aim high*, I thought.

The show seemed accurate and down-to-earth, and I liked that there wasn't a narrator or interviewer in each episode. It was great the way the people on the show told their story in their own words. It was sympathetic and caring, and it celebrated little people in Australia who had done big things. That was Tim! Tim was a great Australian story! I contacted the show and told them all about our news.

A producer named Kristine Taylor responded to my email. If we were heading to America, they were happy to talk about a story. Around April 2004, shortly before we were due to leave, Kristine came to visit me at St Brendan's Primary. We sat in the little Year 1 school chairs and she asked me about our lives.

Kristine was a tiny woman, very demure looking, but she was incredibly smart. She spoke beautifully and thoughtfully, and though she was very direct she listened carefully when I spoke. She also wore a pretty, pastel-coloured silk scarf. Every time I saw a woman in a scarf I assumed they were in a different class. I was terrified of her.

Kristine wasn't there to judge us, however. She was only interested in ascertaining whether they could make a good half hour of television out of Tim's story. Was it big enough? Was there a beginning, middle and end? She was really trying to figure out if there was enough stuff that they could film. I didn't feel like I had to exaggerate; I knew it was a great tale. I felt like we had walked a pretty tough road but we'd ended up somewhere wonderful.

Kristine went away to think about it and I threw myself into preparations for the trip. I had to get the boys' father to sign passport documents, which was a challenge. I had to organise tickets and visas and accommodation and stuff, which was all incredibly new to me. And in the meantime, word was spreading about Tim and the VSA. There were more newspaper stories and some radio interviews, and even a little piece on the local television news. Everyone we knew saw it. Plenty of people we didn't know saw it too, and Tim became a bit of a local celebrity. I pulled up at Cavendish Road to collect the boys from school one day and found a group of reporters waiting for us—one of the articles had mentioned where Tim went to school.

An unexpected momentum had built around our trip. People who read or heard about Tim's story began sending us letters of congratulations and support. One gentleman, on his way home from a trip to America, dropped by our house to give us his leftover U.S. dollars. My friends at St Brendan's all rallied together and collected some spending money for us, and a lot of them let me borrow their clothes so that I would have something to wear to the formal events. Myer donated a suit for Tim to wear to the receptions and a Brisbane radio station gave us a video camera so we could film our trip and keep the memories of it forever. It was really overwhelming. We were swept up in a tide of goodness and it left me floating on air. People were so unbelievably kind; I could never thank them enough.

•

Kristine got in touch and told me they wanted to do the story and my stomach just scrunched up in a ball. It was absolutely huge and I was really excited, but we would be putting our lives on display for the whole country. I don't think I'd really thought it through. I was nervous about how we would be received by our fellow Australians. I wanted to celebrate Tim's achievement, but I was terrified that people would just see us as a pitiful single mother and a kid with autism, and not see how wonderful our life together had become. I didn't want our life to be a sympathy story—I wanted people to feel the joy of it.

The day the film crew arrived to shoot the documentary, our house was turned upside down. There were tarpaulin sheets over the windows, furniture moved around and cords running everywhere; it took them about four hours to set up. The crew was full of perfectionists but they were lovely people. I had no idea how much time and preparation it took to make a TV show.

Kristine met Tim for the first time that day. She wanted him to be spontaneous; she didn't want to talk to him and put ideas in his head or have him rehearse things that he would say later. It worked a treat—he was really natural. It was very strange to have a camera pointed at you, but Tim took it in his stride. He'd become quite used to the attention by this point and I really think that he loved it. Tim acted like a rockstar, in his element. I hadn't really seen him act that way before, proud of what he'd done.

The crew visited us many times over the next few weeks, filming us around the house and interviewing all three of us. Kristine was very direct when she was interviewing me and pulled me up if my answers were a bit fuzzy. But she wasn't mean. She had a plan and she was always busy, so you had to wait to talk to her, but she was absolutely brimming with confidence. I trusted that she knew what she was doing. They wrapped up in Brisbane and we said our goodbyes. Another crew would film us in America.

•

Not long before we were due to leave we got news that the reception at the White House had been cancelled because the president had urgent matters to deal with. The war in Iraq was escalating at the time. I had to break the news to Tim and for one of the first times I saw him really disappointed.

'Why?' he wanted to know. I explained again and saw his face fall. 'Maybe next time,' he said. As a young adult, Tim had become a very steady soul and his emotions didn't waver as much as they had in the past, but in that moment he looked very sad. Thankfully, we got some good news as well. Tim was going to carry the Australian flag into the VSA opening ceremony at the John F. Kennedy Center for the Performing Arts. *Unbelievable*, I thought, *what an honour*. All we had to do was get him there in one piece.

I didn't know how Tim would cope with a fifteen-hour flight. It didn't seem that long ago that it was almost impossible to get him into a car for any length of time. I didn't even know how I would cope; I'd never done such a trip. I was actually terrified of going to America.

I added a bit of a special incentive to get us all across the Pacific—a stopover on our way to Washington. When I went to book the airfares I'd found that flights from Brisbane to Washington were $1700 each, but a five-day holiday package to Disneyland plus flights to Washington was also $1700. We'd be nuts not to go! The boys had grown up with *Saturday Disney*, they loved all the Disney films and we had entered every competition we could to win a holiday to Disneyland, but we'd never been lucky. Now, I could just buy our tickets. It was beyond reality, a dream come true! The boys were jumping out of their skin.

●

We landed in Los Angeles International Airport along with half the world's population, it seemed. There were people everywhere and it was extraordinarily busy. We'd been in the country all of five minutes when we were separated from Tim in the crowd. We stepped out of Customs and he just disappeared.

'Oh no, where's he gone?' I gasped.

Sam and I took off in separate directions to hunt for him and found Tim waiting patiently, totally calm. It gave me an awful scare, mind you. The airline also managed to lose one of our bags—the one that had all the borrowed clothes. Of all the ones to lose. Then we stepped out onto the street and there were two million cars, noise and horns. *What the hell have I done?* I thought. *I can't cope with this.* Tim just stared around with his eyes wide and a big smile on his face.

But all the stress and drama was worth it. Disneyland exceeded our wildest expectations; it was the happiest place in the world. As we walked towards the entrance we heard a whisper of music that got louder as we got closer. The Disneyland sign loomed above us and flowerbeds sprang into view. Not a rose petal was out of place. It was absolutely perfect, absolutely clean.

The boys went crazy. Tim loved the Indiana Jones ride, Space Mountain and Pirates of the Caribbean. We went to the park every day, four days in a row, and he rode them over and over again. I had an absolute ball, too. I think I enjoyed it even more than the boys. No one judged you, no one was unkind and everything ran smoothly. Disneyland was absolutely faultless.

It was the nicest thing we had ever done as a family. We were together all the time with no interruptions and all three of us were really, completely happy.

•

While we were in Disneyland, the news came through that former president Ronald Reagan had passed away; it was all over the television, so were the plans for his funeral. Five hundred thousand people were flooding into the city. A lot was happening in Washington, D.C., in the next week.

When we arrived we were met by men holding signs for the VSA and surrounded by almost five thousand participants— artists, carers, delegates and industry professionals—who had flown in at the same time as us. Together, we clambered onto our transfer buses and we set off across the city. Washington, D.C., was dazzling. It was green as green could be in the height of summer. The streets were lined with grand old oak and cedar trees, and beautiful double-storey houses that looked like something right out of the movies. We were all amazed by the architecture, including so many landmarks that we had only seen on television. I was glued to the windows the entire bus ride.

When we arrived at our hotel, my mouth fell open—the VSA had put us up at the Washington Hilton. The carpets were lush and everything was covered in gold leaf; there were chandeliers hanging from the ceilings and the furniture looked like it weighed a ton. I had never stayed anywhere like it in my life! It was the height of luxury and they'd given it to us for free.

On our arrival there was a letter waiting for us from the Australian Ambassador in Washington, D.C., Mr Michael Thawley. He had invited us to tea at the Australian embassy the next day.

We went for a walk almost as soon as we had landed to find the public exhibition where Tim's work was on display. He'd never had an exhibition before, unless you count his work on the classroom wall at school, and now his drawing was on display at Union Station. It was hard to believe.

There's a replica of the Liberty Bell outside Union Station, with a view up the mall to the White House, and the U.S. Capitol Building and the Washington Monument close by. Standing in the middle of the city was like stepping into the grand heart of America. It really took your breath away. Inside, Union Station soared three storeys high, with these grand columns and gold-leaf details. It looked more like a palace than a train station.

The VSA exhibition was in the middle of the lobby, where hundreds of thousands of commuters passed every day. It was arranged in lovely rows. Sam, Tim and I split up to hunt for Tim's work, racing excitedly down the aisles. Sam found it first and Tim and I came running. When he saw his picture, Tim's face started shining. He rocked backed and forth on his heels as if to say, *Look at this, I've done really well.*

As we were standing and admiring the work, a woman walked up with her little boy. 'Look, this is Laser Beak Man,' she told her son.

I couldn't help myself, I was bursting with pride. 'This is Tim, he's the artist!' I said.

'Wow, we get to meet the artist!' said the mum.

We loitered around the exhibition for a long time and met some of the VSA staff we'd exchanged emails with. Everyone was incredible, so positive and welcoming. It was a very lovely afternoon.

The next day a man arrived in a Lincoln limousine to drive us to the Australian embassy. We were late rising and had to scramble—I had to ask a stranger in the lift to do Tim's tie. Our driver entertained us with stories of all the prime ministers and movie stars he had driven to the embassy and it made us feel extremely special to be in such fancy company.

Two of the embassy staff were standing on the steps waiting for us when we arrived, a man named Ron and a woman called Lori. They had beautiful big smiles on their faces to put us at ease. I really needed it; I was a bundle of nerves. I was incredibly impressed by the building, not to mention the ambassador waiting for us inside. Ron and Lori were delightful, though—he was the Australian Cultural Relations Director in Washington and Lori was his assistant. They were warm and friendly, gentle and genuine and they really put us at ease. They walked us through the foyer, under a ceiling decorated like the Southern Cross, and took us on a tour of the embassy art collection. They were careful to include Sam and Tim, and draw their attention to things that might interest them, while telling us about the people who had come to visit—Keith Urban had been in the week before.

Our tea with Ambassador Thawley was lovely, though it was very formal and refined. We sat across from him in huge leather chairs beside a massive picture window and chatted pleasantly about our trip, then gave him a 'Filthy Disgusting Birthday' card. Mr Thawley burst out laughing when he saw it. He told us to take home the remaining chocolate chip cookies from our tea. They were huge, like everything in America, and Tim just loved them. Then, as our lovely meeting ended, the ambassador said, 'It's been a good week, I've had the Prime Minister John Howard here, the Governor-General and now Tim Sharp.'

Obviously Tim had made a big impression.

All of this was caught on camera by the American crew for *Australian Story*, who had met us when we arrived at the embassy. I coordinated our schedule with Kristine back in Australia, making calls to her from a public phone box every night with a fistful of American quarters. She wanted to make sure they captured all the highlights of our journey.

•

The following evening was the official opening ceremony for the VSA Festival and Ron from the embassy had tickets. I was surprised that he intended to go—he had so many other commitments. I'm glad he did, though. He really took care of us.

It was the night when we would watch Tim carry the Australian flag into the John F. Kennedy Center for the Performing Arts, and for me I considered it the single most important moment in Tim's life. From being told he would never be a part of normal society to here on the world stage representing his country. It made me very emotional just thinking about it.

Unfortunately, when we arrived at the Kennedy Center and collected our tickets, we found that our seats were up on the balcony, very far from the action. 'I haven't come halfway around the world to sit up the back and miss the proudest moment of my life,' I told the girl at the ticket desk. She was very apologetic but there was nothing she could do to help.

'Don't worry,' she said, 'every seat's a good seat!'

Up the grand staircase Sam and I went, while Tim was led away to join the other flag bearers. Then up another staircase Sam and I went, into the dizzy heights of the balcony. We got the video camera out and zoomed it in, taking turns at looking around, using it as binoculars to get the best view we could. Suddenly, in the viewfinder we saw someone jumping around and waving to us. It was Ron from the embassy, beckoning us down.

Ron met us in the foyer and led us into the main part of the hall, just a few rows from the front. 'Can't have you missing the action,' he smiled.

I don't think I've met a more entertaining, delightful, intelligent and charming gentleman in my life.

Finally, the ceremony began. The music swelled, an announcer spoke in a booming voice and the crowd suddenly hushed. 'Ladies and gentleman, we welcome artists from sixty-four countries around the world,' he said.

I was on the edge of my seat, craning my neck towards the back of the theatre, waiting for a glimpse of Tim to come through the doors. I was nervous for him. I didn't know if Tim would get through it because it was more than I had ever asked of him. Between his nerves, the noise at the Kennedy Center and the general exhaustion of the trip, of so many new places and people, I was worried that Tim would be completely overwhelmed. I worried that he'd be too tired to hold the flag up or that he'd have had enough and wouldn't want to go on. I wouldn't be there to encourage him and help him, I didn't know if anyone else would understand if he needed anything. I wouldn't blame him if he felt it was all too much.

'Argentina!' the announcer began, reading through the list of guest countries. I didn't have to wait much longer. 'Australia!' the announcer called.

There was Tim, marching in proudly with the Australian flag held high, a beautiful smile beaming across his face. He walked all by himself, looking so handsome in his new suit—my lovely, talented son. He looked like he was born to do it. A flood of tears filled my eyes. I choked back sobs. It was a powerful, powerful moment for me—I never could have dreamed up this achievement for Tim. I will never forget the smile on his face, not as long as I live.

•

The opening ceremony finished a couple of hours later and we set off to find Tim, who was seated in a separate section with the other flag bearers. The Kennedy Center is a beautiful building on the Potomac River, with an impressive hall of flags and quotes from President Kennedy laid in stone, high ceilings and big columns and lots of different halls. Tim was in one of those halls but we couldn't find him. Ron, Sam and I took off in different directions until Sam finally ran into Tim, waiting patiently with a support worker.

I found the boys and stood with them until Ron came back for us. He came speeding through the crowd at quite a pace—the man could really run.

'Would Tim like to meet Ambassador Kennedy-Smith?' Ron said. He had spotted her with her bodyguards at a side exit. Tim was besotted with the Kennedy family, almost as much as he was with American presidents, so we all took off after Ron on the chase for Jean Kennedy-Smith. She was surrounded by excited participants when we found her, but Ron led us through and introduced us as visitors from Australia.

I hadn't had time to explain to Tim who we were going to meet—I'd just grabbed his hand and started running. When we arrived in front of her and it was clear from her bodyguards and entourage that she was very important, Tim said, 'Are you Mrs Bush?' He still hoped there was a chance he would meet the president. We all laughed, even Ms Kennedy-Smith, and I explained to Tim whom he was meeting.

As Tim knew the whole history of the Kennedy families including the names and dates of their births and deaths, he immediately started reciting these details for Ms Kennedy-Smith and she was duly impressed. We had a lovely chat about the festival and Australia, and she was amazed at how far we had come. She was very gracious and in no rush to get away, which was incredibly flattering. We told her to come and visit us in Australia and we would cook her a nice roast dinner.

After the festival, Kristine's office got in touch with Ms Kennedy-Smith and asked if she would do an interview for our episode of *Australian Story*. Not only did she agree, she said lovely things about Tim and she sent me a signed copy of her book.

Ron and Lori became real friends to us—we kept in contact after we went home. The trip went from amazing to perfect because of their kindness. The boys had a wonderful time visiting the Smithsonian museums, then Ron took them to the Museum of Natural History while Lori took me shopping at Macy's. It was incredible having them as our guides. Just before we left, the embassy staff passed around a hat and Lori presented us with some money. It was so generous but I was very embarrassed. I accepted it so as not to make a scene and tried very hard not to cry. I was deeply touched. They were very decent people.

Tim didn't get to meet the president in the end but he certainly saw the White House. He stood at the gates for a very long time with a satisfied look on his face.

14

Tim Sharp, Artist

When we came back from Washington I had one thought in my mind: *We can't go back to our old life.* I had this irrational feeling that everything we had experienced was a dream; that this amazing adventure would end and things would go back to how they had once been, difficult and sometimes hopeless. Involuntarily, that mantra came to me throughout the day, *We can't go back to our old life, we can't go back to our old life.* I had felt so free in Washington—I couldn't bear to feel trapped again.

The picket fence dream had been taken away from me. I hadn't wanted much, just a husband and a home and a couple of healthy children, but even those modest aspirations had managed to fall apart. I realised now that I'd have to make my own dream, something different. It wasn't going to be easy, but it wasn't going to be ordinary either. Life had given me a second chance and I was grabbing it with both hands. I was going to build another dream for Sam, Tim and me.

•

Our episode of *Australian Story* went to air in September 2004. I had no idea what to expect. After seventy-two hours of filming, who knew what they'd put together. I was worried it would look like a sad, pathetic story. I trusted Kristine but didn't know how she saw things. She had all the power. Seeing yourself through someone else's eyes can be very confronting.

The program was really thoughtful and warm, and I think we came up well. Tim was very shy and nervous about it; he ran in and out of the room while he was on. He had never liked seeing footage of himself. When he was small, he was terrified that the process of having X-rays would leave him looking like a skeleton. With photographs, I got the sense that he felt they were stealing his soul. I was extremely happy for him, though. He came across so well. There were several scenes the crew had filmed with Tim that I wasn't aware of, these beautiful everyday moments, and I was thrilled to see that they'd captured him as a wonderful, life-loving young man.

We had some family friends around to watch the episode with us, a little viewing party, but I found their excitement really distracting. It was a very reflective moment for me.

I watched myself on the screen, saying, 'Sometimes I forget. I forget how hard it was. The day Tim was born was the happiest day of my life. But it only took a few days, and things started to change . . . We went to see a specialist. And that was the first time autism was indicated. And that was the worst day of my life.'

It made me very tired to even think about that time. I felt overwhelmed by everything that had happened, but at the same time my mind was ticking over. *We can't go back to our old life,* I thought.

We'd met people from all around the world in Washington, artists and performers and other people with disabilities, and carers and people who admired Tim's art. Not once did anyone ask me where we lived or what job I had; and at no time did they judge me for my position in society. No one had asked me what disability Tim had. No one asked about his limitations or tried to tell us what he could or couldn't do. They weren't interested in his disability—they were interested in Tim's art. It was an acceptance that we had never experienced before. That was the world I wanted for us.

As soon as the *Australian Story* episode finished the phone started to ring. I heard from friends near and far, including people I hadn't spoken to for years; people who knew exactly where we'd started out. The school secretary from St Brendan's called. She had seen Tim screaming and crying every morning back in his primary school days. 'It's hard to believe it's the same person,' she said. It was a very emotional time.

After the wave of friends had passed, we got the wave of strangers. Strangers started to get in touch and they kept getting in touch for months. We got letters and emails from people who were moved by the story, every time the episode ran. People wanted to congratulate Tim and show their support, and an incredible number of people wanted to buy Tim's art. Every time they re-ran the episode, Tim found a new group of fans.

Tim owned a Laser Beak Man T-shirt that I had had made at a local printer for him to wear when we went to Washington. On *Australian Story*, he was shown wearing it outside the White House. After the show, requests came flooding in; all of a sudden we were in the T-shirt business. It was easy enough to get them made and send them off in the post. A friend built a website for us (for free!) and after that even more orders came through. People sent me cheques or money transfers, and I opened a bank account for Tim. He wasn't out of high school yet, but his career had already started.

•

We had met many people at the VSA Festival who had impressive reputations in the art world, and who believed in the potential of Laser Beak Man. They said out loud the things I dreamt but was too embarrassed to say—they talked of Laser Beak Man books, movies and television shows; action figures, clothing and all the merchandise imaginable. Some of them talked about art exhibitions that could travel the world. They described Tim as an 'Outsider Artist', 'Raw Artist' or 'Naive Artist'. I had never heard these terms before, but they assured me artists who worked in these genres had passionate followers all around the world. They wanted to know why I hadn't done more; they believed in Tim's art so much. I could have told them easily why I hadn't done more; I didn't know what I was doing. This was all new to me.

I think the opportunity to spend time with other artists and get positive feedback had a big impact on Tim, because when we came home from Washington he began to make more art. Not only was he drawing all the time, his drawings were becoming more detailed and distinctive. He was really hitting his stride.

One day we received a call from a woman named Bronte Morris. She congratulated us on the television program and said Tim should have an exhibition now that he was so famous. She had a gallery just waiting for him called Hands on Art, part of Brisbane's arts district in South Bank. She said she'd take care of everything. It seemed like a fabulous opportunity, so I said, 'Why not?'

Tim and I went to meet Bronte, who was the perfect picture of a gallery director, with short hair and black clothes, and a fancy way of talking. I felt totally out of my depth but Tim seemed very happy—he loved Bronte's colourful glasses. There were lots of young people doing workshops at the gallery and it seemed like a kid-friendly place. I could already see Tim's drawings on the wall. *But how do I get them framed?* I wondered.

I told Ron in Washington that Tim was about to have his first solo exhibition—it seemed a bit funny really that he had exhibited in the States but hadn't had an exhibition in his home country.

'Who is going to open it?' Ron asked. I didn't know, I hadn't even thought of that. Ron gave me a ton of good advice about what to do, how to run it and how to present the art, and he insisted that I find someone important to open the exhibition. We didn't know any important people in Brisbane! Our only important friends were in Washington.

I mentioned to Ron that Ms Quentin Bryce, who was the Governor of Queensland at the time, had recently visited Tim's high school. The school had asked Tim if they could give her one of his artworks as a thankyou gift, and of course he said yes. 'Well then,' Ron insisted, 'you should ask Governor Bryce to open it!'

I was shocked by the suggestion; it seemed very unlikely to me that she would do it, but I did as Ron told me. I sent off a letter to the governor's office, including 'Filthy Disgusting Birthday' cards and a Christmas card that Tim had made. The Christmas card featured Laser Beak Man at a control box for TNT, with sticks of dynamite under a chimney that is hung with Christmas stockings. Santa Claus is on his way down the chimney to deliver the Christmas presents. The message on the card is, 'I Told You, No Underpants'.

Apparently, Ms Bryce found the cards pretty hilarious. She was more than happy to come along and open Tim's first exhibition.

•

It was a balmy night on the Brisbane River when Tim's first show opened, early in April 2005. There was a great crowd at Hands on Art, including art-gallery directors and artists Ron had insisted we invite. Ms Bryce made a very touching and wonderful speech, and Tim spent a lot of time by her side. He was very fond of her and a bit in awe, I think. He smiled the whole night.

One of the pictures in the exhibition was called 'Bob's Burger Café' and it featured Laser Beak Man and friends, sitting around a diner. Evil Emily was in it, chopping up chillies, Edward Bigmouth had a pickles jar in his hand and Peter Bartman was mowing lettuce leaves. There were a couple of cows staring in through the window. Another picture was called 'Shakin' That Ass', which showed Laser Beak Man swinging a donkey by its tail. The 'Zebra Crossing' was a black and white piece featuring zebras walking across the road. It was lovely to hear people chuckle out loud as they wandered around the gallery. Every artwork in the show was sold. Tim's debut was a wild success.

Some months later, Sam, Tim and I were invited to morning tea at Government House. The chef made these incredible Laser Beak Man biscuits, cut into shape and decorated in the colours of Tim's superhero. They were absolutely delightful. We felt very honoured to receive such a prestigious invitation and the three of us had a wonderful time. Ms Bryce went on to become the Governor-General of Australia and she was often on television. Every time she came on screen, Tim was pleased to see his friend.

•

At the end of 2005, Tim finished high school. In the months leading up to his graduation, I started meeting with people to find out what support there would be for him and me. As long as he was in school, there was somewhere for him to be during the day and people to take care of him. When school ended, we were on our own.

I was really scared. Tim's world was going to shrink at exactly the moment when the other young adults in his year level would be going off to start their lives, and there was nothing I could do about it. The high school had organised a supported employment trial for Tim at a fruit shop, where he bagged onions all day, and there was another place he went where adults with disabilities painted ceramics. I went to visit Tim at the fruit shop and I got the impression that the owners were making fun of him. Tim had been very distressed by the ceramics workshop, for reasons he couldn't quite explain. I didn't feel right sending him to those places just so that I didn't have to take care of him. I wasn't sure what we were going to do.

It was bittersweet, in many ways, but I was still so very proud of Tim for finishing school. He even went to the senior formal. He went with an Indian girl from the special-education unit named Joyce, who wore a beautiful sari. Tim wore a brand-new Ben Sherman shirt and he bought Joyce a corsage.

The graduation was lovely. The children from the unit were mixed in with the general school population and when they got to 'S', Tim was called to the stage to accept his special certificate. That weekend, there was a graduation party at one of the kids' houses and Tim was invited by some of the girls. There was nothing more terrifying for me at that moment than taking my teenage son to a party and seeing four hundred teenagers all over the street, but Tim was determined to go. I gave him a mobile phone and told him to send me a text message when he'd had enough, then watched helplessly as the girls led 'Timmy' away. Sam and I waited in the car, listening to the music blaring from the house. Tim lasted about an hour. His schoolmates were good kids.

•

Thankfully, Tim's art gave him purpose and gave me some hope for the future. We made a lot of new friends at this point in our lives. I saw an ad for a free legal advice service on a Monday night and went in to meet a lawyer called Michael, who helped me to set up a trust for Tim. We met a photographer named Mark Lutz who helped us with the reproduction of Tim's art and gave me a lot of business advice. People continued to contact us and offer their support, and more and more people were buying T-shirts, birthday cards and prints.

Some women from the Queensland Arts Council had come to see the Hands on Art show and they wanted to take some of Tim's art on tour. They had a touring arts program that travelled regional centres throughout Queensland and they asked Tim if he was willing to have a touring exhibition with them. At the time, Tim was the youngest person they had ever considered touring and the first artist with a disability. Of course we said yes. The exhibition was supposed to last a year, but due to its popularity the tour was extended for three years and went to twenty-seven different regional centres, reaching audiences of thousands. One of the most rewarding things that came out of it were the emails we received from teachers, many of whom were inspired to use art as a way to help kids with disabilities. It gave many people who wouldn't usually have been exposed to it some insight into the mind of a person with autism.

Before I knew it, I was contacted by another gallery owner, Ryan Renshaw, who owned a very well-respected commercial gallery in Brisbane's Fortitude Valley. Ryan was keen to hold another exhibition for Tim in January 2006.

Tim had been very busy creating drawings and his style had really come along—he was getting more adventurous with his compositions. By this stage, we had begun to sell his artwork and prints through the website. Tim was like a little drawing machine, but there was such demand he still couldn't keep up. It seemed as soon as Tim finished a piece it was snapped up by an eager buyer. It was lovely, but it meant we didn't have much artwork around the house any more. And we desperately had to build up a collection in order to hold an exhibition.

Tim's drawings for the Ryan Renshaw gallery were so funny and full of character. 'Bad Hair Day' featured Laser Beak Man as a hairdresser with a chainsaw, next to a lady with a triple-decker bun. There was a picture called 'The Honeymoon', which had a moon, dripping with honey and surrounded by bees. Tim was fascinated by and terrified of bees—if one came close to him he'd scream. He had turned his fear into a very funny picture. There was another drawing called 'Fruit Flies' and I smiled when I saw it, remembering the day it had sprung to life.

'What's a fruit fly?' Tim had asked.

I realised I was always explaining things to Tim but I had no idea what he imagined.

'Why don't you draw one,' I suggested.

Tim drew a banana and a pineapple, with wings. *Wouldn't it have been a shame if I'd told him what it was?* I thought. *I'd never have got to see this.*

My favourite picture in the show was called 'Hubba Hubba', inspired by our American adventures. Laser Beak Man is rowing Michelangelo's *David* across the water, towards New York's Statue of Liberty. *David* is wearing underpants that say, 'I Love New York'. That made me laugh.

Tim's artwork had taken a big leap forward. It was really obvious. Every time he got some good feedback, it seemed to make him more confident. He bloomed and his work just got better and better. His sense of humour was all over the page now, big and joyful and naughty. It told me so much about who he was and how he saw the world.

Tim mulled over everyday expressions. He heard them literally and what other people meant when they said these things wasn't always clear to him. In a way, his pictures showed how he had struggled with language and communication his whole life; how he struggled with the rules of language that everyone else could follow instinctively. That struggle isolated Tim and it kept him separate from me. But in another way, the pictures showed how free Tim was. His point of view was completely unique and that's what made him special. His interpretation of the world wasn't flawed; it was beautiful, smart and funny.

The minute Tim found a way to express that point of view it reconnected him with the world. It brought so many encouraging, enthusiastic friends into his life. And it reconnected him with me. After all the years I had fought to hear him, Tim finally had a voice. I always knew he was intelligent, but he'd found a way to speak to me that I could understand. Every time he drew, he told me something about himself. I was amazed to learn there was so much more to him than even I had imagined. I was surprised, I was fascinated and I was truly, truly grateful.

15

Wayne Bennett and the Powerhouse

The Brisbane Powerhouse was located on the Brisbane River in the much-loved, character-laden inner city suburb of New Farm. As the name suggests, it was an old powerhouse. It was built in the 1920s and operated until the 1970s, when it fell into disuse. The building was neglected and became derelict, a place for homeless people to sleep and wayward kids to party. Then in the 1980s, it was reclaimed by the local council and turned into a really cool centre for performance and visual art.

When it was renovated, the Powerhouse kept its original character, including most of its industrial features—even some of the graffiti and art left behind by the squatters stayed. The building is over three storeys high, made of bleached red brick, and it towers over you. It looks a little scary, as though it has a dark history, but it's always interesting to go in and explore.

It became one of the major arts centres of the city and a really groovy place to hang out; lots of people go there to listen to music, have a drink and watch the river roll by. The Powerhouse is now an iconic and much-loved part of Brisbane life.

The boys and I loved to visit the Powerhouse. It's right next to New Farm Park, which is lined with jacaranda trees and has acres of beautiful rose gardens. It goes right down to the river's edge. The park has a fantastic play area for kids, with bridges and walkways that wind among these huge Moreton Bay fig trees that the boys loved to climb.

Often, we would walk over to the Powerhouse and have a look around. It was a great building for kids. The installation in the foyer had a wheel you could steer that was connected by cogs and rods to a mirror overhead, which reflected light from different angles as it moved. Tim loved it—it was hard to get him much further into the building sometimes. There were so many levels and stairs to climb, and part of the turbine engines was left behind; you could turn the cogs and look into halls where the engines used to be. The walls were bare brick, solid rock and concrete, and there were exposed beams and steel rafters everywhere, as well as massive old windows and an amazing glass lift. Tim called it his 'bat cave'.

You can imagine, then, just how excited he was when he was invited to have an exhibition at the Powerhouse in 2006. Tim was eighteen years old, just graduated from high school, and his career as an artist was still very new. The opportunity meant so much to him and to our family.

•

The Powerhouse came to us, like so many other things, after *Australian Story* went to air. We had also received a call from an oncologist called Dr James Morton. I was raised in a house where specialists were akin to saints and I was surprised that such an important man would call us. I was even more shocked when I heard what he had to say. Despite promising myself that no man would ever make me cry again, Dr Morton soon had me in tears.

Gently, he said, 'Do you mind me asking what your circumstances are? The TV story said you were a single mother with two boys.'

I gave him a shortened version of what we had been through, from Tim's diagnosis to the breakdown of my marriage. Dr Morton was clearly a deeply compassionate man; he seemed genuinely sorry for what we had been through. Having a man treat me with such kindness was a strange shock to the system and I found it deeply touching.

Dr Morton then told me about his circumstances. He and his wife, Louise, had three children. Their middle son, Andy, was diagnosed with autism when he was only two and though his prognosis was not as cruel and final as Tim's had been, they were left without much hope. Like me, they struggled to find support and services. Even though they were smarter than me, had more money than me and knew more people, their journey began with the same suffering and isolation. James told me

Tim with Sheldon Lieberman (right) and Igor Coric (left) from Bigfish TV, producers of the Laser Beak Man TV series.

Everyone getting into the spirit for the launch party of the Laser Beak Man TV series in Brisbane, February 2010.

Tim meeting Cate Blanchett for the first time at his exhibition at QPAC Brisbane, 11 June 2010.

Sam in 2010, looking forward to the plasters coming off his arms after three long months.

Sam after his 200-metre backstroke race at the 2012 Olympic swimming trials in Adelaide.

Sam and Tim at Glenelg Beach in Adelaide, taking a break from the Olympic swimming trials.

Meeting the boys from the Ghost Ballerinas for the first time at Nashville Airport, and seeing Tim's artwork on the cover of their CD. From left: Josh Harvey, Justin Berry, Cameron Burnette and Tim.

For Tim, the best part of the 'I Am What I Am' music festival was making new friends.

Tim's artwork lighting up the William Jolly Bridge in Brisbane as part of Autism Awareness Month, 2012.

Setting up for Tim's 2013 exhibition at the Brisbane Powerhouse.

Tim with Kathy Lette at 'Lynn's Lunch' in 2013. Kathy is holding the picture Tim drew for her featuring her famous corgi dress.

Sam, Tim, Samantha and me in Sydney for TEDx in 2014.

'A Double Shot of Happiness' up on the big screen at TEDxSydney in the Concert Hall of the Sydney Opera House, April 2014. *(Photo: Jean-Jacques Halans)*

A standing ovation after the TEDx talk. *(Photo: Arthur Arnesen)*

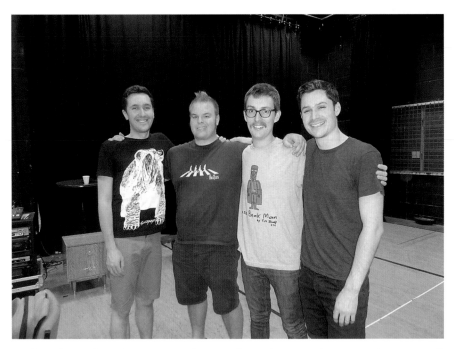

In the rehearsal studio in December 2014, working on the stage adaptation of Laser Beak Man with Nicholas Paine (far right) and David Morton (far left) of Dead Puppet Society, and Sam Cromack of Ball Park Music (in the Laser Beak Man T-shirt).

Tim creating art at home.

that after the diagnosis, he and Louise were walking down the street and she was sobbing. He was trying to comfort her but, for the first time, he had no idea what to do. They were both shell-shocked and feeling so helpless.

Louise found an early intervention centre for Andy that was run by the education department and shortly after he began attending he started to make really big improvements. Things were looking very positive for Andy but the funding for the centre was withdrawn and it was closed. James and his wife were shattered.

James decided he needed to start his own autism centre, to provide a program that benefited the children and wouldn't be shut down. With his own money, he bought an old church, just around the corner from St Brendan's Primary, and established the AEIOU Foundation. AEIOU—the Autism Early Intervention Outcomes Unit—was designed for children five years and younger. Andy was only able to get one year of support before he outgrew the program but James had ensured that other little children would get the help they so desperately needed.

James was in awe of and inspired by Tim. He thought Tim's success was one of the best stories he had ever heard about autism and he wanted to tell the world about it—he wanted other people to know there was a future for their children. I knew how he felt, I had desperately wanted to find role models for Tim when he was little but older people with autism just aren't visible in the community. All anyone ever talks about is the children.

James wanted to support Tim as much as he possibly could. I was overcome by his enthusiasm and his willingness to help.

After we spoke, I looked at the AEIOU website and I was terribly impressed. It was so positive and life-affirming. It talked about the children being treated as children, first and foremost. It was a happy, supportive environment that wasn't all about the *problem* of autism treatment—so much of the therapy was play-based and focused on having fun. I thought back to where we had started, at the cold and clinical Autism Centre, and contrasted it with the bright, happy pictures on the AEIOU website. It made me a little sad to wonder how much better Tim's outcomes might have been, if he'd had access to a wonderful place like that.

James asked if Tim would donate an artwork to AEIOU's next charity event and we were invited to attend as their guests. Tim's artwork raised over $10,000 and we were thrilled with that; it would help so many young children. Tim became an ambassador for AEIOU and James became Tim's biggest supporter. At any opportunity, whether in the media or in a private meeting, James would tell people Tim's story. He bought a lot of Tim's art, as well, and it was a great joy to hear him burst out into laughter when he saw an artwork that he thought was particularly funny—James just loved Tim's sense of humour. He developed the largest collection of Tim Sharp artwork in Australia and displayed it in his offices. I doubt there was a patient who went into those rooms who didn't hear about Tim Sharp and Laser Beak Man.

•

James became my hero. It was so touching for me to see a father who was so involved because it was overwhelmingly mothers who were primary carers for children with autism. I was moved to see a man taking such a proactive role. He was charismatic and forthright, and he put his money where his mouth was, expressing a clear vision for how he felt children with autism should be supported. You couldn't help but be transfixed by his knowledge, his ability to quote facts and figures, and his commitment. And James led by example; if there was a 100-kilometre hike to raise funds for children with autism, he was out at the front of the pack the whole way. Even before the hike was finished, you could be sure he'd already come up with his next brilliant idea to raise funds or implement another program.

Under James' leadership, AEIOU grew from one centre in the old church to many purpose-built centres throughout the state, as well as providing regional support to isolated communities. He also helped establish the Autism Centre of Excellence at Griffith University, ensuring future generations of teachers and community workers could be educated about autism. It was incredible what he was able to achieve in a few short years. He inspired us as much as we inspired him.

•

Not long after the first AEIOU auction, James decided that Tim and AEIOU should have an art exhibition together. He had recently met the director of the Powerhouse, Caz Osborne, who by chance had also been to Washington and had met up with our friend Ron. She was already familiar with Tim's work.

'I've got lots of walls,' she told James and me. 'You'll have the exhibition here.'

The Powerhouse was such a prestigious venue, it seemed that Tim was really coming of age as an artist.

'Who do you want to open it?' James asked.

I really hadn't thought about it, but I quickly answered, 'You.' I couldn't think of another person I respected more.

'What about Wayne Bennett?' he asked.

I laughed out loud. Wayne Bennett was coach of the Brisbane Broncos and one of the most famous sporting personalities in Australia. Wayne Bennett was huge.

'Do you know him?' I asked.

'No,' James told me, 'but I'll get him.'

When he said it, I knew he would. I doubt there is a person anywhere in the world who James couldn't get, especially if he thought they could make a difference to the life of a child with autism. A few days later, James rang to tell me it was all arranged.

My friend Margie, who worked for AEIOU, took care of all the details. Lexus was sponsoring the event and one of their shiny new cars would be on the showcase that night. Melissa Downes, one of the city's most liked and respected television presenters, would compere. Government ministers were coming, sporting personalities, fashion people, TV people and a whole lot of journalists. The media ran several stories on the exhibition and the social pages of the Sunday paper were going to cover the opening. It was going to be a spectacular night.

•

Lexus gave us a car for the evening, so we felt like a million bucks. Tim looked gorgeous in a brightly coloured and patterned Ben Sherman shirt, quite fitting for the colourful artist he was, and he was particularly looking forward to meeting Wayne Bennett. I wasn't.

Wayne Bennett had a fearsome reputation. With an astonishing record of premiership wins, he was one of the best coaches in the history of Rugby League. He was known as a man of incredibly high standards with high expectations of others. He seemed to live a very austere, moral life and never showed off his wealth or success. Despite saying very little, his words held a lot of weight; whatever he said was listened to and regarded in the highest esteem, and Wayne wasn't afraid to be direct. In fact, he was known as a very hard man who didn't suffer fools. Some people might even call him grumpy. For some years, there had been a media campaign to get a photo of Wayne Bennett where he was actually smiling. It was a very hard thing to do. I think it took a premiership win to get the man to smile.

I didn't know what I was going to speak to him about. I didn't like football. I didn't like grumpy old men. I didn't know what I was going to say and I was scared that anything I came up with would antagonise him, and I would cop his wrath. I wasn't exactly scared of him, but my feelings came pretty close.

When Wayne turned up he practically marched into the room, a man on a mission. He was introduced to Tim, who was thrilled to shake his hand, but very quickly got distracted by the waiters carrying platters of food. If it was a choice between conversation and food for Tim, Wayne Bennett didn't stand a chance. He and I were left standing together awkwardly while Tim took off after canapés.

'Show me the art,' Wayne said.

There was another side to Wayne, which is why he'd been asked to open the exhibition. It was well known that he was the father of two children with very high needs disabilities. One of his daughters had a physical disability and his son Justin had several disabilities, including an intellectual disability. There wasn't a sight more tear-jerking than seeing Wayne lead Justin by the hand, out onto the football field, in front of a cheering stadium. Although he was very guarded about his private life, Wayne never tried to hide his children.

As we wandered around the exhibition together, he asked me some very direct questions about my life and I answered him as honestly as I could. In response, Wayne told me about his life, which sounded very much like mine. He told me what day-to-day living was like and it broke my heart; the difficulties he faced were enormous. He explained that his children were his priority but that it was difficult to juggle work and home life. At the same time, it was plain that Wayne's dedication and commitment to his family were rock solid. He spoke of his incredible respect and admiration for his wife. It was clear from the look in his eyes that she was more of a hero to him than any sporting star he had ever met.

Wayne was nothing like I expected. He was a warm and genuine man who really cared, and he talked easily about his weaknesses and his emotions. It made him very real and very human to me. We had so much in common. We both worried what the future held for our children. We shared the same fears and struggles, even though we came from completely different situations in life, and we both felt there wasn't anyone else around who understood what we'd been through. It was often the loneliest feeling in the world, but for a moment we could lean on each other.

Others, like James, had some empathy for my situation, but Wayne Bennett was the first person that I truly felt understood me and what my life was like. It was an uplifting conversation—I had never experienced meeting a kindred soul like that before. And I could never have imagined that finding someone who shared your journey would make such a difference.

I could have stayed talking to Wayne all night, but the opening was due to start and there were people wanting to meet him and talk to him. I was so glad we had the time that we had; those few minutes were truly inspiring.

•

The evening was perfect, as promised. Tim doesn't like to make speeches because microphones scare him, but I tried to encourage him to say a few words. He was simple, short and truthful, as ever, 'Thank you very much for coming to see my art everybody. I am very happy. I love it.'

I made a speech thanking everyone for their support then James spoke, followed by Wayne. Without warning, in the middle of his speech, Wayne called me back onto the stage and asked me questions about my life with Tim. He took me by surprise and I was nervous at first, but it was a very warm and honest conversation. I think he wanted people to understand how much we had been through to get to that moment. A lot of people didn't have a clue. Later that night, and long afterwards, people came up to tell me how amazing and powerful that exchange had been. I knew just what they meant.

Tim gave Wayne an artwork as a way of thanking him for coming and opening the exhibition. With his gift, Tim did what few people had been able to do: he put a huge smile on Wayne Bennett's face.

Tim just loved seeing Laser Beak Man take over the Powerhouse. We all joked that it was his headquarters, but it wasn't really a joke—it just felt right. Laser Beak Man lived in Power City; the Powerhouse is where he belonged.

The artwork for the exhibition was Tim's best yet—brighter, more individual and funnier than ever. It had started selling before they even opened the doors. One of the pictures was called 'Hang Ten' and it featured a surfing Laser Beak Man and ten pairs of board shorts on a washing line. 'Sweet Dreams' saw Laser Beak Man flying over a city, dropping a cloud of lollipops and sweets, and 'Peking Duck' had ducks peeking nervously through the Great Wall of China, watching Laser Beak Man cook.

By far and away, the most popular picture was his drawing of The Wiggles. It was called 'Laser Beak Man Tells The Wiggles To Shut Up' and it was wickedly funny. Tim had drawn it after I'd forced him to listen to *The Wiggles: Christmas Classics* CD one too many times. Dorothy the Dinosaur was roasting on a spit in the picture and Captain Feathersword was walking the gangplank of a pirate ship while Henry the Octopus swam in a pool surrounded by sharks. The Yellow Wiggle was on a conveyor belt heading for a giant axe that was chopping up fruit salad and the Blue Wiggle was about to be squished by a giant hot-potato masher. Laser Beak Man was standing happily in the middle of the drawing. He'd just shot the Red Wiggle out of a cannon.

One of the other fabulous pictures that debuted at the Powerhouse was 'Laser Beak Man and the Barbie Queue'. It showed Laser Beak Man at a grill, cooking sausages, with a long queue of bouncy blonde ladies lined up behind him. They have numbers in their hands, like you get at the deli counter when you're waiting for your turn.

James bought Tim's 'Mona Lisa' drawing, which became one of his most famous works. Someone had given us an art book that featured Da Vinci's smiling lady and I had explained to Tim that people liked it because they didn't know why she was smiling; it was a mystery. I'd asked Tim why he thought she smiled and he drew me an explanation. In his picture, the Mona Lisa posed beside a nearly finished portrait that was being painted by Laser Beak Man the artist. In order to make Mona Lisa smile, Laser Beak Man had turned around and dropped his pants, and was flashing his bare bottom. James bought the picture for a friend who was a proctologist. That artwork still hangs proudly on his waiting room wall.

•

Tim and I went into the exhibition every day of its two-week run. It was lovely to meet people as they came through the gallery and hear them as they chatted to each other and admired Tim's work. It felt like home to us and Tim was really happy to hang out there. He wandered about wherever he wanted and talked to the staff, and everybody was lovely and friendly and excited about his work. The more compliments Tim received, the more his confidence seemed to grow and develop.

'These are wonderful, Tim!' people would say.

Tim would smile and say, 'I know!'

His honesty was so natural, without conceit or pride, that people actually found it charming. They always smiled.

'You are so modest, Tim.' I laughed.

'What does modest mean, Mum?' he replied.

I wasn't very good at explaining modesty or irony. After that, when people told Tim he was good or clever or talented, Tim replied, 'I know! And I'm modest.'

Somehow he found a way to make people laugh even more.

16

Sheldon, Igor and the ABC

Our lives became a blur of activity. Tim's show at the Brisbane Powerhouse sold out and before long we were inundated with commissions. We got emails and orders from all over the country—I lost track of how people had found out about us. Tim continued to act as ambassador for AEIOU and we got other requests to support charities, so we donated work wherever we could. One piece went to the Rugby League player Luke Priddis, whose son had been diagnosed with autism. Luke started his own foundation to support children with autism, and he asked Tim if he would donate an artwork for its charity gala night. The artwork was purchased for $10,000 by the radio announcer Alan Jones in a spirited auction at the event.

Later, we began making annual donations of artwork to Brisbane's Mater Hospital, who auctioned the drawings to support their Little Miracles foundation. It was so lovely to be able to give back to the hospital that had saved Sam's and my life.

Tim had developed quite a decent profile. It wasn't a particularly huge shock when he was asked to participate in an exhibition celebrating International Day of People with Disability, late in 2006, but boy were we thrilled by the location. The exhibition was held in November, in the Sydney Opera House. When we arrived for the opening of the exhibition, Tim was so excited that he ran towards it, all along the quay and up the steps to the very front doors. I was laughing as I ran to keep up. The Opera House is like a boat out there on the gleaming harbour, one of the most iconic buildings in the world, and now it was home to an artwork by the famous Tim Sharp.

•

Life seemed to be full of all these amazing opportunities all of a sudden. James Morton nominated Tim as Queensland's representative for Young Australian of the Year in 2006 and he was chosen as one the finalists. The premier of Queensland made a speech about Tim in parliament, praising his achievements and recognising what a good role model he was, especially as he had overcome so many of his own challenges. Tim was included in the *Who's Who of Australia*—a list of influential Australians—and there was an article about our family in *Who Weekly*. I was rather pleased to find the photo of us sandwiched between photos of George Clooney and Brad Pitt.

In 2007, we received a lovely message from the National Museum of Australia in Canberra asking if they could include Tim in their Eternity Gallery exhibition. The Eternity Gallery was a beautiful space, with an exhibition that explored different human experiences. It looked at joy, chance, devotion, hope, loneliness and thrill through the lives of prominent Australians, and Tim's story would be told under the heading of 'separation'. The curator, a woman named Rowan, said that they wanted to show how autism had separated Tim from society and how his art had brought him back. I found it quite interesting that Rowan selected that word for Tim. It had a very strong meaning for me because I felt I had been fighting that separation his whole life. I was so glad she wanted to put a positive spin on the story. How lucky we were that Tim found this gift that brought him back to the world.

The exhibition included video, photographs and a piece of Tim's art. It was a positive story and was very well told, and it was just incredible to walk through the beautiful glassed-in gallery and see Tim's story beside Robert Menzies, Lindy Chamberlain, The Wiggles and Ben Lee. He was in illustrious company.

Through our association with the National Museum of Australia, a publisher contacted us about using one of Tim's artworks on the cover of a publication they were preparing called *Teaching Values in Australian Schools*. It was to be distributed to every public school throughout Australia. They chose Tim's artwork 'Sweet Dreams', a whimsical and beautiful piece that reflected the idea of spreading a good message, which is exactly what they wanted to do.

Shortly afterwards, we heard from another young man who had seen the exhibition at the museum. Giles Bowen was a teacher's aide at an autism school in Wollongong and he contacted us to say how much he liked the exhibition and how much it had inspired him. I thanked him for taking the time to write—Tim read all the messages he received but left all the replying to me—and said we hoped to make it to Wollongong one day. Giles responded in a flash, saying the school held an annual art show and he invited us to attend. *Of course*, I thought, *why not?*

Giles introduced me to the principal of the Aspect South Coast School for children with autism, a man named Bruce Rowles. Bruce invited us to attend their exhibition in 2007. The gallery that hosted the exhibition was at the local surf club on North Wollongong Beach. It was a beautiful setting but it didn't beat the crowd—some of the loveliest people we'd ever met. The show wasn't just for the children at Bruce's school, although their work was marvellous. Artists from around the region who had autism came to exhibit their work and the quality was really quite extraordinary.

Tim and I arrived a few days before the exhibition to speak to the media and meet some of the locals, and then we went to visit all of the classes that were supported by the Aspect South Coast School. The school operated a base centre and then satellite classrooms within mainstream schools as well as a special school, where the students with autism were supported by specially trained teachers. South Coast ran programs from playgroups to kindergarten, through primary and high school and even into adulthood. It was one of the best and most successful programs I had ever seen. The staff members were incredibly devoted; it was obvious how much they loved the kids in their care.

It was a very emotional experience for me seeing how the children were drawn to Tim when we visited their classrooms. Even when the teachers warned us that the children might not be interested, the kids seemed thrilled to meet him. Some of them were only beginning their autism journey and their needs were very high, but watching them come up to Tim, to take his hand or want to sit on his knee while he encouraged them to draw, brought tears to my eyes.

One of the men who came to the South Coast exhibition loved Tim's artwork so much that he offered him a free parachute jump. We were due to leave for Sydney in just a few hours, but the gentleman insisted there was plenty of time; he owned the company and could arrange for Tim's jump to take priority. I must have asked Tim a hundred times if he was sure he wanted to go and each time he told me that he certainly did. Off he went with the parachute group to the airfield—there was no room for me to fit in the bus. It was one of the first times he had ever gone off without me or someone else he knew and I was stunned by how confident and happy he seemed. Meanwhile I was a blubbering mess. I telephoned Sam and said, 'What have I done? I think I've killed your brother!'

An hour later, Tim floated happily to earth with a huge smile across his face, and landed safely with two feet firmly on ground. It had been the longest hour of my life. He asked immediately if he could do it again. I said, 'I don't think my nerves could take it.'

We had such an amazing time in Wollongong in 2007 that we agreed to come back the following year, and every year after that. Tim supported the South Coast school by donating his art, including a Laser Beak Man picture that was painted onto a surfboard and raffled off for thousands of dollars. The school community said thanks by giving Tim some other incredible experiences like a motorbike ride down the Princes Highway and a helicopter ride over the south coast. Tim loved it there and I got a lot out of it, too. We made some incredible, lifelong friends and seeing the children in the program grow and develop was one of the best gifts I had ever received.

•

Over the next couple of years, we travelled regularly around the country to meet people and exhibit Tim's work. There wasn't a grand plan, but somehow people found us and we were never short of opportunities. People loved Tim's art and wanted to share it, but we were also asked to talk about disability and inclusion, and how important it was for Tim to have a voice. He was invited to talk at charities, businesses and schools—everything from kindergartens to high schools. At first I was nervous about going to the high schools, thinking the kids might be cynical and not care about Tim's experience, but teenagers turned out to be Tim's biggest fans, admiring all that he had achieved and falling in love with his art.

Tim's adult life had taken shape very quickly. When he wasn't exhibiting or speaking somewhere, we were at home, with a very orderly kind of routine. Every day, Tim had a plan for what he wanted to do. He liked to do some exercise with his Wii video games, watch a movie, do some writing, read up on some facts and figures, then sit in the sun with our newest dogs Coco and Sugar. Some days he liked to cook and do household chores like hanging out the washing, though he couldn't always tell if the clothes were properly dry. I had to appreciate the effort.

When Tim was ready to draw he announced it, 'It's time to draw, Mum!'

He worked at our dining-room table, which was four feet long by two-and-a-half feet wide, and had great sentimental value for me. My mother had given me the table when I left my ex-husband; she had bought it when she and my father were married. It was pine, seventy years old and covered in countless coats of paint, but I could never bring myself to get rid of it. When it was time to eat, the artwork was moved out to the old table-tennis table in the garage, then brought back in when Tim was ready to work again. He didn't need a gallery or a studio, he was happy in his favourite chair, always facing the same way.

From the very first time he had picked up a pencil at our place in Cleveland, I was always with Tim when he drew. Having me there with him was more than a habit—the familiarity of routine was how he learned to do things. If he first did something in a particular way then that was how it stuck in his brain and how he remembered and focused. He still grabbed my hand when we crossed the street, just like he used to grab my fingers when he was a baby, to march and wobble around the backyard. He still coloured with the same kind of crayons that he had started using in primary school—he went through hundreds of wind-up crayons every year. It was one of the things that made his art so unique.

As he got older, I tried to get him to start drawing without me. 'Go ahead and do it. I'm cooking,' I'd say, but it wasn't any use. Tim needed me beside him, and he needed me to watch him. If I tried to read a book or talk on the phone, he would put his pencil down. *Move it along*, I'd laugh to myself, *this is taking forever!* I had so much to do, but the truth is him drawing was really beautiful to watch. Tim had good hands, just like the doctor had said when he was born. His hands flowed across the page so gracefully and it was so wonderful to watch a line transform into an image; I could never get enough. But the colouring, don't get me started. It was *so* laborious. People told us that when they looked at Tim's art they could see the intensity in every single stroke of colour, but unless you'd seen it up close you'd have no idea. It took forever, and the further along he got with a drawing the more I'd hold my breath. All that work and if he made one mistake . . . it was like watching him tightrope walk across Niagara Falls. My nerves were shattered by the end of it.

The concentration really wore Tim out as well—he couldn't go more than half an hour before he got tired and had to have a break. When he started to flag, he would get confused and reach for the wrong colour, which is about the only time I made a useful contribution. 'Did you want red or green there?' I would ask.

I only ever checked to see if he was using the colour that he'd intended because the one time I tried to make a creative suggestion it was a disaster. Tim had been drawing a sunny beach scene and I told him he should use a bit of purple in the water. It looked awful. When Sam came home and saw the drawing he said, 'What's with that purple spot?'

All Tim said was, 'I know what I'm doing, Mum.'

He rarely made mistakes. He told me he could see the pictures in his head so he knew exactly what to draw.

●

After high school, Tim had ten hours a week with a carer, supported by the government, but I still had to cut back my hours at St Brendan's to stay at home and look after him. For the rest of his life, as long as I was around, he would need me to care for him. As gifted as he was, he still couldn't cross the road alone. If you told him your birth date, he could tell you in a split second how old you were, but he couldn't manage money. He couldn't order a pizza by himself. I couldn't leave him at home alone.

Tim could become extremely anxious when put under pressure or frightened. At times like that, if he was holding a pencil, his lines would jump like the line of the Richter scale as an earthquake hit. He needed constant reassurance and help with processing and planning, and other people's questions or conversation often confused or tired him. He was still extremely vulnerable.

I didn't mind being there for Tim—I loved him so much—but it didn't seem right that a young man was so bound to his mum. I worried about what would happen to him when I was gone. All the money he made from his art went straight into a trust fund and we got by on my pension and part-time work. It gave me a little bit of comfort to know that Tim had money in the bank to help support him when I no longer could. I worried that it wouldn't be enough, but at least it was the start of something.

•

In 2009, we were invited to return to the Brisbane Powerhouse for a show. Tim had been working hard and had a lot of art to exhibit, which was just as well—he had already been booked to exhibit at another gallery in Brisbane and the two shows would overlap by a few days, but we weren't going to miss our chance to return to our favourite gallery.

The other exhibition was at South Bank and was opened by the premier of Queensland at the time, Anna Bligh. Tim and I were back at the Powerhouse a few days later, meeting and greeting people as they came to see Tim's work. Tim loved to just wander the halls and look at his art, so perfectly exhibited on the Powerhouse walls. He loved to explore the building, talk with old friends, meet new people and accept kind compliments. He was totally at home there and it was a wonderful thing. I love seeing him that happy and relaxed. He just loved speaking to people who enjoyed his art—and there were a lot of people who did. The exhibition sold out very quickly and we were getting enquiries from art collectors from around Australia, and overseas as well.

I was chatting with a couple of gallery visitors one day when I noticed two women in a heated argument. They were fighting over a piece of Tim's art called 'The Chick Magnet' (with no sense of irony). It was getting serious and I was sure one of them was going to grab the art off the wall and march away with it, but the situation sorted itself out as the two women launched into a bidding war. Tim was the winner.

The Powerhouse show included 'I Love A Sunburnt Country, A Land of Sweeping Planes', which was inspired by the lines of the Dorothea Mackellar poem. In Tim's drawing, Uluru is in the background and Laser Beak Man is on top of a plane, with a broom in his hand. 'Wild Night Out' showed Laser Beak Man driving around the city in a convertible, surrounded by lions and giraffes, and 'Wee Wee Wee All The Way Home' featured the three little pigs in three out-houses. Laser Beak Man was standing next to some nice-looking women in 'Let's Go Clubbing', holding a bunch of golf clubs.

'A Double Shot of Happiness' was my absolute favourite. It was an obvious pun and it wasn't really meant to be funny, but gee did it make you smile. Laser Beak Man stood in the middle of the picture with six-shooters in each hand. Exploding from the guns were two brilliant clouds of colour filled with smiles and love hearts and music notes. It was the most joyful thing I'd ever seen. That picture really made me happy, because Tim didn't lie. If Tim drew an explosion of happiness, I knew that's what was in his heart.

•

One day, while I was sitting at the Powerhouse at our little merchandise stall, I saw two men come down the stairs and wander into a rehearsal room. One of them was tall and lean with longish black hair and deep, soulful eyes. The other was very short and fair, with a physique just like a dancer. His eyes were light and full of life.

A few minutes after they went in, they came out of the room again. It was obvious they were at the Powerhouse for a reason, but they stopped for a moment to look at Tim's art, then they looked a little bit closer. The two men went from one artwork to the next, looking carefully and occasionally smiling. I was always pleased when I saw that reaction from people.

Tim was standing in the middle of the gallery and the two men walked over to speak to him. I was happy for people to talk to Tim, and he enjoyed it for the most part, but sometimes it got confusing for him. People asked him the most ridiculous things, especially when it came to commissions. Sometimes, he agreed to whatever people asked him just to stop them talking, then I had to tell them afterwards that it wasn't going to happen.

A lady had walked up to the merchandise stall and I was trying my best to help her while also trying to pick up a few words of Tim's conversation. It seemed like the two men were making some effort. They walked Tim over to one of his art pieces and were gesturing and pointing, and I could see he was giving one-word answers to their questions. When the woman left, I went straight over and introduced myself as Tim's mum, but the men weren't really interested in speaking to me. They were asking Tim the story behind each artwork. They wanted to know 'why this' and 'why that', which was very hard for Tim. He got confused quickly when there were too many questions. His most common answer was that he liked it and it made him happy—he let the art speak for itself. But I was impressed that the men weren't pushing Tim. They were patient as he struggled to find the words, especially when it was clear that it was difficult for him.

I stood back and waited. I was pretty certain they weren't trying to push him into doing something or asking too much of him. I was Tim's protector, but something told me he didn't need protecting this time. The men spent a long time with Tim, just looking at the art. And when they were done, they came over to introduce themselves. The small one was Sheldon Lieberman and the tall one was Igor Coric, and they were animators. They wondered if Tim might like to work with them.

Sheldon owned a digital design company called Bigfish TV and Igor worked for him. They were very successful animators who had won awards and did all kinds of commercial work, including promotional work for the Powerhouse. They had been asked by ABC television to submit four ideas for animated series for a new ABC channel for children, ABC3. They thought Laser Beak Man would make a perfect television character.

Tim heard this and his eyes lit up, and mine nearly fell out of my head. Tim had wanted Laser Beak Man on TV right from the very beginning—he often asked me when it would happen but I had no idea when or how. Suddenly, here was the opportunity, standing right in front of us. I think I might have overreacted. I got so excited that I must have been embarrassing, but it was the chance of a lifetime. They were offering us Tim's biggest dream. I was thrilled and so was Tim, though he was a lot calmer than me.

Igor and Sheldon were looking for creative inspiration when they had come into the Powerhouse that afternoon. In fact, Igor had just flown in from his home country of Serbia so that he and Sheldon could do more work on their ABC proposal. It was also a huge opportunity for them and they wanted to present the very best proposals they could. They were very keen to have their animations on the new television channel as well. They were extremely excited when they found Tim, though maybe not as excited as me. When they left I jumped in the air and hugged Tim, and made sure that he understood that Laser Beak Man would soon be on television. I bypassed all the possibilities that something could go wrong or that it may not be accepted; I didn't mention that at all. I believed with all my heart that Sheldon and Igor would do a great job and the ABC would love it. I was convinced the whole thing was fate.

•

The process of bringing Laser Beak Man to TV began very quickly. Igor and Sheldon selected artworks from the show, which were photographed at a very high resolution by a professional photographer at a nearby studio. Things had to be done perfectly from the very beginning. The images went off to Bigfish TV where the production team got to work cutting up each and every piece of each artwork so that every element could be individually animated. They were cut up digitally, not by hand, and it was an intensive and time-consuming process. Igor was busy writing scripts and storyboards while Sheldon worked on the sound and music. Every time they came up with something, they asked Tim to come to their offices to see whether or not he liked it.

Once or twice a week, we would go over and check on their progress and learn about the process of animation. Tim was amazed by the Bigfish studio, which was in a converted church and had retro toys strewn all over the place. The staff always smiled and said, 'Hi Tim!' when we arrived. It made me happy that he was the man of the hour, the creative brain behind their project.

The process was far more detailed than I had imagined and the Bigfish team were working incredibly hard—there were only a few weeks until their submission to the ABC was due. The animations were to be interstitials, which were forty-five-second clips that would come on between half-hour shows, but there would be a whole series, eight in total. For now, they were just working on the pilot.

Sheldon and Igor said the basic joke in each picture was obvious but when you looked at the pictures another layer revealed itself. They would interpret a little bit of action behind the scenes and then they would ask Tim what he thought. Ninety-nine per cent of the time, Tim agreed with them exactly. Sheldon and Igor treated Tim with a lot of respect and I trusted them completely. Sheldon in particular was unlike any man I had ever met. He was incredibly intelligent and his words were very measured, but his mind was lucid and funny. His quirky observations revealed a very different way of seeing the world, which Tim found absolutely fascinating. Their connection is what made the project work so well.

•

'The Chick Magnet' was the very first Laser Beak Man cartoon and it was just perfect. All the elements of Tim's drawing sprang to life, creating a little story. An angry chicken looked on as Laser Beak Man used a magnet to play with her little chicks, bouncing them off the footpath. When the chicks and their mum walked off in a huff, Laser Beak Man turned the magnet on himself, flying off-screen.

Sheldon and Igor hadn't tried to turn Laser Beak Man into a crime-fighting superhero, they had just let the natural humour bubble to the surface. They had even used Tim's handwriting in the credits, to make sure they had the right feel. The thing that really brought the drawing to life, though, was the music and the sounds. Tim was very clear from the beginning that Laser Beak Man didn't speak, so Sheldon had asked what sound he might make. Tim made a noise, a kind of humming sound and a chuckle, and that became Laser Beak Man's voice. Knowing how much Tim struggled with language, it seemed right that his hero didn't have to rely on words. He did have a theme tune, however, a neat little bongo rhythm. It captured the spirit of Laser Beak Man perfectly.

'That's good,' Tim said, when it finished. That was all I needed to hear.

Bigfish submitted four animation projects to the ABC but they only accepted Laser Beak Man. We barely had time to celebrate before the team got cracking on the rest of the episodes.

Every week, Tim and I would spend time at the studio. The guys would ask him his opinion and he would tell them what he thought. It was lovely; there was a wonderful feeling of collaboration and camaraderie among the whole team. We would gather in the editing room at the back of the building to watch clips and there were often so many people in the room that some would stand and some would sit on the floor. We'd watch the clips and wait for a reaction, all eyes on Tim. Everyone knew when an episode was a winner because Tim would chuckle or laugh out loud—that was a success for all of us.

Sheldon went out of his way to cut production costs so that Tim would be able to get as much money from the TV series as possible. I think he knew that Tim's ability to earn an income was limited and he was determined to help him as much as he could. The series was *Laser Beak Man* by Tim Sharp from the very beginning, and the majority of the profits went to Tim. But even though the budget was tight the work they did was just brilliant. Each episode that Bigfish produced made Tim's artworks dance. Laser Beak Man sat in a bathtub in 'Soap Opera' while all kinds of drama escalated around him and bubbles rose up to the ceiling. In 'Red Hot Mamma', Laser Beak Man threw a bucket of hot water over a steaming woman with a baby in her arms. 'The Frequent Flyers Club' saw a flock of birds settling into an airport lounge next to Laser Beak Man, before settling on an aeroplane and lifting it into the air with the flapping of their wings. They were funny and cheeky and a little bit strange. Tim grinned from ear to ear when he watched them.

•

Laser Beak Man went to air as part of the ABC3 test broadcast on Boxing Day in 2009. Sam, Tim and I gathered in the lounge room to watch his television debut—a forty-five-second film called 'The Black Sheep of the Family'—and we were spellbound. Although we'd seen the animation many times, actually seeing it on the television as part of a broadcast, introduced by two hosts who raved about it, was a surreal and shocking experience. We sat there in silence, stunned smiles on our faces.

On Monday 8 February 2010—the night before *Laser Beak Man* began its regular run on television—I threw a big party for Tim and the team at a venue right opposite the Powerhouse. It was a thankyou for Sheldon and Igor, for Bigfish TV, and all of our friends and supporters. We screened all of the animations and the team got a standing ovation. It was beautiful to listen to that endless applause. There was a lot of love in the room.

Sheldon had Laser Beak Man masks made and we took some great photos of everyone being Laser Beak Man for the night, and later he gave a very lovely speech. He talked about the beauty of the relationship he had with Tim, how much it had affected him. He explained that he wasn't a spiritual man, but there was something very spiritual about that relationship and the work they had done together. I knew exactly what he meant. It was something that couldn't be defined but it was a force around all of us that drew us close. It felt like Laser Beak Man was a gift that Tim had given to all of us.

After the party, I received a thankyou letter from Igor that touched me deeply. *I will always think of Tim as my biggest hero*, he wrote. *I never thought of how many challenges he had to overcome and how many there are to live with, so seeing him stand there alone against all of us really changed me forever.* Later that year, when Sheldon and Igor won Tropfest with an animation called 'Testicle', Sheldon wore his Laser Beak Man T-shirt for the whole world to see.

•

Tim was twenty-one years old when his animation was first screened on ABC3. He was the first person in the world with autism whose art had been made into a television series—he had paved the way for other artists and animators with autism. By January 2011, the series had been sold to Cartoon Network Asia Pacific and it would be seen throughout Asia, New Zealand and Australia. Laser Beak Man was international!

It was such an incredible achievement for Tim. It would have been an amazing achievement regardless, but the fact that Tim had autism made it all the more wonderful. And yet, seeing Laser Beak Man fly around the globe wasn't the really special part. Seeing Tim surrounded by other artists who valued his opinion brought tears to my eyes. Sheldon and Igor were such generous collaborators, completely without ego or selfish motives. They didn't just help Tim to realise his dream of getting Laser Beak Man on TV, they allowed him to work with his peers, to make something bigger than he could achieve on his own. That experience was priceless. It made me feel differently about the world.

17

Cate Blanchett and QPAC

In early December 2009 I was trying to mow the yard and was halfway through when the mower coughed and spluttered and then just stopped. I played around with the spark plugs and got it started again but seconds later it spluttered and died again. I was kicking the tyres and cursing when the home phone rang, and Tim came out to tell me that the call was for me. I wanted to get the mowing done before it got dark and I knew that anyone who called at 6 p.m. was a telemarketer. *Just what I bloody need,* I thought, scowling at the grass.

'What do you want?' I barked down the telephone line.

'Oh hello,' said a nervous voice. 'Is that Tim's mum?'

The very kind woman on the other end of the line was Rosemary Myers, the Artistic Director of Brisbane's Out of the

Box Festival. She was calling to see if Tim was interested in having an exhibition as part of the 2010 event.

'Hi, nice to hear from you,' I said sheepishly.

Out of the Box was a biennial arts festival for children under eight, held at the Queensland Performing Arts Centre. When it was on it took over the whole arts precinct at South Bank, with artists and theatre groups from around the world flying in to perform. When the boys were young, I'd taken them along to one or two shows. It was hard for Tim to cope with the outings but Sam really loved them, and I was very impressed with the professionalism of the festival. It really was world class. We had a real affection for the Powerhouse but QPAC was where the international stars came to perform and it was very impressive to us. I was delighted that Tim would have an exhibition in such a prestigious venue.

●

The publicity team at Out of the Box organised some media coverage for Tim to help promote the festival, including a feature spread in *The Courier-Mail*. A journalist named Frances Whiting was coming around to our house to do the interview. I'd been a fan of hers for years. Frances was a clever and witty woman who was very relatable, although I knew her best as a humourist. I was sure she'd understand Tim's sense of humour but I didn't want her treating his backstory too lightly.

I needn't have worried. Like so many journalists who had interviewed Tim, Frances was keen to portray Tim in an accurate and sensitive way. She drank tea and ate scones with Tim, and they quickly built a rapport. Tim even invited her to see his bedroom, much to my surprise. He wanted to show off his most prized book, DVD and CD collection.

Even more surprising, Tim wanted to show Frances the contents of his 'writing books'. He carried A4 notebooks with him everywhere he went and could fill a book a day with lists of all the different subjects he was interested in or ideas for his art. When I could pinch a sneaky look at them, it was fascinating to me to see how active Tim's mind was. He didn't ever repeat an entry, and filled each page entirely. He made lists of music, movies, world leaders, world events, television series, historical events, famous people, Shakespearean quotes, geographical locations and internet sites. He did a lot of research!

Tim got a real kick out of the photo shoot for *The Courier-Mail*—he had the whole parade of stylists and wardrobe people, the art director and the photographer. He had several clothing changes but he was a complete natural, posing for the camera like a supermodel. It put a huge smile on my face to see him so confident. He did everything he was asked without complaint and he even managed to have fun with it.

The article came out just before the festival started, in the *QWeekend* magazine. It was four pages long and included some great colour photos of Tim and his art, and a picture of Tim and me. It was as good a piece of work as the *Australian Story* documentary, capturing the real Tim with dignity and celebration. The article actually made me cry in a few places because of Frances' obvious affection for Tim, her sympathy, and her ability to see his inner beauty.

Tim read it and said it was good. He didn't make too much of a fuss over it. He never did about much, really; he doesn't dwell. But I caught him once or twice going through my old scrapbooks, looking at the articles about the famous Tim Sharp.

•

Tim made a lot of new pictures for the QPAC show; he had twenty pieces of art on display. 'How To Make A Friend' was one of his drawings, which had Laser Beak Man bent over an ACME box with assorted body parts ready to assemble and a hammer and drill for the job. There was a big heart and a friendly smile, ready to make the perfect friend. In another picture, 'Don't Leave Me', Laser Beak Man was standing under some autumn trees that were shedding for the winter. 'The Block Party' was a bunch of toy blocks having a party and 'I Adore You' showed Laser Beak Man offering a door to a very unimpressed girl. My favourite was 'Row, Row, Row Your Boat' which had Laser Beak Man lounging on a boat on a lake while a blonde lady worked the oars; he's singing 'Life's a butter dream' and dreaming of a slab of butter. Tim had misheard the song lyrics 'Life is but a dream'.

Tim's drawings were a big hit—he sold virtually everything on the walls. A very nice woman bought a picture called 'Smartie Pants', which had Laser Beak Man throwing millions of Smarties into the air. In the foreground, there were three people holding the waistband of their trousers open to catch the Smarties. She told us she had been bullied at school because she was bright; the other kids called her smarty-pants. She said Tim's picture made her happy because it turned those words into something colourful and positive. A drawing called 'Eat It', which had Laser Beak Man at a table with the word 'It' in front of him on the plate, was bought by the Mater Hospital eating disorder clinic. I thought that was a bit grim, but I supposed everyone needs to laugh at themselves sometimes.

Creating art could be a lonely business and Tim didn't get a lot of feedback on a day-to-day basis. He loved spending his days at the exhibition. There were hundreds of kids and families pouring in through QPAC every day, coming in and out of shows, and lots of people had seen the article about Tim. Lots of people came in for a chat, including a ninety-year-old gran who climbed up the stairs and said, 'I must meet the next great artist before I die!' She was divine.

Somewhere in the promotional material they had said that Tim might draw for people if he was asked. Initially, we thought Tim could do one Laser Beak Man outline while everyone watched, but everyone who visited us wanted one. We had children and adults lining up thirty- and forty-people deep, all wanting their own Laser Beak Man drawing. Whole school classes would gather wanting one! As usual, Tim was very obliging, but it was exhausting for him. I had to keep a very close eye on him to make sure he could rest.

Our contacts at the festival were Tara and Adam, two vibrant and enthusiastic people who were not much older than Tim. They were so friendly, always leading him off to look at something or other on the site. Tim's exhibition was hung in the foyer outside the Playhouse Theatre, where a lot of the children's theatre productions were performed, and they often took Tim into the theatre to watch one of the shows. I stayed outside, chatting with people who came by to look at the art.

One morning, when Tim had disappeared into the theatre, I noticed a bit of commotion among the QPAC staff. Everyone was bustling about, trying to look busy, but there was a whiff of excitement in the air. There was someone very special in the building. All of a sudden, the bigwigs of the festival were walking through the foyer—Rosemary and the QPAC director, and a cluster of their staff—with a familiar blonde woman at their side. *Oh wow*, I thought to myself, *that's Cate Blanchett!* I tried really hard not to stare. I learned later that Cate was in town on official business. She was Artistic Director of the Sydney Theatre Company at the time and they had a show on at the festival. She had brought her three sons along to see it.

The first thing Cate did when she walked into the foyer was look at one of Tim's drawings; it was hanging right in front of her. She moved over to another picture then looked at a third, which made her laugh out loud. I was quietly tickled about that. *It's such a pity Tim isn't here!* I thought. He would have jumped out of his skin. He was a huge movie buff and he was really into the Lord of the Rings trilogy. Cate was one of his favourites.

One of the QPAC bosses came over to me and told me Cate wanted to meet Tim.

'He's in the theatre!' I said. 'I'll go and get him.'

'I'm afraid she doesn't have the time to wait,' came the reply.

'I'll be two minutes!' I insisted.

I was off like a shot. I swear I hadn't run that fast since I was ten years old. The room was filled with mothers and children and I zig-zagged between them all—I felt like I was skipping over the top of their heads like a sheepdog over sheep. I had to climb three flights of stairs to get to the theatre door and I took them three steps at a time. I banged on the door and asked the usher to grab Tim, then I ran him back downstairs at the speed of light. We ran towards Cate Blanchett and came to a screeching halt at her feet. I'd never seen Tim's eyes so wide.

'Hello, Cate Blanchett,' he said.

I left Tim talking to Cate, thinking how nice it was that she'd waited for him. Tim knew her whole filmography by heart and I'm sure he told her the year every one of her movies had been released. They took a walk around the exhibition together and I watched out of the corner of my eye, wondering what on earth Cate had to say to Tim. I was impressed with her body language; she dealt with him very respectfully. She looked directly at Tim when he spoke to her and she was patient with him; she didn't try to put words in his mouth. She had a very gentle manner. When they made their way back towards me, Cate asked if she could buy our Wiggles drawing, which was in every exhibition. It was one of the only pictures we'd kept and when it wasn't hanging in a gallery it was hanging over our kitchen table.

'I'm sorry,' I told Cate. 'That's not for sale. But Tim could make you another one.'

Tim wasn't precious about his art. If someone wanted him to create a new version of an existing picture, if they were friendly and they took the time to get to know him, he was usually pretty happy to do it. Each copy was a little bit different from the original. He made someone a version of 'A Double Shot of Happiness' that only had one 'p' in the title. I was very embarrassed and asked them to be patient while Tim made another one but the buyer was delighted. They thought the mistake made it even more special. Cate was happy to have her own version of The Wiggles and Tim was delighted to make it.

'You know,' I told Cate, as we were getting her details. 'Tim has always wanted to see Laser Beak Man in the flesh. I'm sure it would make an excellent play.' She agreed that it was an interesting idea.

•

I took a picture of Tim and Cate Blanchett that day and we put it on his Facebook page. 'Who's the skinny blonde with the superstar?' someone commented. It was all very funny. Tim even started referring to her as his 'BFF'. He worked hard on Cate's drawing and we sent it off to her office a few weeks later, thinking that was the end of our brush with fame.

We had an email from Cate shortly afterwards, thanking us for the work.

'The boys will be thrilled,' she wrote. She said she hadn't been able to stop thinking about Laser Beak Man and she wondered if we would come to Sydney to meet with her to discuss the idea of a Laser Beak Man play. *Would we ever!* I laughed to myself. Tim enthusiastically agreed.

It wasn't until August 2010 that we went to Sydney to see Cate. I'd worked myself into a bit of a state by then. It had always seemed inevitable that Laser Beak Man would come to life in a full-length story, either on film or on the stage. He was a larger-than-life character with a lot of colour and humour who got himself into so many strange situations, and had a unique story to tell and an entertaining way of looking at life. Everywhere we went, people would ask when it would happen; there was a lot of faith in the idea. I just never could have dreamt that it would come about by a chance meeting in such unplanned circumstances. I felt a lot of responsibility to make it happen, but I had no idea what proposal I was going to present or how to pitch a Laser Beak Man show. I felt totally out of my depth. It wasn't just that Cate Blanchett was this big Hollywood star, but also that the Sydney Theatre Company was as posh and prestigious as you could get. *Always biting off more than you can chew*, I told myself. I printed lots of Tim's artworks and burned a DVD of the ABC3 series, and decided to figure out the rest when we got there.

The Sydney Theatre Company is housed in one of the old wharf sheds in Dawes Point, just around the corner from the Sydney Harbour Bridge. It was quiet there in the middle of the day and there were very few people wandering past as we waited. It was odd to me that Cate Blanchett worked there, in such an unassuming place.

When we were brought into her office, the first thing I noticed was the Laser Beak Man cards pinned to the wall behind her desk. It was a modest office with a beautiful view over the harbour and a few comfortable sofas. She invited us to grab a seat beside her and a few other people from the company. Tim gave Cate a big hug but I think he was quite nervous. Barely a second after we sat down he said he had to go to the toilet and Cate popped to her feet. 'I'll take him,' she said. I thought that was quite lovely.

Before the meeting had even started, Tim began playing with a pair of black-rimmed glasses that were left on the table in front of him. He put them on and pulled some very serious faces—I think he was trying to look intelligent and studious. I was horrified and sent him telepathic mother messages, *Put those things down!* But Cate started laughing when she glanced up at Tim. 'Hey, those are mine!' she said. Everyone smiled and I breathed a sigh of relief. The tone of the meeting was set.

We weren't there to sell Laser Beak Man; they were already sold. It was clear that Cate was in charge and she was very keen to propel this idea of Laser Beak Man onto the stage; she had many ideas and was determined to get just the right people to work with us. If anything, Cate was trying to convince us that she understood the character. She saw him as a classic superhero in an urban setting, a bit like the characters in *The Incredibles*. She loved the fact that his humour appealed to both adults and kids, and that the art didn't talk down to anyone. I got a good sense of her care for Tim and her determination to ensure that he would be looked after, and that no one would lose sight of the character he had created. It was exciting and comforting to see her passion and enthusiasm for the project. I knew Tim would be in safe hands. The other people in the room were young, fast and terrifically smart, and just as enthusiastic. They spoke in a language that was new to me but was incredibly exciting.

The best thing about the meeting was that Cate directed all her questions to Tim. She didn't treat me like I was an interpreter; she let him speak for himself. And if he took a long time to answer or the question was a bit too complex, she waited patiently until he found the words he was looking for. She had good instincts. She was very respectful. Meanwhile, I said a lot of dumb things, I think. Cate asked me how much time we could commit, which was really considerate. 'I'd walk across the Simpson Desert if I had to!' I replied. I think I said that a few times, as a matter of fact. It was very embarrassing.

We left that meeting floating on air, this great adventure with Cate Blanchett and the STC stretching out ahead of us. I took Tim to a pub across the road for a hot chocolate (and a scotch to calm my nerves). The idea of Laser Beak Man live on stage was thrilling, but just as important was that feeling of connection, of finding another guardian angel, like Sheldon and others before him, who saw that Tim was precious and wonderful.

•

Between QPAC and Cate, and the *Courier-Mail* article, 2010 was turning out to be a very dramatic year. Little did I know what was to come. Shortly after our meeting in Sydney, I got the phone call every mother dreads. Sam was in hospital.

As much as Tim had loved swimming as a toddler, Sam had hated the water. He would cry and resist it, linking his arms around my neck with a vice-like grip as I held him in the pool. He was terrified that I would let him go. He grew to love it, of course, and he was a natural swimmer. He cut through the water like a dolphin. From those early swimming carnivals, he'd gone from strength to strength, competing at state level and then the national championships. At sixteen years of age he was the fastest in the state in the 200-metre backstroke. He was on his way to compete in the Olympics.

In 2010, by the time he was twenty, Sam was training for two hours every morning and then another two hours in the afternoon, six days a week, every week of the year. I never once had to wake him or insist that he go; he was always ready and willing, wanting to get down to the pool. When he finished high school, he took a job as a swim coach for a prestigious girls school.

Sam was focused on the 2012 Olympics qualifying trials in Adelaide. He never missed a training session, he was doing more gym work and working on his fitness, he was very strict about his diet. He didn't go out clubbing or to parties with his friends, preferring to do everything he could to improve his performance.

After six months of dedication to his program, Sam went to a swimming competition and achieved his best time ever in the 200-metre backstroke. That night, he went to a club in Fortitude Valley with his mates—a well-deserved night out. They'd only been in the club half an hour when Sam went to the bathroom. When he emerged, a bloke just ran at him. Sam found out later that his attacker's girlfriend had told him that Sam had asked her to dance. It wasn't true, but it didn't matter. The boyfriend flew into a jealous rage and launched himself at Sam, pushing him back three metres. Sam tried to brace his fall but he was pushed so hard that both of his wrists were broken.

The next day, when we made the police reports, the police told us there had been many similar incidents that had resulted in much more serious and permanent injuries. They said the chance of finding Sam's attacker was slim as there was no security footage of his face and the club owners hadn't bothered to get his name. That man walked away not realising how much he had affected someone else's life, although he probably wouldn't have cared.

Sam was devastated. Both arms were in plaster from thumb to elbow and he couldn't get back in the water.

There was so much Sam couldn't do. I had to cut his food up for him. He couldn't drive a car. He tried as hard as he could to do as much as he could, but most things were just impossible. But worse than the physical damage was the psychological damage.

One day when his arms were still in plaster he decided to walk down to the shop and get himself a treat. He wasn't far from home when a well-built young man who looked a little unkempt came walking towards him. Sam turned around and came home. He had felt threatened. Another time we were joking around and I gave Sam a little shove and uncharacteristically he became quite unsettled by it, telling me never to do it again.

Worst of all, with two arms in plaster, Sam was unable to train. It was such a blow. He needed to be working constantly if he was going to make the Olympic trials, but there was very little he could do. It was an exercise in patience. Instead of giving up, he took himself down to the pool every day and sat on the side, kicking his legs. He stayed near the water, though he couldn't get in, and he waited for his bones to heal.

He wore the casts for three long months. The day after they were removed, we flew to the United States for the screening of the *Laser Beak Man* television series at a film festival in Austin, Texas. As soon as we arrived, Sam made his way down to the Austin University swimming pool and asked if he could join their squad. A week later, we made our way up to New York and again Sam did the same thing. He went to the University of New York in Greenwich Village and trained with their team every single day.

Once we got back home, Sam immediately went back into full training and some months later qualified for the state championships, then the nationals, then the Olympic trials. Tim and I went to Adelaide to watch Sam compete in six races at the trials, and though he didn't qualify for the Olympics he was a champion in my eyes.

•

Sometimes life throws you curve balls; that's what we learned from Sam's experience. Ultimately, that's what happened with Cate Blanchett and the STC. We had to take it in our stride.

On 1 February 2011 the Laser Beak Man play got a green light. It was nineteen years to the day after I'd packed my two sons into the car and driven away from my miserable marriage. *We had nothing*, I thought to myself. *Look at us now!* But things didn't turn out the way that I'd hoped. Cate said there was a theatre company she'd wanted to work with for a long time and she thought they'd be a great partner for Laser Beak Man. They were based in another state and specialised in making theatre with people with disabilities. The artistic director had a very good reputation and a very strong vision for his company, but sadly his vision did not marry with Tim's.

Over the next year, Tim and I travelled interstate regularly to work on the Laser Beak Man play. It was a very interesting process, seeing people workshop ideas and try different things to bring Tim's characters to life, but ultimately it was a disappointment. The final script was very dark. It had nothing to do with the spirit of Laser Beak Man and Tim found it very upsetting. I hadn't seen him so distressed since he was a little boy, struggling to communicate, and it really broke my heart.

We parted ways with both the STC and the disability theatre company and their play became something else altogether. It was such a pity, but it was a good lesson. A lot of opportunities may come your way, but they're not always the right ones. You have to stay true to yourself, in the end. Tim had to stay true to his own creative vision.

18

The Ghost Ballerinas

We heard from a lot of people around the world. Some of them found Tim's art on the internet and then tracked him down through our website. Some people heard about him through the media and some found him on Facebook. I was amazed at how small the world had become. It was quite humbling to think of how far the news of Tim had spread.

A lot of people shared their own experiences with autism and they wanted to let Tim know how much he had inspired them. Their contact was always welcome. Tim loved to know that people in other countries liked his work and I was always touched by their kind, supportive words. They always said such lovely things.

There were constant requests for Tim to appear at events, or for a donation of artwork to support a good cause. Occasionally, the request was truly unusual, like when a couple in Kalgoorlie, Western Australia, asked Tim to illustrate their wedding invitations.

One of the most exciting requests we received arrived in September 2011, from a gentleman in Nashville, Tennessee:

Tim,

I manage a band called The Ghost Ballerinas here in Nashville, TN. I just came across your beautiful artwork and had an idea to get you to do the cover for our next album, coming out soon.

We intend to call the album either 'Play Me On The Radio' or 'OD on Happiness', which are both names of songs on the album. Would you be interested in working with us? Your artwork for 'Double Shot of Happiness' would have been perfect or maybe something that other people haven't seen yet? Please listen to our music. You can get a free download of our first CD.

Our new CD will be out soon and we need to get the album artwork done as soon as possible, so let me know.

Thank You,
Jonathan Britt
The Ghost Ballerinas

I replied to let Jonathan know how much Tim loved music and how much he would love to work with them. Tim watched the Ghost Ballerinas' videos on YouTube and he really loved their sound. He was very proud of his CD collection and the idea that his art would grace an album cover was a very big thrill.

We exchanged several emails with Jonathan, who was the band's manager, and he told us about their lead singer, a guy called Cameron Burnette. Cameron had been dating Jonathan's daughter for several years. He was born with only one ear and he had spent his school days wondering why everyone else was so smart, and wishing he was as smart as them. It was a very touching story.

Once Tim had agreed to do the artwork, Jonathan sent through another request:

> What is the chance Tim could come to America and see the
> band perform sometime? I know this is very preliminary, but he
> has such a great story and I am thinking outside the box. For
> us, things are about building relationships. We like 'connections'
> and reasons why we do what we do.

Likewise for us, all the best things we had ever done had been about relationships and connections. I already felt that Jonathan and The Ghost Ballerinas were on our wavelength and this only confirmed it. Certainly we'd try to get to Tennessee, if the right opportunity came up.

Jonathan wanted to provide Tim with as much information as he could before Tim started on the album art. He emailed information about all four band members, their attitude and their hopes for the album. A few days later Jonathan and Cameron gave us a call. Hearing their magnificent Southern accents come down the line was just amazing—I had never spoken to someone from their part of the world. Tim didn't usually talk much on the phone, but he chatted away to Cameron like they were old friends. It was such a thrill to listen in and know he was connecting with someone who was 15,000 kilometres away.

I asked Jonathan how they'd found us and he told me they had searched the internet for 'happy, colorful art'. Tim Sharp's name had popped up. When I spoke to Cameron, he was incredibly excited. He said talking to Tim was like talking to a real superstar. He'd met some stars in the music industry and he said Tim was right up there for him. We felt the same way! There was such a positive buzz around the project. We knew we were onto something special. The first phone conversation with Jonathan and Tim lasted nearly two hours.

The Ghost Ballerinas offered to pay Tim for his artwork, but we couldn't accept their money. There was something really magical happening between us—it was much more than just a financial transaction. There was an artistic respect between the band and Tim, and they were very considerate of his feelings. We wanted to support them as much as they wanted to support us.

Soon after we spoke, Jonathan shot a video of the band members introducing themselves to Tim. They thought it would help to have a visual introduction, which was incredibly considerate. To our surprise and delight, the video included a special gift. The band had been working on a new song. They played us the very beginning of a tune about Tim and Laser Beak Man. It wasn't finished yet but it sure sounded great!

Jonathan and I exchanged emails every day and there were more and more telephone conversations between us all. The relationship grew stronger and we became closer the more we learned about each other.

When I'd heard the name 'The Ghost Ballerinas' I thought it sounded quite whimsical and enchanting. I loved the story behind the name even more. Many of the old Southern mansions were used for ballet lessons during the Civil War era; the doors and windows would be flung open in the heat and people walking by could see the ballerinas dancing. As the war raged on, many of the mansions were ransacked and burned and many civilians died, including many of the young girls. When it was over, people told stories about passing the shells of those big old houses and seeing the ghost ballerinas dancing, hearing music floating through those grand homes. It was said that the ghosts of the girls would dance forever as they waited for their loves to return from the war. I could see the story so clearly in mind.

We told our friends and collaborators back home about The Ghost Ballerinas and they were amazed at how the boys had reached out to Tim; how artists were collaborating across the seas and how the friendship was growing.

When he finished the artwork, Tim was actually a little worried about whether the band would like it. He never worried about that sort of thing! He sent the next email himself, with the artwork attached.

hello jonathan and cameron and the boys from the band

thank you for sending me your music. i love it. you rock. you are really good friends. this is the artwork i have done for you. hope you like it. i'd like to go to nashville one day and see you there and listen to you play. you make me happy because we are good friends.

thanks
from tim

Tim needn't have worried about the response to his artwork. It was clear how Jonathan and Cameron felt when the next email came through.

Tim,

BRILLIANT!! Cam is so excited about your painting!!!!!!!!!!

Perfect! He will send you a message today.

We were working late yesterday. The band will see it today when we get together for band practice tonight. I know they will love it!! That is SOoooooooo awesome!! It couldn't be any better.

You did Soooooooooo Gooooood, Timmmmmmmmmm!!!

In Cam's words, "THAT IS SO BAD ASS!!" :) :) :)

LOVE
The Ghost Ballerinas

We assumed that after Tim delivered the album artwork our relationship with The Ghost Ballerinas would slow down considerably, but no one really wanted to let the friendship go. The Laser Beak Man tune that we had heard was a playful thing that had sprung out of a jam session but the band had continued to work on it and a great song had taken shape. It was going to be included on the album. The boys emailed us a copy of the song and Tim listened with a huge grin on his face. The lyrics incorporated the titles of nine of Tim's artworks.

I met a superhero who can really fly
Drives 'em all crazy, he will blow your mind
Picking up chicks, he's on the run
He's a double shot of happiness, the lucky one

I wanna be like Laser Beak Man
I wanna do all the things that he can
'Cause we could use another, we could use another
Superhero tonight

Come on everybody, let me break it down
He's sailed the seven seas, he's coming to your town
He's a man with a plan, he's got a friend named Tim
And all the single ladies wanna be with him

He wants to be like Laser Beak Man
He wants to do all the things that he can
'Cause he could use another, he could use another
Superhero tonight

You know, babe, he's got you on his mind
And what counts is on the inside
He'll take you by the hand, fly you in the sky
You're his Red Hot Mamma, he's your real shy guy

We want to be like Laser Beak Man
We want to do all the things that he can
'Cause we could use another, we could use another
Superhero tonight

Jonathan and I continued to exchange emails and he told me so much more about himself and the band, and their plans to reach out to the world and make good friends and strong connections. He really believed in The Ghost Ballerinas and he wanted to help them, but he also believed the band could help others. I liked the way he thought. He sounded like a good man to me.

Jonathan and his family had some experience with autism. His daughter Sophia had worked with children with autism and they had friends whose children also had the condition, so it felt like they understood us. When Jonathan found Tim's art, he was pleased to learn that Tim had autism. He felt it had a meaning for him and I felt it had a meaning for us. Something about our shared experience in this area kept the two of us talking.

It was all of the connections and serendipity in our lives that led Jonathan and the boys to decide that they wanted to do something to support people with autism. Jonathan called me one day full of excitement; they had decided to do a benefit concert. Not just a concert, as matter of fact, but a whole music festival—a music festival inspired by Tim!

Jonathan was a man of action so when the band decided they wanted to do it, the festival immediately began taking shape. He worked tirelessly on the project and it was clear it would be a very professional event with a lot of great talent on the bill. He sent us demos of the bands that were going to play, bands and musicians who were coming from all over America. He organised car washes and other fundraising activities to get some cash and get the project started, and he took care of all the media and marketing. He wanted the festival to have a real rock'n'roll attitude. It was to be called the 'I Am What I Am' music festival. It was named after one of Cameron's songs.

It was all very exciting and sounded wonderful and it was tempting to make the trip over for the event but I hesitated. It would cost thousands of dollars for Tim and I to travel to the United States. I had never had any luck getting funding from the government sector—it was so time consuming that I had given up trying. With such short notice, it was unlikely there would be any funding available for this trip. I didn't want to borrow any more money and I probably couldn't anyway. I also didn't want to keep dipping into Tim's money for travel. I knew it was good for his career but he might need it for something else in the future. Arts Queensland had made a short film about Tim that screened at the Metropolitan Museum of Art in New York City in April 2012, but we didn't go over to see it. There were so many amazing opportunities coming up, but if we did everything there would be no money left.

One day, I had to reorganise some of Tim's art and there were a lot of pieces that were slightly older or torn, which had been a bit damaged in transit. It was unlikely that we would exhibit them again. Before that moment, I hadn't really decided what to do with them, but I had no intention of getting rid of them. I started to count them and there were more pieces than I'd expected, and I realised the value of the work was quite high, despite the damage. It was still great art and they were still Tim Sharp originals, no matter what shape they were in. A light bulb must have switched on over my head all of a sudden; I realised the solution to our problem was right before my eyes. We'd have a one-day-only factory outlet sale to take Tim Sharp to Tennessee! I put a post on Facebook and there was a tidal wave of support.

The day of the sale we opened our home and invited the Tim Sharp fans inside. So many people came through the door including a couple named David and Bec Marriner, and their beautiful little daughter, Drew. Drew had autism and they were struggling through, but Tim gave them faith. We had the most amazing chat with this couple then, out of the blue, David said he would pay for our airfares. Dave and Bec could see the benefit of the trip, not just for Tim but for so many other families searching for hope and inspiration. They were happy and very willing to support us because this was the kind of future they wanted for their daughter, a future that so many other people hoped would be available for their children.

Of course I burst into tears. What else could I do? Their generosity was overwhelming. Tim just smiled and said, 'Thank you', safe in the knowledge that he was headed to Tennessee.

•

Flight delays and missed connections meant that our trip to Nashville took nearly thirty hours, which was so much more than I could ask from Tim. He handled it like a trouper, however. We arrived five hours later than we were supposed to, late at night, so I assumed we'd take a taxi to a hotel somewhere and call our friends in the morning. We were both very frazzled.

Slowly, we made our way down to the baggage-claim area. As we went down the escalator, Tim and I spotted something at exactly the same time—a Laser Beak Man T-shirt! Tim took off running—not something he often did—into the open arms of his friends, The Ghost Ballerinas. Cameron, Justin, AJ and Josh were waiting for us, and of course my good friend Jonathan. There was a whole bunch of other people as well; their friends and family, who had all come out to meet us. They had waited hours for us and were holding up a sign: *Welcome to Tennessee, Tim and Judy and Laser Beak Man.* We were thrilled to see them; it was an incredible welcome. The sight of them brought tears to my eyes.

I was amazed that our Southern friends weren't much taller than Tim; in my mind they were seven feet tall. I fell in love with their accents and couldn't believe we had arrived in that part of the world, but for Tim it was like coming home. He walked off with the boys as though he had always hung out with them. They took him in like one of the gang.

•

The next morning we woke up in Murfreesboro, about thirty minutes outside of Nashville, near Jonathan's home and close to where the festival was being held. I pulled back the curtains and saw magnolias outside the window and a clear blue sky overhead. Just across from our hotel was a sight that I knew would thrill Tim—an IHOP (International House of Pancakes) restaurant. He started the day with a big helping of chocolate-chip pancakes with chocolate syrup while I enjoyed a root beer. We truly were in heaven.

Back at the hotel, we found our room had been filled with gifts including a handmade quilt from Justin's mum, Tennessee T-shirts and caps, and gifts from local autism awareness groups. There was a big basket filled with local goodies and the best present ever—a copy of The Ghost Ballerinas' CD with Tim's artwork on the cover.

Our hosts were incredibly generous. Justin and his mum, Kendra, took the day off and took us out to see the countryside, to Jack Daniels country, and to a town called Lynchburg. The town was as pretty as a picture, and had old men sitting on benches on the front porches of cafes, talking to the local policeman. There were pretty little gardens around old buildings and an old historical jail that Johnny Cash had once visited. Charlie Daniels, the famous fiddle player, lived down the road and the town was surrounded by rolling hills and lush green vegetation. We saw the U.S. flag on display outside almost every house.

They showed us where the festival would be held in the township of Shelbyville, at the local showgrounds. Like Lynchburg, Shelbyville was full of character and had a huge equestrian centre where the National Tennessee Walking Horse Championships were held every year. There was a big open shed at the showgrounds with owls hanging over the entrances.

While we were inspecting the site, a tough-looking older lady drove up to us on a ride-on mower. Her name was Miss Helen and she'd been busy all morning making sure everything was in tip-top order for the festival; she was excited about helping all the kids with autism in her area. She was a very impressive and imposing woman. When somebody walked by and said a minor cuss word, Miss Helen quickly told them off. 'Jesus don't want my ears to be hearing words like that! Don't you be saying such things around me.'

I hadn't heard anyone talk like that before. Her accent and the way she expressed herself were music to my ears. We were truly in the South.

•

By the time the day of the festival arrived, we were deeply in love with the South. We loved the architecture, the landscape and the great Southern cooking, but the best thing of all was the people. I'd never met such hospitable, warm and gentle folk in my life.

When we arrived at the showgrounds that Saturday morning it was a hive of activity. Within an hour a rally of about 100 motorcyclists had turned up to show their support. They had all paid a fee to enter and were going to ride out of the showgrounds and then out through the hills, to raise money and awareness for autism. They'd be back in time to watch the bands. We cheered them off as they left in a cloud of denim, leather and tattoos, these big men with mean, solemn faces. They obviously had big hearts.

Meanwhile, the crowd had started to gather. There were three stages where over fifty bands and performers would play during the day and night. Local vendors had set up food stands while character actors walked through the crowds, dressed in superhero costumes. One of the stages was called the 'Laser Beak Man Stage' and a local artist had created a huge hand-painted banner of Tim and Laser Beak Man to hang on its back wall. It was so beautiful and so much effort had gone into it. Yet again I felt a lump rise in my throat.

Before the music started, a prayer was said and the American national anthem was played, and the audience took off their hats and held them over their hearts. Then Tim was brought on stage and given a huge welcome. He waved and the crowd cheered him on.

Tim made some wonderful friends that day. A crowd of kids scooped him up and took him to see one band after the next—the day started with some really loud rock music and Tim was absolutely delighted. I went to help in the kitchen where a group of volunteers was preparing food for the bikers and the many other helpers. Tennessee was called the Volunteer state for historical reasons, but the culture was alive and well.

Tim met a lot of band members during the day and some of them invited him onstage to play. He had a go at the drums and guitar, and though he definitely couldn't play either, he was having a ball. The bands carried him and it didn't sound too bad at all. It was one of Tim's greatest dreams to have his own band. He even had a name for his band and wrote song lyrics in his A4 notebooks. So this was yet another dream come true, playing with his new friends on a stage. I took about a hundred photos of Tim Sharp, the rockstar, because I didn't think anyone would believe it.

Finally, the moment we had been waiting for came. It was time to hear The Ghost Ballerinas play. The boys had organised dancers to perform on stage when they played the Laser Beak Man song and Tim sat right beside them on stage, grinning like crazy. A young man with autism played drums for that one song and he was brilliant; he was really getting into it. The Ghost Ballerinas rocked.

The headline act at 'I Am What I Am' was a 'hick hop' artist called Big Smo. He rolled up in a long white Cadillac with a number plate that read, *Prayer changes everything*. I wasn't familiar with hick hop and I didn't like rap, but Big Smo won me over. The crowd just loved his Southern references and local pride, and my foot started tapping all by itself. Big Smo was hugely popular. He called Tim up onto the stage during the set and Tim was recognised as the inspiration for the festival. I watched him and listened to the cheers, my heart bursting with pride.

The last performance of the day was late in the night, when The Ghost Ballerinas returned to the stage to close out the festival. They had so much energy and enthusiasm, and they put on a great show. Tim kicked off his shoes and started dancing in the sawdust as the boys tore up the stage. I watched with pride and happiness and joy, so glad we had made the trip.

•

The festival was a huge success. Jonathan and the band raised $30,000 that day and the whole thing ran as smooth as butter. It was an alcohol-free event but that didn't seem to stop anyone from enjoying themselves. It ran all day and all night without a hitch.

What impressed me most were all the teenagers and young adults with autism who came to the festival, who were hanging out with young people their own age. They did exactly what young people like to do—listen to bands and go to concerts. Many of those kids had never had the opportunity before. It was such a safe and supportive environment that no one bothered them or looked twice at them, no matter how challenging their behaviours were. And I know it was a relief for their families to be out, doing what everyone else got to do, without judgement or comment. There was true acceptance and inclusion at that festival.

The next day we went to Jonathan's house, a beautiful brick home with a sprawling garden. We read the reviews of the festival in the paper while Jonathan fielded phone calls of thanks and congratulations, and we reflected on all the wonderful things that had happened. Tim and I would be heading home soon and neither of us was really ready to go. We wanted to bask in all that Southern goodness just a little bit longer.

On our last night in Nashville, Jonathan and The Ghost Ballerinas took us to the recording studio downtown where the band had made their album. We got to meet the engineers and producers, and Tim went into a recording booth. He even sang a tune with Cameron. Afterwards, we went out to dinner with the band and their family—Jonathan's beautiful wife, Marianna, Cameron's girlfriend, Kimberley, and many of his other friends. Again, they showered us with gifts. I had to buy another suitcase just to bring everything home.

I felt quite sad leaving Jonathan and Marianna and our Tennessee family. There wasn't a day that we didn't talk about them after we got home. Of all the things Tim has done and the places he's visited, he always says Nashville was his favourite.

•

Once school had finished, there were so few opportunities for young adults with autism. They were forgotten by the system, left to live in isolation with little or no social contact with people their own age, not involved in the activities of their peers. The music festival and the friendship that Tim had formed with The Ghost Ballerinas broke him free of that life sentence. Together, they had proved that connections could be made. There was something else, if only people made the effort.

I wanted to hold music festivals like the one in Tennessee all over the world, every year. I wanted to form the Double Shot of Happiness Foundation after that trip, to encourage other young adults to ask a young adult with autism out for one social event a year. They could buddy up and make a real difference in the life of another person with autism. Imagine going from isolation to having perhaps six social events a year, and having the chance to do something that was totally normal for your peers. I wanted every young adult with autism to have this opportunity.

I had seen with my own eyes how art could break down barriers and bring people joy. I never ceased to be amazed by its power. It united an artist and a band across eight thousand miles. I wanted to see it bring the whole wide world together.

19

The Conversation Hour

Tim turned twenty-five years old in 2013. It had been ten years since our Laser Beak Man journey began. If anyone had told me in the beginning what wonderful things were in store for us, what extraordinary opportunities and marvellous people lay ahead, I never would have believed them.

The year began with Tim's inclusion in *The Sunday Mail*'s 'Happy List', which recognised those who brought joy to others, acknowledging fifty Queenslanders who helped to 'make the world that little bit better through their kindness, compassion, good will, effort, altruism or sheer warmth of personality'. I couldn't think of a better person than Tim for that honour.

Tim had become a bit of a celebrity in Brisbane over the years. As well as his exhibitions and all the media coverage, his artwork had been selected to light up the William Jolly Bridge in

2012 for Autism Awareness Month. It was such a hit they invited him back in April 2013. The William Jolly Bridge is a famous landmark, a 500-metre span that crosses the Brisbane River and joins the suburb of West End with the city. Tim's artwork was splashed across it with these magnificent light projections that covered the entire bridge. It looked magnificent on that scale. We invited families and friends of people with autism to join hands across the bridge, to show their support and connection. Over five hundred people participated—one for every metre of the bridge.

We were given some wonderful photographs from professional photographers who captured Tim's art on the bridge. It was amazing to see so many of them come along, set up with their tripods and cameras with big lenses, helping to spread the message of autism awareness. A friend suggested we aim bigger next time and mocked up a picture of Tim's art on the Sydney Opera House. It looked extraordinary. *Definitely worth pursuing*, I thought to myself.

I found that I was asked more and more often to attend public events and speak. I had been on such a long journey with Tim, with so much heartache and so much joy, that there were many things I felt I could share with the world. But it was always humbling to be asked to speak and I was always a bundle of nerves.

In 2013, Dr Morton and his wife, Louise, asked me to appear at the annual lunch for the Lynn Wright Memorial Foundation, which was established in honour of Louise's mother.

Lynn had been one of the greatest supporters of Andy Morton in his struggle with autism. She had had so much faith and commitment to her grandson and was prepared to do anything to help him. I was sad that I'd never had the opportunity to meet her.

The foundation raised funds to provide scholarships for struggling families facing financial hardship. Although the costs were subsidised by the government, there were still out-of-pocket fees of nearly $20,000 a year for each child. As someone who was financially vulnerable when my child was diagnosed with autism, I felt the work of the foundation was very dear to my heart. It would have been devastating to think that money was the obstacle to getting help for my child.

The renowned author Kathy Lette was also invited to speak at 'Lynn's Lunch' and we were seated next to each other for the day. Like me, Kathy had a young adult affected by autism to care for so we quickly found common ground. It was a revelation and a comfort for me to share the daily struggles I faced with someone who understood exactly what I was talking about, despite how different our lives were in so many other ways. Although Kathy's and my situation were worlds apart, we had the same fears and worries, both battling against a world that seemed to forget young adults with autism.

It was a heartfelt conversation between two mothers but there was no resolution, no answers. All we could do was offer each other support. Both Kathy and I were committed to changing the situation but we didn't really know how. We were both getting older; we could feel ourselves getting tired and our heads getting heavier with the worry of how to make the best lives for our sons. We realised that both our sons had more opportunity than many others but without the work we did to give them those opportunities there would be very little for them, just like so many other people with autism who remained silently apart from society and isolated in private homes.

Kathy spoke first and of course brought the house down with her witty, quick-fire observations that appeal particularly to women. She was hilarious and had everyone in fits of laughter. Her story about her son was in contrast very touching, honest and moving. When it was my turn to speak, I decided to tell more of our story than I had ever told before. Although I did not go into a great deal of detail, I spoke about my marriage. I explained that we had struggled through the years to survive but I also shared the great joys of our life, all the heartache and triumph of Tim's journey.

Kristine was there filming a follow-up to the original episode for the ABC's *Australian Story* and she told me women in the audience had wept as they listened to me speak. She had tried to make her way to the stage with the camera when I had finished but they had struggled to get through the crowd. The entire audience had risen to its feet to give me a standing ovation.

•

In April 2013, I heard from a producer at the Richard Fidler Conversation Hour on ABC Radio National. As the name suggests, every day for one hour Richard Fidler had a conversation with someone of interest on his program. Featuring everything from international stars to local heroes, it was always a fascinating hour of radio.

When Michelle, the producer, explained where she was calling from I asked her if Tim would have to wear headphones for the interview. It was off-putting to sit opposite someone while their voice came to you through headphones and Tim didn't like it at all. I wondered if there was another way we could do it to make it easier for him.

'But we don't want to interview Tim,' Michelle said. 'We want to talk to you. We want to hear your story.'

I was genuinely shocked. We had done hundreds of interviews all around Australia and they were all about Tim. Of course I spoke for him when he couldn't speak and I filled in a lot of the gaps about his life, but ultimately it was Tim's story, not my own. I was just the storyteller.

'Nobody wants to know about me!' I laughed. It was true— other than asking me my age and the name of my other son, and noting that I was a single mother, no one had ever asked about me. Only Kristine from *Australian Story* had shown any interest, but she was a uniquely insightful woman. I assumed that once we had started the preliminary interview, Michelle would lose interest. I assumed she'd redirect the conversation towards Tim. Our first half-hour chat sprawled into a two-hour conversation and she convinced me that I had a good story to tell. I was not worthless and my life wasn't boring. My story could help others.

As I spoke to Michelle about my marriage, fear began to rise in me and I became very nervous. It had been twenty-one years since I had left my husband but I was still scared of him.

'I can't talk about this on radio in case the boys' father hears it,' I said.

I had knots in my stomach and I felt sick. I was also bitterly disappointed with myself that after all that time he still had the ability to control my life. I feared the repercussions if I spoke publicly about what he had done to me. He was still holding me back.

•

Michelle and I had several interviews over many hours. We discussed what I did and didn't feel comfortable revealing on-air and she never pressured me into talking about things I wanted to keep private. But the further along I went, the more I felt sure that I should talk about my marriage. It was a crucial part of my story, which impacted on everything that came afterwards. I spoke to Sam, who by this stage had formed his own opinions about his father, and with his blessing I decided that I would be brave and I would be honest. I did not want to go on national radio and denigrate the boys' father, but it was important to me to stand up and say, *This happened, this mattered.*

I sat in the studio across from Richard Fidler, who was a gentleman and wonderful conversationalist, and he asked me about my ex-husband. I felt the muscles in my stomach tighten and heard a voice in the back of my head warning me to be careful. I wondered what would happen if the boys' father was listening; if just a few short words about our life together would make him want to take revenge. I was scared, but this was my life and my story. It was time to step up and claim it as my own.

The hour went by so fast. Speaking to Richard was like speaking to a friend and we got so deeply into things. Ten minutes before the hour was due to end, I took a quick glance at the clock and realised I had only got through the first five years of Tim's life. All the best was yet to come! I whizzed through all the highlights in the time remaining and hoped the audience would understand how blessed I really felt.

As soon as the interview had finished, my phone started ringing. I got calls and text messages from friends all over the country saying 'good job' and 'congratulations' and sending me their love. When we got home that day, there was a flood of emails waiting, hundreds, the 'Likes' on Tim's Facebook page had gone through the roof. The Laser Beak Man website was inundated with people wanting to buy art, T-shirts and cards, and it all got too much: the website crashed.

Many types of people were affected by my story. The people who got in touch with me afterwards were either connected with autism, or had serious marriage issues, or were single parents. Some connected with the story of Sam's birth and there were many others who said they were just inspired by Tim's success.

So many people said so many wonderful things about us as a family.

The interview was so popular that Richard Fidler's team included it on the podcasts they make available to Qantas as part of their in-flight entertainment program. Richard also included it in the USB of his favourite programs of the year, which was sold in ABC shops around Australia for Christmas. I was so overwhelmed and encouraged by the support. It was wonderful for my self-esteem. It gave me the strength to look in the mirror and feel finally that I was doing okay.

20

A Double Shot of Happiness

Tim created art whenever he could. His public commitments made it difficult to find enough time, but whenever we were home he made new work. There was so much demand and such a long list of people waiting for commissioned artworks, it was difficult to build up enough drawings for a whole exhibition. In fact, by 2013, it had been three years since Tim's last big solo show. We were well overdue.

The Brisbane Powerhouse invited us back for a third time and Tim was delighted to return to his headquarters. As the exhibition drew closer, it was all we could talk about. There was a new Artistic Director at the Powerhouse, Troy Armstrong, whose mind spun like a fast-bowler, churning out new ideas every minute.

Tim exhibited thirty-two pieces of art at the Powerhouse and sold twenty-eight off the walls. His T-shirts and cards were so popular that they sold out, and the compliments flowed in daily. As with every exhibition we had done before, I could see Tim gaining confidence with every conversation and I could see how that confidence was expressed in his artwork. The ideas were clearer, the colours were bolder and the composition was stronger with each passing show. It was amazing to see how he had continued to develop.

Tim welcomed each and every person who came into the gallery.

'Hello, I'm Tim, what's your name?' he said, holding out his hand.

He signed autographs and posed for photographs in front of his artwork, always gracious and incredibly polite. Long conversations and complicated questions were hard for him, but he never complained. He took everything in his stride and did everything that was asked of him. He revelled in the many moments of joy and pleasure he got from meeting new people and making new friends. Of particular joy for Tim was when people his own age came to see his art and took the time to get to know him, like Kitty and her brother Edward, who took Tim for hot chocolate.

An elderly lady came to the exhibition one day, moving with the assistance of a walking frame. She came towards Tim and I saying, 'Love, love, love, love!' with a great deal of excitement. I thought she meant that she loved the art and I was very happy about that. But as her carer explained, it was a little more complicated.

The woman was born with an intellectual disability. At fifteen, her parents had given her up to the church to be cared for, as they could no longer cope. She was put to work in the laundry of a hospital run by nuns, and the life she lived was brutal and lonely. It wasn't until she was sixty-five that she moved into a home of her own, with carers who took her out socially and helped her to find some joy in her life.

The carer told me that the woman had never learned to read and that the only word she could recognise was 'love'. Tim had an artwork on exhibit that was inspired by the Beatles song 'All You Need is Love' in which Laser Beak Man is walking up a slight incline, pulling a red wagon that carried the word 'love'. It was a simple artwork but its message was powerful. The elderly woman was obviously deeply affected by it and her response deeply affected me. She stood before me with a huge smile on her face, saying 'love' over and over again. She was so happy with Tim's art. It was a beautiful thing to see.

On another afternoon, a young boy came to the exhibition with a woman by his side. I had developed quite a strong radar for autism and I knew before she told me that the little boy had the condition. I watched him as he went to each and every piece of art and stood in front of it, moving closer and closer until his nose almost touched the glass. He stood as his eyes moved over every inch of every artwork. While he did this, his carer watched, then walked over to me with tears in her eyes. 'I have taken him everywhere, to everything I can think of,' she explained. 'He never shows any interest in anything, he just always runs away. This is the first time I've seen him happy and enjoying something.'

She was so excited that she called the boy's parents and told them to come to the gallery to see their son. It was a major breakthrough and a revelation about the power of art. The little boy was usually so violent he wasn't allowed at any school and his parents required full-time support to be able to keep him at home. Yet here he was, happy and peaceful, enjoying Tim's art. We took a photo of Tim with his arm around the little boy and the boy's head resting on Tim's shoulder. I was so moved I had to cry. I cried a lot at those exhibitions.

●

The Powerhouse show brought in new fans, from New York, Amsterdam and Edinburgh. Some of the people we met worked in the arts and wanted to exhibit Tim's work around Australia and overseas. Troy introduced us to a woman named Jenny Simpson who went on to organise an exhibition of Tim's work at the State Library of Western Australia. We were also contacted by representatives from the ABC's 'Mental As' initiative, who wanted Tim to become an art ambassador for Mental Health Week. Tim would join a prestigious list of artists for the event, including Ben Quilty, Reg Mombassa, Del Kathryn Barton and Euan MacLeod.

There were many generous-spirited and talented artists who were keen to speak with Tim when they visited the

Powerhouse, and at least one conversation grew into a thrilling new collaboration.

Nicholas Paine and David Morton from Dead Puppet Society came to see Tim's show and told us they wanted to work with him. We had seen Dead Puppet Society's most recent production, *Argus*, and were most impressed. It wasn't like the puppet shows I had grown up with, which were usually very childish. It was funny, clever and heartwarming; their work was very innovative. We spent a lot of time talking with Nicholas and David and I was delighted when they said they were interested in developing a theatrical puppet production of Laser Beak Man. Tim's superhero was destined for the stage after all.

Not long after the exhibition ended, Nicholas and David travelled overseas with their production company and ended up having a residency in New York City. While they were away, they prepared a script for Laser Beak Man that they hoped to develop and produce. Tim smiled a lot when he read the first draft. I laughed out loud and at times I cried. It felt to me like they had got inside Tim's head and captured the soul of both Tim and Laser Beak Man. I was thrilled that they understood my son so well.

These two young men who had come into our lives were very sensitive and expressed a strong desire to work inclusively with Tim. Though they were overseas, they were keen to know Tim's reaction to everything they did. We communicated via the internet, answering questions and helping them with materials, giving feedback and talking through their ideas. They were an absolute joy. Nicholas and David's youthful enthusiasm was exhilarating and it was balanced by their maturity and thoughtfulness towards Tim.

In late 2013, the boys applied to develop *Laser Beak Man* as part of an artist-in-residency program at the New Victory Theater on Broadway, in New York City. In May 2014, they called to let us know that they had been accepted. I saw the tears in Nicholas's eyes when he told us the news via Skype. Tim smiled that beautiful smile of his and I thought my heart would burst with pride and elation. Nicholas was twenty-five, Tim was twenty-six and David was twenty-seven. These very gorgeous and talented young men were bringing Laser Beak Man to Broadway. As soon as we got the news, Tim and I booked our flights to New York to be there for the final production work and its first appearance on stage in June 2015. There was more exciting news when we learned that the Jim Henson Foundation had awarded a grant for the development of *Laser Beak Man*. Shortly afterwards, we heard that the Sydney Opera House, QPAC and the Arts Centre in Melbourne would be hosting Dead Puppet Society's *Laser Beak Man* in 2016.

•

I was surprised by every achievement and every opportunity that came our way. With every great thing that happened to us I thought, *That's it, it doesn't get any better.* To my delight and profound gratitude, I always seemed to be wrong.

It was November 2013 when I received an email from Edwina Throsby, the Editorial Director of TEDxSydney, saying she had some ideas she wanted to discuss with us. She said she had heard me on the Conversation Hour and she had been very impressed. I was familiar with TED because I'd seen many TED Talks on the internet. Even Tim was a fan—he followed the TED channel on YouTube. 'TED' stands for technology, entertainment and design; it is a non-profit organisation based in the United States that is dedicated to spreading great ideas through engaging, illuminating talks. I associated TED with intelligence, integrity and innovation; it is a globally renowned brand that is making the world a better place.

Edwina mentioned that the next TEDxSydney event would be held at the Sydney Opera House in April 2014. My heart was racing at the thought that we might be asked to speak.

I called Edwina and she was interested in our story, but she explained that speaking at a TED conference was a lot more complicated than simply being asked. Our nomination had to go before a board and we would have to wait a few weeks to find out if everyone agreed. She simply wanted to know if we were interested. 'We are!' I gushed. 'We absolutely are!'

The weeks that followed were ridiculously long. Christmas was getting closer and I didn't think it was possible to have to wait for the board's answer through the holiday season, when all the offices would be shut down and everyone would be on holiday. And I really had no idea how it would go. I had seen many of those talks and they were very professional, with a lot of really powerful stories being told. We were just a mum and son from Brisbane, battling through. I wasn't sure if we were TEDx material.

Edwina telephoned a few days before Christmas to tell us that the committee had unanimously agreed that Tim and I would be part of the program. We were so excited we nearly danced around the room—it was the best Christmas present ever! Shortly after the celebrations, the hard work began.

I had to write the presentation myself, which would be reviewed by a TEDx curator, Madeleine Hawcroft. I knew exactly what I wanted to say and how I wanted to do it. I very much wanted Tim to have the opportunity to speak. I wanted to show his art and his unique intelligence, to tell his story so that people would understand the significance of his achievements. I also hoped that I could adequately show the depth of my love and admiration for him.

I asked Tim what he wanted to say and his words came very quickly. He wasn't very clear at first but in the weeks that followed, he made changes to his words, leaving out some bits and adding more. As he did, it became free flowing for him and sounded more like his natural speech. I was so proud of him for doing this. What he wrote about me was so beautiful and it really moved me.

Madeleine was really pleased with our work. She sent it back with only one slight alteration.

•

We were booked in for a Skype rehearsal with a public speaking coach in April. It was my birthday and I was terrified; it felt like I was sitting an exam. I was so anxious I couldn't sleep the night before and, to make matters worse, I barely knew how to use Skype. I didn't know if I could get it working properly. Worst of all, I was worried that the committee would change their minds; that they'd see our presentation and say, 'Thanks, but no thanks.' We passed with flying colours, much to my relief. And once we were finished, Tim insisted that the people on the other end of our conversation wish me a Happy Birthday. It was a very Happy Birthday after that ordeal was over.

Tim and I practised our presentation at least twice a day, every day. Tim had always been very frightened of microphones so I borrowed a headpiece mic and amplifier from a friend. Twice a day, we blasted our neighbours with our TEDx talk. Eventually, Tim got so excited that he overcame his fears. He wore the mic like he didn't even notice it was there. It was an extraordinary achievement for Tim, who had spent his whole life standing side-on to microphones, who hated hearing his own voice so loud. No matter how much I had coaxed him in the past, he couldn't bear it, yet here he was doing it as if he always had. It was clear TEDxSydney meant as much to him as it did to me.

•

The harbour looked magnificent on the morning of 26 April, with its deep emerald green waters and bobbing ships. The sky was clear and blue and the Harbour Bridge framed the whole glorious picture. Sam and his girlfriend, Samantha, arrived in Sydney, and I was happy. Our family was together.

When our taxi pulled up in front of the Sydney Opera House, Tim quickly jumped out. A gigantic smile filled his face and he started running towards the magnificent white sails, just as he'd done the first time he saw it. It was an absolute joy to watch. Backstage, Tim got out his iPad, kicked off his shoes and lay back on the couch, cool as a cucumber. We had a three-hour wait until we were due to speak. I didn't know if I could survive. Several times I asked Tim if he was nervous or scared. 'No! I'm excited and happy,' he said.

He told me to relax.

Tim loved sitting in the chair to have his hair and make-up done, while I was a bundle of nerves. I knew the event was sold out and there would be 2500 people in the audience, and we were told there would be over 30,000 people watching via a live stream. I had also been told that more than 13 million people viewed the TEDxSydney talks and content online. I was glad that Tim was enjoying himself but that didn't help me much.

Finally, it was close. We were moved from one room to the next, and then up some stairs, then mic'd up and taken into the wings of the stage. All of a sudden I thought I was going to have a heart attack. I actually wasn't sure I would survive until it was our turn to speak. I sipped on water but it felt like my mouth was filled with sawdust. My hands were shaking and my heart was beating way too fast, so loudly I thought the audience would hear it. My biggest fear was that I would forget the words and just stand there silently. But it was too late. Edwina was on the stage, introducing Tim and me to a full audience at the Sydney Opera House.

Tim and I walked onto the stage hand-in-hand and my nerves began to drop away. By the time we'd stepped onto the circle of bright red carpet in the middle of the stage, I felt totally calm and comfortable. *These people want to hear what you have to say*, I thought. *Just relax and enjoy it. It's a once-in-a-lifetime opportunity and you have a good story to tell.* I felt the intangible force of love filling the room that day.

Tim took his position in the chair next to me and we began. 'I live with two superheroes,' I said. 'The first one does not wear a cape, he is my son.'

Tim said, 'Hello, everybody. I'm Tim Sharp. I'm a world-famous artist.'

As Tim spoke, I scanned the audience, hoping that I might see Sam. Every chair was filled in every row, in the balconies above, to my left and right, and all the way to the back of the hall as far as I could see. I spotted Sam six rows from the front and I felt very emotional. I was so proud and touched to have him there. I couldn't look at him again or I wouldn't make it through.

When I introduced the character of Laser Beak Man, 'A Double Shot of Happiness' appeared twenty feet high on the screen behind us. I burst into chuckles; it looked so amazing. We had never seen that drawing loom so large and certainly not at the Sydney Opera House. Tim went on to introduce a few of his most popular pictures and every time one appeared on the screen the room erupted in laughter. They got his sense of humour instantly and they absolutely loved it. Every time Tim spoke, I wanted to burst into tears. He was so perfect and so calm.

I went on to tell my story. I talked about the day that Tim was born. I talked about my screaming baby and the doctors who told me I just had to work harder. I told them about the child psychologist who treated us so cruelly, who diagnosed Tim and told me to put him away. I talked of the dream I had that one day I would hear my son say, 'I love you.' I told them how Tim had started drawing and how his drawing had changed our lives.

When I was done, I was pleased with how it'd gone. The audience was extraordinarily attentive and very responsive. They had made me feel comfortable and welcome, like they genuinely cared about what I had to say. I could feel their support and enjoyed it immensely. It was then Tim's turn to talk.

Even though I had heard it hundreds of times before, what he said that day moved me deeply. I could feel the tears flooding my eyes again and I didn't think I'd be able to hold them back.

'Every day is a good day for me. Every day is a happy day for me. My mum and I are a team,' he said. 'She is my mum and my best friend. She is beautiful and excellent. I love my mum.'

I broke down as the audience rose to its feet. I was so ecstatically proud of Tim. He was perfect; he'd done a perfect job. I thought my heart would burst out of my chest.

It was impossible to explain the significance of that moment. The journey Tim and I had been through—from utter hopelessness to that shining spotlight—was both incredibly difficult and incredibly beautiful. I was so grateful that we had had the chance to tell our story, in our own words. I was so proud that people around the world would be able see the splendour of my son and to honour him. 'Love is all you need,' Tim had said. I felt overwhelmed with love.

Tim and I walked off the stage hand-in-hand, the same way we had walked on, the same way we had walked through all the moments of our life together.

•

The next morning, I sat across from Tim as he ate his chocolate croissant at the little French cafe down the road from our hotel. I couldn't remember seeing him look so blissfully content, so I took out my camera and took many photos of his beautiful face. He kept telling me how happy he was, how much he loved giving the talk and that he wanted to do it again.

As I looked at him, I recalled all the wonderful things that had been said to us the day before. I recalled my talk and the reaction it had received. My last line had been the hardest one to deliver. My voice had started to quaver as I fought back my tears. I couldn't say it without pouring everything I held in my heart into those few words.

'Tim, you are a superhero for Sam and me,' I'd said. 'You are my very own double shot of happiness.'

Afterword

I made a decision when Tim was small not to tell him he had autism. I made that decision for a few reasons. It's a complex condition that is hard enough to explain to anyone and I wasn't certain I could explain it to Tim without confusing him or making him feel inferior. There were so many generalisations made about autism and I was concerned that I would tell him things about it that didn't affect him or mean anything to him; I didn't want him thinking he had problems that he didn't. Until the day when he could actually tell me how he experienced the world, I could never be sure how his autism affected him and I didn't want to influence his own, individual interpretation of life. I didn't want autism to become an explanation or reason for Tim's whole existence.

Over the years, in countless meetings with doctors and counsellors and therapists and specialists, people tried to explain away everything Tim ever did as a product of autism. I wanted to scream with every ounce of my breath, *That's not Tim! Tim is not autism! Not everything he does is autism; he is Tim!* Hearing so many people diminish him and write him off in that way only made my resolve stronger. I would not define my son by his condition.

Tim sat in many of those meetings but he never asked me about autism. He asked me once in high school why he had to go to the special unit when Sam didn't, but I didn't know what to tell him. I didn't want to emphasise a difference.

It wasn't until Tim's art started gaining recognition that autism became an issue for us. I cringed whenever I heard the words 'autistic artist Tim Sharp'. I knew they were just trying to highlight what Tim had overcome but I would have preferred that he was just 'artist Tim Sharp'. I wasn't in denial and I wasn't ashamed—I had battled the condition his whole life and I knew exactly how he had struggled—I just wanted people to see Tim before they saw autism.

I was forced to raise it with Tim because of all the media attention. I broached the subject when he was sixteen.

'They say,' I started, shifting the blame to some nameless person, 'that you have autism, Tim.'

'What does autism mean?' he wanted to know.

I answered him in the simplest way I knew how. 'It means you have trouble talking.'

'I don't have trouble talking,' Tim replied, indignant that I had even suggested it. 'I'm a good talker.'

'It also means you have trouble making friends,' I added.

'I don't have trouble making friends,' Tim said. 'I have lots of friends.'

It was a happy revelation for me to realise that he saw himself in such a positive way. I was proud that he was so sure of himself.

'I'm not interested in autism,' Tim told me. 'I don't have autism.'

When we go to schools and organisations to speak, I often talk about autism, ability and acceptance. Tim is happy to go because he understands that it helps people but he normally leaves all the autism talk to me. He prefers to talk about his art. It almost feels like a betrayal to talk about the things that were said on the day that Tim was diagnosed. It feels cruel to stand beside him and repeat the horrible things that psychologist said. But Tim knows that the psychologist was wrong. I try to be respectful and protect Tim's feelings, but I believe it is important for people to realise how significant his achievements are, how he defied the predictions and judgement of people who thought they knew best.

It is good for people to meet Tim and see what a fine, well-adjusted gentleman he is. Everywhere we go he charms the pants off everyone, challenging the misconceptions and stereotypes about people with autism. By being himself, that's how Tim changes the world.

For parents of children with autism, all I can say is never lose sight of the person. Not everybody with autism has a creative gift like Tim, but everyone with autism is an individual. Trust that there is something unique in this world that will bring your child happiness and joy.

I know it's hard. To this day, I find it almost impossible to explain the distress that a child with autism goes through, the crying and the rages and the wordless misery. It is a genuine response to pain, and the difficulties we cannot imagine or understand, that affects these children with such severity and keeps them separate from us. It is a cruel and insidious condition that robs our children of the very essence of their humanity, the ability to connect and communicate with other people. Those words still ring in my ears, *Within one's self.*

We have met so many brave and dedicated parents beginning their own journey with autism, who came to meet Tim because he inspired them. It makes me want to try even harder, to help Tim rise up even further. I know how desperately I needed inspiration when he was a little boy. Every day was like trying to pull myself out of quicksand.

I wish I had known then what I know now. I wish that someone had told me that there was no magic about the age of three or the age of four, or any other age that was supposed to be a milestone. I wish that someone had told me that there was no one thing that would provide all the answers and make all the difference. I wish someone had told me to be patient; that progress is a culmination of all the little things coming together; that everything helps but not one thing will be the answer. I wish someone had told me that it wasn't my fault. I wish someone had convinced me that I didn't have to blame myself for everything. I wish someone had told me that it would get better.

In my extreme lows, I often received a kind word from someone who probably never realised the impact they were making on our lives. Kind words are a very powerful encouragement and I think we should say them more.

•

I know that we are lucky. Often young artists ask me what they should do to get started. They want to know how Tim has achieved what he has, how to make connections. I can't answer them. People give me credit for a lot of things but it's a bigger picture than me. Tim has brought so many wonderful guardian angels into our lives and they have guided us through.

I have never had a grand plan, never mapped out how Tim's career should develop. In fact, to me it always feels like divine intervention. I believe in God, I often say 'God is good' and believe it all comes from Him, but still I struggle to fathom how we could be so blessed and receive so much good in one lifetime. It is more than I can explain or understand, but I embrace it all. I think about it an awful lot and I am thankful for it every minute of every day. It has helped me find a place for Tim in this world. It has helped me to be exactly what I always wanted to be—a loving mother to Tim and Sam.

But nothing is as simple as it seems. Tim has an amazing life, travelling and meeting wonderful people, with opportunities that I could only dream of. Yet without art, it would be difficult to provide him with the engaging and varied lifestyle that I want for him. And to a certain extent, Tim's life is what I create for him. He relies on me for everything.

When he was a little boy, I always wanted to meet an adult with autism to see what lay ahead, but there were none around. Now I understand why. Parents of adults with autism are just plain worn out by having to do everything for their children, long past the time that other parents have hung up their spurs. Once the five-day-a-week routine of school is gone, there is nothing to fill those hours. Your responsibility becomes greater and you realise, then, that it will never end. I am older now and very tired.

The desperate, chilling thought of what will happen when I am not here is almost debilitating. I try to plan for Tim's future, but it has so many variables and relies so much on others to provide for and sustain Tim. I can't rely on the government or autism agencies when I'm gone; I have seen too much of how they operate now. I know no one will ever love and care for my son the way that I have done. Of course Sam will protect his brother, but he will have his own family to look after, too. Taking care of Tim is a full-time job.

I am terrified of leaving Tim here alone without me. It honestly wakes me up in the middle of the night sometimes. I don't have a solution to this problem but I know that one is needed.

•

Tim, for what it's worth, seems happy. In summer, he likes to swim and go to the beach. He likes to see a movie and he likes to go to the shops to buy games, DVDs and books. We ride our bikes sometimes or drive to new places, and everywhere he goes he strikes up a conversation and makes new friends. When we're at home, he doesn't have much need for conversation. He'll go hours without speaking to me while he sits in his room reading or writing, gathering information on his iPad, making lists or learning about something new.

I struggle with his silence sometimes and wonder if he is lonely or wants more in his life than I can provide. Sometimes, I can't hold back my curiosity.

'Are you all right, Tim? Are you happy?' I ask.

Quick as a flash he tells me, 'I am always happy, Mum. I have a good life. I like it.'

I wish I was more like him sometimes. Tim says what he actually means. There are no games. It's not hard work. And because he has this instinct to look for the good in everything, it's never a battle to be around him. His company never leaves you tired or drained; it always leaves you happy. Tim is very pure. He lives in the moment and just doesn't worry. He's figured out the meaning of life.

So I try not to worry too much about what the future holds. I try to focus on my time with Tim, which is filled with peace. It is such a blessing to be able to sit silently beside him, holding his hand, knowing that he loves me and he knows that I love him.

'We're a good team, Mum,' Tim always says.

I totally agree.

Acknowledgements

Thank you to Simone Ubaldi for your writing talent, which turned my manuscript into something special; it wouldn't be the book it is without you. Thank you, Kathryn Knight, for all of your writing help. It has been a joy to work with you. Thank you to all the enthusiastic and caring people at Allen & Unwin for your excellence and commitment to Tim's story, and to the superb Tom Gilliatt at Allen & Unwin for the opportunity of a lifetime.

Thank you for the gift of true friendship, Debbie, David and Brooke Johnson, Kaye Wathen and Wendy Ariel.

To the many treasured friends introduced from one suburb, our 'Moorooka mates' from 1995 to 2013, thank you for your unshakeable belief and your commitment to Tim, and all you have done for us. Friends, teachers, co-workers—we love youse all.

Thank you to Kristine Taylor from *Australian Story*. Look what you started! Without you taking the chance on us, most of this wouldn't have happened. I don't think even you could have written this amazing script. It's been a blast.

Thank you to our TEDxSydney family, particularly Edwina Throsby, Remo and Melanie Giuffré, Mick Garnett and Madeleine Hawcroft. Thank you to Richard Fidler, Pam O'Brien and Michelle Ransom from the Richard Fidler Conversation Hour for the life-changing encouragement.

Thank you to our loyal, passionate and devoted Laser Beak Man family all over Australia and around the world, including our Tennessee family. Love y'all.

Thank you to Margie Lawrence, Dr James and Louise Morton, Shirley Wright, Mark Lutz, Anne Dowd and Len Phillips, Sheldon Lieberman, Mitch Ellems, Michael Drummond, Jonathan Bell, Trish Wright, Glenn Rogerson, Graham Young, Ann Schindel, Kelly Rogers, Peter Leask, Chris De Klerk, Arthur Frame, Rose Pearse and Kathy Crawford for your help and support throughout the years. It will never be forgotten and will always be appreciated.

Eternal thanks to my dearly loved mother, Myra Hoey Unsworth (1925–2005), for being the greatest teacher I have ever had in the lessons of love and life.